THE
WOLF
AGE

'The turbulent age that straddles the first millennium is brought to life in a history worthy of a modern television epic'

Financial Times

'A vivid chronicle… Tore Skeie's book has won awards in Norway, and it's easy to see why. This is exemplary popular history'

Neil Price, author of *The Children of Ash and Elm*

'An impressive depiction of the Viking world in the tenth and eleventh centuries. Tore Skeie deploys his scholarship with a light touch, not so much evoking this bygone age as fully inhabiting it'

Michael Jones, author of *The Black Prince*

'Gripping and compelling. This is the story of Medieval Europe and its neighbours like it has never been told before, where there's no hero nor villain, just men fighting for power and glory. Skeie masterfully tells their complex stories and brings these men back to life'

Estelle Paranque, author of *Blood, Fire and Gold*

'Hugely readable… richly imagined, vividly described'

Carolyne Larrington, author of
Norse Myths: A Guide to the Gods and Heroes

TORE SKEIE is one of Norway's most acclaimed historians, having written several prize-winning and bestselling works of medieval history. Tore is known for his eye for historical and human drama, while his books have been praised both for their thrilling style and the way they challenge traditional nation-oriented historical narratives. *The Wolf Age* was a bestseller in Norway, won the prestigious Sverre Steen award and is the first of Tore's books to be translated into English.

ALISON MCCULLOUGH is a Norwegian to English literary translator based in Stavanger, Norway. Her previous translations include *The Therapist* by Helene Flood and *Theatre of the World: The Maps That Made History* by Thomas Reinertsen Berg.

THE
WOLF
AGE

The Vikings, the
Anglo-Saxons and
the Battle for the
North Sea Empire

TORE SKEIE

TRANSLATED FROM THE NORWEGIAN BY
ALISON MCCULLOUGH

PUSHKIN PRESS

Pushkin Press
65-69 Shelton Street
London WC2H 9HE

The Wolf Age was first published as *Hvitekrist. Om Olav Haraldsson og hans tid* by
Gyldendal Norsk Forlag in Oslo, 2018

Revised edition first published by Pushkin Press in 2021
This edition published in 2022

This translation has been published with the financial support of NORLA

3 5 7 9 8 6 4 2

ISBN 13: 978-1-78227-835-1

Maps drawn by Line Monrad-Hansen

Designed and typeset by Tetragon, London
Printed and bound in The United States

www.pushkinpress.com

For my grandparents

Brothers will fight
and kill each other, [...]
—an axe-age, a sword-age
—shields are riven—
a wind-age, a wolf-age—
before the world goes headlong.
No man will have
mercy on another.

THE FORETELLING OF THE COMING OF RAGNARÖK
AND THE END OF THE WORLD IN *VǪLUSPÁ*, "THE
SEERESS'S PROPHECY", TENTH CENTURY

When sitting among his friends his countenance was so beautiful and
dignified that the spirits of all were exhilarated by it. But when he
was at war he changed in colour and form and he appeared dreadful
to his foes.

SNORRI STURLUSON ON THE GOD-KING ODIN,
THE MYTHOLOGICAL FOREFATHER OF ALL
NORDIC KINGS, *YNGLINGA SAGA*, 1220S

I was with the lord, who gave gold to his loyal men and carrion to the
ravens.

OLAF HARALDSSON'S SKALD SIGVAT TORDARSON,
BERSǪGLISVÍSUR, C.1031

CONTENTS

CHAPTER OVERVIEW

1241

The meeting at Sauðafell—Reykholt—'Thou shalt not strike!'—the historian and the politician—the masterpiece

A REGIME FACING RUIN

God's messenger—the royal murder in Corfe—Æthelred—foreign ships—a kingdom forged in the fight against idolatrous foreign barbarians—the Battle of Maldon 991—Harald Bluetooth's kingdom—Sweyn Forkbeard—Olaf Tryggvason's conversion—"Satan's bonds are now indeed slipped"—the St Brice's Day massacre in 1002—"like a fire which someone had tried to extinguish with fat"—the great famine of 1005—Eadric Streona's palace coup—the Danes "lighted their war-beacons as they went"—"that victory on which the whole English nation had fixed their hopes"

THE WARRIOR'S GOOD LIFE

"That immense hostile host"—*Óláfr inn digri*—Olaf's background—Vik and the wider world—a new time and a new God—under Olaf Tryggvason—"east on the salt sea"—"gold to his loyal men and carrion to the ravens"—in the Danish king's army—the plundering of Tiel—the first attack on Canterbury

FIRE AND SMOKE

Between Córdoba and Constantinople—the hunt for food—plundering
in the south—"God help us all. Amen"—the siege of London—the
Battle of Ringmere—"spoiling some wretched people of their property
and slaying others"—the second attack on Canterbury—Archbishop
Ælfheah's martyrdom—peace

MIDGARD

New alliances are forged—the Frankish kingdom—Normandy—in the
service of the Norman Duke—Ringfjord—"duke of the pirates"—plundering the Loire Valley—about slaves and the slave trade—the caliphate
of Córdoba—the caliphate's crisis—about ships, seafaring and the mighty
sea—the Vikings and Saracens in al-Andalus—Cádiz—Córdoba burns

HVÍTI KRISTR

An invasion is planned—conquest—Æthelred's flight—the Sermon of
the Wolf to the English—a king's death—in Rouen, winter 1014—about
ceremonies—Olaf Haraldsson's baptism—"he would be to them a loving
lord"—reconquest—the hostages on the beach

TO NORWAY

The old North Way—the history of the Jarls of Lade—about Harald
Fairhair's kingdom—Olaf Tryggvason's victory and defeat—Eric
Håkonsson, Jarl of Lade—the meeting in Oxford in 1014—Edmund
Ironside's rebellion—yet another invasion—Olaf and Cnut—Saudungssund

BROAD ANCESTRAL LANDS

About the thinking of the kings—to Vik—"afterwards you took the
tongue of he who lives furthest north"—"the generous one"—about
things and the hailing of kings—Sigvat the Skald—about skalds, skaldic
poetry and sagas—the war in England, winter 1016—the new Jarl of
Northumbria—the Battle of Nesjar

TWO KINGDOMS

A life lived "with great toil and under great difficulties"—'*Flet Engle, Flet Engle!*'—the Battle of Assandun—peace in Gloucestershire—the death of one...—"ONLAF REX NORMANNORUM"—chieftains in the north and south—the construction of Borg—a foreign, Christian king—the travelling king—about the Christianization of Norway—about brutality

THE GREAT

Cnut consolidates his power—a head higher than everyone else in England—Cnut and Denmark—Olaf and the Swedes—the *thing* at Moster—Olaf's poverty and Cnut's shadow—the feud with Thorir Hund—Thorkell the Tall's fate—the fate of Eric Håkonsson, Jarl of Lade—"Olaf the Stout never surrendered his skull to anyone in the world"

SILVER COINS FOR THE KING'S HEAD

"Olaf caused his ship, the *Bison*, to tread the waves"—a new war is planned—switching sides—European complications—Olaf, "feller of the Danes"—the trap in the Øresund—a journey through Europe—the long march home—in Rome—at Cnut's court—"all the inside of your hall is agreeable to me"—the death of two brothers—"they greedily accepted his bribes"—"Little joy will the army have tonight in Jæren"—the power dissolves—eastwards, again—a shipwreck—towards Stiklestad

OVERVIEW OF PERSONS

THE WESSEX KINGS

ÆTHELRED, King of the Anglo-Saxons, both weak and strong, uncertain and despotic.

Edgar "the Peaceful", his father.

Edward, his brother.

Ælfgifu of Northampton, his first queen, mother to many of his children.

Edmund Ironside ⎱
Eadwig   ⎰ his blinded sons.

Emma, his second queen, sister of the Duke of Normandy, later Cnut's queen.

Edward ⎫
Alfred ⎬ their children.
Gota   ⎭

PROMINENT ANGLO-SAXONS

Eadric Streona, Ealdorman and Lord of Mercia. A master at forging alliances—and at breaking them.

Beortric, his brother.

Wulfnoth, Beortric's rival.

Byrhtnoth, Ealdorman of Wessex and a general in Æthelred's army.

Ulfcytel "the Brave", Ealdorman of East Anglia, army general, probably King Æthelred's son-in-law.

Wulfhild, according to uncertain sources Eadric's wife, Æthelred's daughter, later married to Thorkell the Tall.

Ælfhelm of York, ealdorman and central figure in the north.

Wulfheah ⎱
Ufegeat ⎰ his blinded sons.

Uhtred of Bamburgh, Ealdorman of Northumbria, first allied with Sweyn, later with Edmund Ironside.

Siferth ⎫
Morcar ⎭ Northern English thanes, Eadric's enemies.

LEADERS OF THE ANGLO-SAXON CLERGY

Ælfheah, Archbishop of Canterbury.

Wulfstan, Archbishop of York and fierce rebuker of the Anglo-Saxons' lack of piety.

Eadnoth, Bishop of Dorchester.

IN NORWAY

OLAF HARALDSSON, Viking, warlord and King of the Norwegians.

Harald Grenske, his father, the King of the Danes' under-king in Vik.

Asta Gudbrandsdatter, his mother, daughter of a prominent man from the Uplands.

Sigurd "Syr", his stepfather, petty king in Ringerike.

Harald Sigurdsson, his young half-brother.

Astrid, his queen. Daughter of Olof Skötkonung.

Ulvhild, their daughter.

Alvhild, according to the sagas Olaf's mistress.

Magnus, their son.

Bjørn "Stallare", *hird* leader and army general.

Tord, *hird* member and standard-bearer.

Grimkil, Olaf's English *hird* bishop, likely of Norse descent.

Siegfried ⎫
Rudolf ⎬ *hird* clergy.
Bernhard ⎭

Olaf Tryggvason, Olaf Haraldsson's predecessor—as King of the Northmen, as an enemy of the Jarls of Lade, and as a rival of the king.

THE JARLS OF LADE

ERIC HÅKONSSON, Jarl of Lade, ally of the Danish kings, regarded as their Norwegian prince. Jarl of Northumbria from 1016.

Håkon Sigurdsson, his father.

Sweyn Håkonsson, his brother.

Gyða, his wife, Sweyn Forkbeard's daughter.

Håkon Ericsson, his son and heir, Cnut's loyal servant.

PROMINENT NORWEGIANS

Erling Skjalgsson, uncrowned king of Western Norway, the most powerful man in Norway after Olaf.

Aslak "the Bald" from Fitjar, Erling Skjalgsson's second cousin.

Aslak of Finnøy, Olaf's man.

Erlend of Gjerde, Olaf's man.

Thorir Hund, Hålogaland's most important chieftain, Olaf's *lendmann*, but not his friend.

Asbjørn, his nephew, Olaf's reluctant representative.

Hårek of Tjøtta, Olaf's man in Hålogaland.

Arne Arnmodsson from Giske, a prominent man with many connections along the coast to the north and south, Olaf's man.

Kalv Arnesson, his son, Olaf's most important man in Trøndelag, with his seat at Egge.

Sigrid, Kalv's wife, Olve of Egge's widow.

Finn Arnesson, Arne's son and Kalv's brother, Olaf's man in Trøndelag, with his seat at Austråt.

Torberg Arnesson ⎫
Arne Arnesson ⎭ Finn and Kalv's brothers, also Olaf's men.

Olve of Egge, leading heathen man, killed by Olaf.

Tore ⎫
Grjotgard ⎭ Sigrid and Olve's sons, Kalv's stepsons.

Einar Thambarskelfir, Chieftain in Trøndelag, from Gimsar in Gauldal.

Eyvind Aurochs-Horn, Olaf's man in Aust-Agder.

Brynjulv Ulvalde, Olaf's man in Ranrike.

Tord from Steig, Olaf's man in Gudbrandsdalen.

Dale-Gudbrand, heathen chieftain at Hundorp in Gudbrandsdalen. Tord from Steig's rival.

Kjetil Kalv, Olaf's man in the areas around Lake Mjøsa, with his seat at Ringnes in Stange.

Gunnhild Sigurdsdatter, his wife, according to the sagas Olaf's half-sister.

Torgeir from Garmo, Olaf's man in Ottadalen.

THE DANISH KINGS

CNUT SWEYNSSON, "the Great", king of many kingdoms around the North Sea.

Sweyn Forkbeard, his father.

Gunnhild, his mother, also called Świętosława, of the Polish Piast dynasty.

Harald Bluetooth, his paternal grandfather.

Gorm the Old, his great-grandfather.

Harald Sweynsson, his brother.

Gyða Sweynsdatter, his sister, wife of Eric Håkonsson.

Estrid Sweynsdatter, his sister.

Ælfgifu of Northampton, his first queen, daughter of Ælfhelm of York.

Sweyn Cnutsson, their son, who as a young boy becomes his father's under-king in Norway.

Harlad Cnutsson, their son.

Harthacnut ⎤
Gunnhild ⎦ Cnut's children with Emma.

WARLORDS IN THE DANISH KING'S SERVICE

Thorkell the Tall, a headstrong Danish warlord, after 1016 the Jarl of East Anglia.

Hemming, his younger brother.

Eglaf ⎤
Ulv ⎦ warlords in Thorkell's army.

Lacman, a warlord in the Danes' service in England, Olaf Haraldsson's partner in Norman service.

IN SWEDEN

ANUND JACOB, the young Swedish king, Olaf Haraldsson's brother-in-law.

Olof Skötkonung, his father.

Ingegerd, his sister.

Astrid, his sister, Olaf Haraldsson's queen.

Ragnvald, a jarl and possibly ruler of the Swedish kingdom during King Anund's childhood.

Ulf, King Anund's army general, perhaps Ragnvald's son.

IN NORMANDY

Richard II, Duke of Normandy, a Frankish prince with Norse roots, brother to Emma, Queen of the Anglo-Saxons.

Robert, Richard and Emma's brother, Archbishop of Rouen.

Richard I, their father.

Gunnhild, their Danish-born mother.

OTHER EUROPEAN FIGURES

Robert II of the Capetian dynasty, King of the Franks.

Conrad II, Prince of Franconia in Bavaria and from 1027 the German Holy Roman Emperor.

Pope John XIX.

Unwan, Archbishop of Hamburg-Bremen.

William V, Count of Poitou and Duke of Aquitaine.

Odo II, Count of Blois, Chartres, Châteaudun, Beauvais and Tours. The Duke of Normandy's rival.

Solomon, lord of his castle at Dol.

Ulric Manfred II of Turin, Prince of Lombardy.

Alfonso V, King of León.

Sancho III, King of Navarre.

Mieszko I, King of Poland, from the Piast dynasty, and Cnut's uncle.

Bolesław I, his son, Cnut's cousin.

Stephen I, King of Hungary.

Yaroslav the Wise, Grand Prince of Kiev and Novgorod, married to Ingegerd, Olof Skötkonung's daughter.

THE CALIPHATE OF CÓRDOBA

Hisham II, Caliph of Córdoba.

Almanzor, "the provider of slaves", vizier and Córdoba's true ruler.

al-Malik, his son and successor.

Muhammad II ⎫
Sulayman II ⎭ rival caliphs.

SKALDS

Sigvat Tordarson, Olaf Haraldsson's most important skald and his trusted man. Composed poetry for a number of kings and prominent men.

Tófa, his daughter.

Tord Sigvaldeskald, Sigvat's father, a merchant and skald who served Olaf in England.

Ottar the Black
Torarin "Praise-mouth"
Gissur Svarte, "Gold Brow"   travelling skalds who composed poetry for various figures
Tormod Bersason, "Coal-black skald"
Torfinn Munnen

THE
WOLF
AGE

Pennies featuring royal portraits

TOP: Æthelred, King of the Anglo-Saxons
CENTRE: Olaf Haraldsson, King of the Norwegians
BOTTOM: Cnut, King of the Danes, Norwegians and Anglo-Saxons

1241

THEY CAME ACROSS the desolate yellow wetlands, like a caravan through the desert. The company consisted of around thirty men on shaggy-haired, hardy horses, the animals' backs so low that the men's feet almost dragged on the ground. They had ridden a long way, below silent mountains and flocks of birds, through valleys in the Uplands. Their destination was the farm at Sauðafell, which lay on a wet, grassy plain at the end of a fjord on Iceland's wind-battered west coast. When they arrived, they were received by Snorri Sturluson.

In the evening, while the servants and attendants warmed themselves, resting in the farmhouses, Snorri gathered some of his visitors around him. A ship had recently arrived from Norway carrying beer, and this was brought into the house. A young man poured the beer into drinking bowls. As the autumn dark descended outside, the men exchanged news, made plans and drank. We know this because one of the men would later write down his memories of this meeting in a saga about his kin and the age in which he lived. He was one of Snorri's many nephews, and one of the people who knew him best. He had grown up in Snorri's household, and been taught to read, write and narrate by the master himself.

He doesn't tell us much; gives us just a few glimpses of what must have been a long evening spent around the fireplace. It was in many ways an ordinary night—they often met like this, on the numerous farms owned or controlled by Snorri—but in retrospect the evening would take on an especially poignant significance. It would be the last night they spent together.

The year was 1241, and it was mid-September. Snorri was sixty-one or sixty-two years old, a more venerable age in the 1200s than it is today, but not so old that he couldn't have had many more years ahead of him. He was a greying man, reportedly ruddy-cheeked and fat—stalwart, as chieftains should be—his physique the result of a nobleman's life spent consuming great quantities of the best food and drink. On this particular evening he was very cheerful, the saga tells us.

This last piece of information is a surprising one—not only because the sober and minimalistic Icelandic family sagas rarely shed light on people's states of mind in this way, but also because everything else we know about Snorri's situation at this point in his life indicates that he didn't have much to be cheerful about.

Just two weeks earlier, he had lost the woman with whom he had lived for the past few years. She died following a period of illness, and we know that he grieved deeply for her.

Her death was just one misfortune among many.

One year earlier, Snorri had made a fateful mistake. He had spent his entire adult life purposefully and shrewdly seeking out wealth and influence, and over the course of several decades had managed to work his way up from a relatively modest position to become Iceland's most prominent chieftain, a kind of uncrowned king of his home island. But in an attempt to become even mightier and richer than he already was, he had become embroiled in secret plans to stage a coup against the King of Norway. The mutiny was unsuccessful, however, and Snorri's allies across the sea had all been killed or forced to flee, or had surrendered. Snorri's role in the conspiracy had been discovered, and its consequences were catching up with him. The King of Norway, now stronger than ever, openly considered him a traitor and enemy, and had recently bought himself the loyalty of important Icelandic men with promises of future positions. Under pressure from the king, the network Snorri had laboriously built up around him over the course of his long life began to unravel. The situation was so dire that Snorri was soon no longer regarded as the most prominent man in Iceland. His old rivals and formerly loyal supporters found themselves united in their opposition to him, driven by a mixture of jealousy, political opportunism and bitterness at his notorious greed and conceited lifestyle. A new era was dawning, and Snorri's rivals were the new men. Snorri was in mortal danger. He must have known that his life was at risk.

As they sat there, talking and drinking beer, Snorri produced a curious letter he had received a few days earlier. It was written in so-called "beggar's script"—a form of code composed of runes, which was sometimes used to convey secret messages. Snorri was unable to read beggar's script, and so had attempted to decipher the letter's contents without success. He passed the letter around. None of the others managed to read it either, but they agreed that it seemed to be some kind of warning. Perhaps a threat. And yet Snorri's nephew tells us that Snorri was in a very cheerful mood. Did he laugh at the irony in receiving a warning that couldn't be read, perhaps?

The next day, Snorri accompanied the group of men when they left Sauðafell. Together they rode into the timeless landscape of Western Iceland, over black sand and yellow fields, crossing shallow, ice-cold rivers that ran towards the sea through sharp curves. They rested at another farm, ate a meal together, and then went their separate ways. The main company went in one direction,

Snorri in another. Accompanied only by his servants, he rode down a wide, barren valley towards his home farm.

His companions would never see him again.

The journey was not a long one, and so Snorri probably arrived home that same evening. His farm, Reykholt, was situated on a low ridge, on a gently sloping wooded hillside with a view of a quiet river, and surrounded by small patches of cultivated land and pastures for cows and sheep. It was a monument to its owner's unique character and unrivalled status.

The farm was among the largest in Iceland and without question the most extravagant, built just as much to impress as to function as a comfortable and luxurious home in this weather-beaten land. Many years earlier, Snorri had ordered that a several-metre-high wall of turf, soil and stone be erected around the farm, wide and long enough for 200 men to stand on it simultaneously. The wall had a gate that could be raised and lowered, and even a tower, giving the site an appearance that was a cross between a large Icelandic farm and a small castle of the type in which English and French nobles lived.

White steam carrying the odour of sulphur rose from a hot spring just a stone's throw beyond the walls. Through an ingenious arrangement of underground pipes, possibly inspired by Arab bathing and irrigation systems, the spring supplied naturally heated water to both a bathhouse inside the farm's walls and the brick baths outside, where Snorri often sat with his friends.

Inside the gates were clusters of turf-roofed buildings of various sizes, clumped together as if in a narrow village: storehouses, a brewhouse, a church, buildings that contained beds and workplaces for an entire community of farmhands, priests and servants, and an elegant feast hall decorated with woven tapestries and other gifts Snorri had accumulated on his travels. The biggest buildings were constructed from the trunks of large trees that did not grow naturally in Iceland, and which had therefore been felled and de-limbed in a forest in Norway before being transported across the sea at great cost.

Reykholt had long been a natural centre of religious, political and financial power, but over his long life Snorri had also made his seat into Iceland's foremost secular centre of learning. It was a place for magnificent feasts and scholarly study, where disputes about power, money and property merged with music and the telling of stories to form a natural whole. A group of priests lived and worked on the farm permanently to help Snorri with various tasks, including his writing. Sundry musicians and entertainers came and went; distinguished guests often slept under Snorri's roof.

At the centre of the site was the writing studio, a small workroom containing quills, ink and a collection of books. This was where Snorri had written, or dictated to his literate priests, his blood-spattered works about the triumphs and defeats of gods and men.

Snorri was a rare combination of prosperous politician and gifted poet in one and the same person. He belonged to a distinctive and already several-hundred-year-old Icelandic narrative tradition that collated, cultivated and disseminated knowledge of the past. He was a skald, a successor of the Icelandic court poets who had served the ancient Viking kings—men who were close to power, and who described it through poetry. Snorri could recite hundreds of old skaldic poems by heart, and was able to retell long, complicated stories about the events of former ages in a way that rendered his audiences spellbound.

Over the course of his long life, Snorri collected and systematized an enormous amount of knowledge about the events of former times—from older historical works, from the old poems that had been passed down orally over hundreds of years, from the stories told by elderly members of the community, and from countless sources that have since been lost. Today, his works about skaldic poetry and mythology are our most important single source of knowledge about the pre-Christian Scandinavians' mythological histories. His collection of sagas about the Norwegian kings, *Heimskringla*, extends from the distant mythological past, when dwarfs and giants wandered the earth and the one-eyed godking Odin ruled among men, up until a few years before Snorri himself was born—it is the most comprehensive historical work to have been written in Scandinavia during the Middle Ages. Like the other saga writers, Snorri supplemented what he knew and believed with guesswork and invention, filling out the story by making things up, so that his writing approached fiction in terms of its form. Knowledge of the past was therefore artistically and logically woven into complete stories, with which to entertain, educate and elevate the Nordic people of the 1200s.

There was one particular period of history that interested Snorri intensely—the period around 200 years before his birth, towards the end of the era that is today known as the Viking Age, when Christianity was beginning to take root in Scandinavia and the Nordic kingdoms were formed. It was a time far from Snorri's own, a time that had left behind no books or written testimonies other than a few runic inscriptions of poetry and commemorative words for the dead.

But memories of the old ancestors' accomplishments lived on through fantastical oral narratives, which excited and astonished Snorri and his contemporaries. These were stories from a time when Nordic adventurers travelled to far-off regions of the world to return home with incredible riches in the form of silver and gold; a time when bands of Nordic warriors were able to subjugate renowned kings in foreign lands through incredible feats of ingenuity and brutal violence. It was the time in which the legendary Danish King Cnut—the mightiest Nordic king ever to have lived—took control of large and rich England, and came to rule over an enormous kingdom that spanned both mountains and seas. It was also the time in which the roving Viking Olaf Haraldsson conquered Norway, with the help of English noblemen and chests full of plundered silver. When he was finally killed, Olaf was made a Christian saint, and in Snorri's time he was celebrated as the reigning royal dynasty's holy forefather.

These were feats that would have been impossible in Snorri's time, and which therefore seemed almost infinitely impressive. It is not so strange, then, that even in Snorri's day the Viking Age seemed like a foreign and distant past, exotic and magnified—a time populated by singular heroes who were nobler, braver and wilder than any of those who came after them. Many people believed that their ancestors had quite literally been giants—bigger, taller and more powerful than the people who came later. At the end of the 1100s, a Norwegian monk wrote that the distinguished warriors of old "were brave and strong, much more robust in body and mind than men in our miserable times, though far inferior to their own predecessors […] We can almost see the whole human race generally diminishing day by day, and there are few men who are taller than their fathers." These mythical and exaggerated qualities have clung to depictions of the Viking Age throughout history, enduring all the way up to our present time.

Today, Snorri is remembered as the greatest of all the ancient saga writers, and no other individual has had a greater influence on future generations' notions about the ancient Scandinavian past. This is because Snorri, like all literary masters throughout history, was able to capture something fundamental and universal in his narratives. None of Snorri's contemporaries described the logic of violence and power with such precision as Snorri did. He understood how the powerful operated, because he himself was one of them. His practical experience enabled him to convey the human in the political and the political in the human like no one else. While the kings' sagas were stories about the past, they were just as much studies in and practical handbooks on the timeless art of power. Snorri was concerned with the use of power on a practical level—with the unwritten rules of the game, with what worked and what didn't work. With great victories and grave errors.

For this reason, it is hard not to see the irony in how Snorri met his own end. When he returned to Reykholt, the farm was almost deserted; with the exception of a few servants and one or two priests, Snorri was alone on the great farm during the last few days of his life. Despite the threatening letter he had received a few days earlier, nothing indicates that he expected something was afoot: he instructed no guards to keep a lookout at the wall; no one barred the gates in the evenings.

Snorri was unaware that his enemies had gathered in secret, and that they were now hiding in the Uplands. He was unaware that their spies were keeping the farm and residents of the valley under close observation.

On the evening of Sunday, 23rd September 1241—which just happened to be the feast day of Saint Maurice, patron saint of swordsmiths and soldiers—a group of 400 men rode into the valley further north and blocked the road, in case Snorri's people should come to his aid.

The following night, another group of seventy armed men set out for Reykholt under cover of darkness. Unnoticed, they led their horses all the way up to the farm walls, where they dismounted and walked unhindered through the open gates. Many of them knew the farm and its various buildings well—they had been there before, as Snorri's guests. The intruders walked purposefully to the main house, where Snorri slept in a bedchamber on the first floor. They tried the door. It was locked from the inside.

Snorri must have been woken by the noises outside. Considering his age, he was able to move remarkably quickly, because in the brief period of time it took the intruders to break down the door he managed to make his way out of his bedchamber, down a flight of stairs and out of the building through another exit. He was likely naked or in his nightgown.

As the intruders searched the farm's buildings and fear and confusion spread among his servants, the fat old man crept into one of the smaller adjacent houses, unseen. Inside, he bumped into one of the farm's other residents, one of the priests who served him in the farm's church. They whispered to one another in the pitch-darkness.

Just a few metres away, on the other side of the wall, a spiral staircase wound its way down to an underground passage that led under the wall and out to freedom. Snorri had requested its construction so that he could walk dry-shod and sheltered from the unceasing wind to the warm baths outside the walls. But he didn't use the passage now—an old man on the run without warm clothes would not last long out in the freezing Icelandic autumn night. Instead, he crept down into a narrow cellar that was used as a storeroom and hid there.

This is where he was when the intruders found the priest. From his hiding place, Snorri would probably have been able to hear the conversation going on just above his head, as his loyal priest tried—in vain—to save him. The intruders' leader was summoned. When he asked the priest where Snorri was hiding, the priest said that he hadn't seen Snorri anywhere. The intruders did not believe him, and so he tried to negotiate. He would tell them where his lord was, he said, but only if they swore that they would spare Snorri's life.

We are not told how the priest revealed Snorri's hiding place, only that he did so. Perhaps he inadvertently cast a glance in the direction of the entrance to the cellar; maybe he succumbed to fear of his own death and pointed to it. Perhaps he told the men where Snorri was because they lied to him, promising to let Snorri live. The intruders found the entrance regardless, and five men descended into the dark.

Later, those who had been at Reykholt that night—both the murderers and Snorri's servants—gave their accounts of what had happened, and their stories found their way into the saga written by Snorri's nephew. As was the custom of the Icelandic saga writers, Snorri's nephew recounted what he knew of his uncle's last night in great detail, soberly, without condemnation and without comment.

When the first of the men walked towards Snorri with his sword drawn, Snorri said: 'Thou shalt not strike!' This was the Fifth Commandment, *Thou shalt not kill*, as formulated by the Icelandic priests of Snorri's time. 'Strike him!' said one of the men. 'Thou shalt not strike!' repeated Snorri. The first man cut him with his sword; another came forward and cut him again. It was the first blow, they said later, that caused his mortal wound. And so he died, by the sword, as so many had done in his sagas.

þan þær reſ hwadaðæg þharaoneſ ʒebynoðıo· þaþ
æ beoꝛıcıpe hıſ cnıhtum· ʒemanʒþam daʒeþohte
la ealdoꝛ· Ɂþæ nabæcerʒıa· Ɂheʒeꝛecce þæꝛ þa byþl
ere note þehe æþhæꝛoe þone oþeꝛ ne hehet hon· onꝛ
ıoꝛeþeꝛ ꝛoþfæꝛt nyſ aꝛuno00 Ɂþeah hwæþeꝛe þ
on foꝛʒeat ıoꝛeþeꝛ æꝛ ende·

ꝛ þam ʒꝛaþum þharao mætte þæ þheſ tooe bean
ꝛ þæ þheʒe ꝛaþe ʒán up oꝛ þam flooe ꝛeoꝛon fæꝛ
e· Ɂþımán læꝛ uoe on moꝛıʒum lanoe· hım þuht
ꝛaþe cuman oþþe ꝛeoꝛon oxan up oꝛ þæꝛe ta· þaþ
e hlæne· Ɂhı todon be þæ ꝛe ta oꝛ þun onꝛʒꝛenum
þaꝛætte oxan ʒꝛ þæ ton hı· Ða apoc ꝛuꝛao
mætte oþeꝛ ꝛþeꝛn· Hım þuhte þæ heʒe ꝛaþ
ꝛ eaxan on ánum healme fulle· Ɂfæʒene· Ɂh
ꝛeoꝛan lyþꝛe Ɂfoꝛ ꝛꝛunc ene· Ða ꝛ þæ ton ta
Ða apoc þharao ꝛꝛ oꝛ ame:

A REGIME FACING RUIN

IN THE YEAR 975, a comet came into view above Anglo-Saxon England. It appeared on one of the first days of August, when the summer was at its hottest and farming peasants were at their most hungry, busy reaping and grinding the first corn. High up in the firmament, they saw a hazy but intense ball of light with flames radiating from it on one side, "like golden hair on a human head". It fell slowly sideways, towards the north-east.

Among those who observed this strange phenomenon with both interest and unease were the learned Benedictine monks who wrote the annals that would eventually be collected and compiled and known as the *Anglo-Saxon Chronicle*. It is this work we have to thank for much of our knowledge of England during what, for us, is a very distant age. In a society where almost nothing was written down, these humble servants of God with their cowls and shaved heads kept tabs on the course of history outside monastery walls. In the form of brief notes and comments, they recorded information about kings' travels through the kingdom, about bishops' Church meetings, about nobles' endless petty feuds—and about unusual natural phenomena.

A comet was a disconcerting sight—an ancient and well-known evil omen. For the monks, a comet was God's messenger, a warning of impending catastrophe. The God who was worshipped in

Western Europe at this time was an unpredictable deity, good and warm one moment, wrathful the next—an almighty judge and strict father who demanded absolute obedience, and who often punished his weak and sinful children. The Lord made his will known through the Northern Lights, solar eclipses and comets— anomalies in the perfect and orderly world system he had created and set in motion at the dawn of time, in which the stars followed their repetitive and predictable orbits and where daybreak followed daybreak, winter followed winter. The monks were always careful to document such events, because together they constituted a network of signs which might, if studied together, reveal God's plans for humankind.

A nervous, uneasy atmosphere was already pervasive in Anglo-Saxon England. Just two weeks previously, the realm had lost its king. King Edgar, who would be remembered as Edgar the Peaceful, died in the summer of 975, having governed his kingdom for sixteen years. These years—as Edgar's popular name suggests—had been good ones, a long and unbroken period of peace that later generations would look back on as a flourishing golden age.

Whether the king died suddenly or slowly, due to illness or by other means, is not known. But a king's death was always a dramatic event in any European kingdom at this time, quite simply because there were really no set procedures dictating exactly how sovereignty should be transferred to the next generation. It was not a given that the king's eldest son would inherit the throne, and the matter was often subject to complicated negotiations between political factions.

Anglo-Saxon England was fragile. The royal dynasty was ancient and distinguished, stretching back many hundreds of years, and its mythological origins incorporated Odin, various figures from the Old Testament and Jesus Christ himself. But its power over a united English kingdom went back only a few generations. The right to the throne rested with a council—the so-called *witan*, or "council of the wise men"—which was dominated by a handful of ealdormen, the heads of the most prominent noble families in the land. These were tremendously rich and obstinate men, some of them the descendants of rival royal families who had been forced to submit to the throne just a few generations earlier, and the leaders of large and extremely powerful groups dotted around the English countryside. Many of them were rivals, openly feuding with each other.

An especially problematic and potentially dangerous situation arose if the heir to the throne was a child. Edgar the Peaceful left behind no adult heirs, but he did have two boys, the elder around twelve years old, the younger eight or nine. The two boys were born to different mothers, high-born women with their own familial networks and connections all across the large, densely populated country. The dead king's court divided into two factions, each supporting their kin and heir.

For a time, open war seemed about to break out, but the ealdormen and Church leaders finally managed to come together around the elder of the king's sons. His name was Edward. As the crown was set atop his head before nobles and churchmen, the comet moved slowly and soundlessly across the sky above them. It remained visible for many weeks. In mid-November, around eighty days after it was first sighted, it finally faded and disappeared.

Agonizing conflicts made their mark on the new king's reign from day one. The high lords of the council built up their own private bases of power; a huge number of items from churches and monasteries across England were confiscated in the king's name. King Edward himself was reputed to be quick-tempered, moody and unstable. Too immature to bear his power and status with dignity, the boy king repeatedly exploded in scandalous public outbursts of rage, and humiliated and beat servants of both high and low birth within the royal household.

In the spring of 978, just three years after he was crowned king, Edward's rule came to an abrupt end. Now around fifteen years old, the king led a hunt through the expansive wooded hills that ran along the coast of Wessex. Afterwards, accompanied by a small party of men, Edward set out to visit his younger half-brother, who lived with his mother and his own household on a nearby royal estate in the small village of Corfe. When the hot-blooded young king rode into the courtyard, he quickly got into a scuffle with a group of thanes—high-ranking Anglo-Saxon men who were lower in status than the ealdormen—from his little brother's household. In what was probably a spontaneous quarrel that got out of hand, the thanes surrounded the king's horse on foot. They grabbed the king by the arms and dragged him from his saddle as he howled and screamed, then stabbed him to death with their knives.

One month later, just after Easter in the year 978, a group of ealdormen, thanes, representatives from the peasants and townspeople, and the kingdom's ten bishops and two archbishops gathered for the crowning of a new king in the small market and church town of Kingston, a short distance south-west of London. A contemporary observer noted that the new king, who was twelve or thirteen years old, was handsome, and conducted himself with great dignity when the crown was set on his head. His name was Æthelred.

His brother had left him a kingdom that extended from Wales in the west to the North Sea in the east, from the English Channel in the south to the River Tweed and the land of the Scots in the north, and which was home to around a million subjects. He ruled over a machinery of power that consisted of royal judges and administrators centred around the country's cities—the envy of other kings all across Europe.

The *Anglo-Saxon Chronicle* states that yet another evil omen appeared at the time of Æthelred's coronation. In many places in England a bloody cloud was seen at night, "oftentimes, in the likeness of fire; and it was mostly apparent at midnight, and so in various beams was coloured: when it began to dawn, then it glided away".

One year later, on a summer's day in 979, seven Viking ships were seen off Wessex. They slipped silently along the coast before they put ashore in a bay in Dorset, not far from the royal family's hunting grounds. The *Anglo-Saxon Chronicle* briefly states that they killed many people, and took others with them as prisoners when they returned to their ships and sailed away. This was the first Viking attack to be recorded in the *Chronicle* for several decades.

The next year, 980, they returned. Southampton and the Isle of Thanet at the mouth of the Thames were attacked; the Vikings pillaged valuables and food, and took people as captives.

More attacks followed. Over the next few years, the *Anglo-Saxon Chronicle* gives descriptions of Viking raids along the coasts, some small, others larger. Æthelred grew up and took control of his kingdom in the shadow of this slowly growing wave of violence. In 985, when he was eighteen or nineteen years old, he took the young daughter of a Northern English nobleman as his queen; over the following years she gave him several children. By this point, the Viking attacks had become an annual occurrence in the kingdom. Small groups of peasants under local leaders fought against the foreigners.

The attacks in themselves did little damage to Æthelred's kingdom—the Viking fleets consisted of just a few hundred men—but they spread great fear and unease among his subjects. This was due not only to the immediate threat the Vikings posed to the people who lived along the coasts, but also to the fact that the attacks played out against an unpleasant historical backdrop—one that was imprinted on the Anglo-Saxons' self-image and identity. The kingdom in which they lived had been forged in a battle against the Vikings.

Two hundred years had passed since the first gangs of Scandinavian robbers crossed the sea and began to ransack out-of-the-way monasteries towards the end of the 700s. They came from many different places in Scandinavia and the surrounding areas, but the Anglo-Saxons referred to them under the collective term "Danes". Encouraged by their own success, the Danes returned in the first decades of the 800s in ever-larger, braver and better-organized groups, causing ever-greater devastation and suffering.

At this time, there was no united Anglo-Saxon kingdom—what would eventually become England consisted of a number of smaller rival kingdoms with no common defences against the Danes. Paralysed by the Viking warriors' mobility and resoluteness—and their own lack of collaboration—the kingdoms were overrun, one by one, as their horrified inhabitants saw armies driven away and massacred, monasteries burnt, gold and silver stolen, valuable illuminated manuscripts destroyed and young men and women carried off as slaves. The Danes built permanent bases for their ships on the islands just off the English coast, and in the mid-800s they began to overwinter in large camps on the mainland. What had begun as single opportunistic attacks developed into the systematic looting of large areas—and eventually into conquest and colonization.

The Danish armies brought women and children with them. In what is best characterized as a migration, tens of thousands of Norse settlers established themselves on the north-east coast of

England, in the area that would become known as Danelaw—"the area in which Dane law holds sway". The new arrivals mixed with the local population; since the Anglo-Saxon and Norse languages were similar, they were to some extent mutually comprehensible. Many of the Danes became Christians, and quickly adopted local customs while simultaneously continuing a number of their old traditions. The city of York, which like many other cities in England had originally been a Roman settlement, became the centre of power in this new English Viking kingdom.

In the end, only one of the old kingdoms remained—that of the West Saxons, Wessex, where the celebrated Alfred the Great was king. Alfred was King Æthelred's great-great-grandfather. Towards the end of the 800s, he led first a desperate defence and then a successful counter-attack against the Danes, which changed the course of the war. Under the leadership of Alfred and his West Saxon warlords, the Anglo-Saxon armies reconquered the lost city of London and forced the Danes to retreat.

After Alfred's death, his sons and grandsons continued his fight, and in the early 900s the West Saxon kings became conquerors. They expanded Wessex's borders to the north and east, wresting control of the lands of their old Anglo-Saxon rivals from the Danes—and eventually conquered the Danelaw, too. In the 950s, under West Saxon leadership, the Anglo-Saxon armies fought the last remaining Norse king of the Danelaw, whose seat was in York.

This was how the English kingdom inherited by Æthelred was born. His forefathers had not permitted the areas captured by the Danes to re-emerge as independent kingdoms, but instead forced them to submit to West Saxon supremacy. Influenced and inspired by the royal ideology of Charlemagne, and by memories of the long-lost Roman Empire—whose ruins were still visible all across the English landscape—the West Saxon kings attempted to build an English empire. Over the course of just a few generations, a corps of bright and talented administrators in their service developed one of the most advanced systems of royal power in Europe in order to govern these new areas.

The kingdom was divided into shires—administrative units centred around cities where judges enforced common laws in the name of the king, and the king's officials attempted to regulate trade on the markets. Learned clergymen, who were effective organizers, established a common Church organization that linked various areas of the country together across local identities; faith in God was the unifying ideology that held the entire construction together. It was at this time that Anglo-Saxon scholars began to refer to the kingdom using the name it still bears today, *Engla lond*—Land of the Angles.

Keen to be seen as liberators rather than conquerors, the Wessex dynasty encouraged its new subjects to forget their former conflicts and instead focus on the common battle that united them—they were a God-fearing civilization, forged in the fight against idolatrous foreign barbarians. And of course, nothing has a more uniting effect than a mutual external enemy.

It isn't hard to explain what attracted the new wave of attacks that made their mark on Æthelred's first year of rule. His forefathers' victories over the Danes and the unification of the English kingdom were followed by a period of economic development which, in the context of Europe in the 900s, was almost inconceivable. England had the most thriving wool production in Europe, and in the latter part of the century an ever-increasing demand for wool products on the continent turned many Anglo-Saxon farmers into merchants. Grazing sheep could be seen all across the kingdom's green landscapes—there were probably more sheep in England than there were people. On farms and in small villages from north to south, wool was tied up into large bundles, bound to packhorses and mules and transported in convoys to the ports on the south coast, where merchants arranged fleets of ships that ferried balls of wool, woollen clothing, finely woven fabrics and embroidery across the sea to the Netherlands. And in the opposite direction, huge volumes of silver flowed into England.[1]

In the cities, the Wessex kings developed a system of royal mints which for its time was extremely sophisticated—the most advanced in Western Europe. Under the leadership of mint masters with a royal licence, the mint workers hammered the silver into small, thin coins, matte in colour and smooth to the touch, and featuring Christ on one side and the reigning king on the other. Æthelred's kingdom had more than seventy mints, most of them situated close to the city markets and kept under constant observation behind walls and palisades. The Crown enforced strict punishments for counterfeiting. By law, any mint master who produced coins that were too light would have a hand cut off and nailed to the workshop's gate, to serve as a warning and deterrent.

Every few years, all the coins across the kingdom would be declared invalid as a form of payment on the Crown-regulated city markets. In order to be able to buy goods at the market, people would have to exchange any coins they owned at one of the mints, where the currency would be melted down and minted again using new, valid dies. For every ten coins that a person handed in, they would receive eight or nine in return. The rest were collected by the master of the mint, who in turn forwarded them on to the Crown as a form of tax. Maintaining control of the country's silver was the cornerstone of the Wessex kings' power.

Between five and ten million coins were produced at each re-minting, and the Anglo-Saxon kingdom became a society in which millions upon millions of tiny silver coins and bullions[2] were in circulation. There was probably more silver in England than in any other country in Western Europe.

Æthelred was young and inexperienced, and in all likelihood Europe's richest monarch. It was a dangerous combination.

Vikings with bases in Ireland, Scotland, the Isle of Man and Normandy were probably behind the sporadic attacks that occurred at the start of Æthelred's reign. But then, in the summer of 991, a new fleet of warships came to England's coast—one that was fundamentally different from its predecessors. It was the biggest Viking fleet to be seen off England since the days of Alfred. People who saw it from land counted more than ninety large warships, in addition to smaller accompanying vessels. This fleet had not come from a nest of bandits on the periphery of the English kingdom, but directly from Scandinavia.

The ships sailed along the east coast as a group. Then, to the terror of the local population, they put ashore, and an army of several thousand men disembarked. As the local people fled before them, the Danish warriors plundered the village of Folkestone, setting its buildings ablaze. They then sailed on to the small ports of Sandwich and Ipswich, where they did the same.

Æthelred, now a grown man in his mid-twenties, dispatched an army to defend the coast under the leadership of one of the most prominent men in his regime, an ageing, white-haired ealdorman from Wessex by the name of Byrhtnoth. When the Danish fleet arrived in Essex at the start of August, Byrhtnoth and his army followed it along the coast. And when the Danish warriors came ashore just outside the village of Maldon, Byrhtnoth lined up his army on a plain on the other side of the beach. The battle that followed was immortalized in a poem composed by an unknown poet a few years later which remains one of the age's most important works of Anglo-Saxon heroic poetry:

Then Byrhtnoth marshalled his soldiers,
riding and instructing, directing his warriors
how they should stand and the positions they should keep,
and ordering that their shields properly stand firm
with steady hands and be not afraid.
Then when he beheld that people in suitable array,
he dismounted amid his people, where he was most
     pleased to be,
there amid his retainers knowing their devotion.

Then stood on the shore, stoutly calling out
a Viking messenger, making speech,
menacingly delivering the sea-pirate's
message to this Earl on the opposite shore standing:
'I send to you from the bold seamen,
a command to tell that you must quickly send
treasures to us, and it would be better to you if
with tribute buy off this conflict of spears
than with us bitter battle share.
[…] pay the seafarers on their own terms
money towards peace and receive peace from us,
for we with this tribute will take to our ships,
depart on the sea and keep peace with you.'

Rather than pay the proposed tribute, however, Byrhtnoth chose to fight the superior force—he consequently paid with his life, and the lives of his men. Along with his personal bodyguards and large parts of the army he led, he fought to the death.

Æthelred called a meeting of his *witan*. "It was decreed that tribute, for the first time, should be given to the Danish-men, on account of the great terror which they caused by the sea-coast," states the *Anglo-Saxon Chronicle*. On Æthelred's orders, the men in his service quickly gathered together the enormous sum of 10,000 pounds of minted silver coins and unminted silver bullion—around 3.5 tonnes of silver in total, which must have been transported to the coast in chests using wagons. The chests' contents were likely inspected and weighed in the presence of the Danish leaders, before they were carried aboard the ships and taken away.

And so began that which has been termed England's second Viking Age. Because the Danes would soon return.

*

During the decades in which the Wessex kings tightened their grasp on England through political power reforms and the control of silver, there had also been significant events on the other side of the North Sea. At some point in the 940s—a time in which Scandinavia's modern inhabitants can only glimpse historical figures and the lives they led through the foggy landscapes of myths and legends—a Viking king known as Gorm the Old died in North Jutland, in the north of Denmark. He was buried by his son in a pagan burial mound in Jelling, where his family had its power base. This son was Harald Bluetooth—the man who today is regarded as the founder of the Danish kingdom. He is thought to have been given his characteristic nickname because he revealed a rotten tooth when he smiled.

Harald Bluetooth inherited his father's interests intact, and spent his life expanding them. He rejected his forefathers' ancient faith; he and members of his family were baptized, and he appointed bishops and built churches on the Danish islands. On his orders, his parents were exhumed from the mound in which they had been buried; Harald had them laid to rest in new graves through a Christian ceremony held in a newly constructed church in Jelling, and thereby stepped into the Christian community of European kings. He fought with great armies against the aggressive German Emperor Otto I, and succeeded in stopping the emperor from expanding his territory northwards. With a secured southern border, he built a kingdom of a kind and scope never before seen in Scandinavia.

Harald Bluetooth expanded his realm by waging continuous war. In the 970s and 980s he subjugated Norse kings, jarls and prominent men in the north, east and west with his ever-growing army, war expeditions and threats of fire and destruction, thereby creating a kingdom of an extent unprecedented in this part of the world. Towards the end of his life, his dominion extended across the Danish islands and along the shores of the Baltic as well as the southern, western and northern coasts of the Scandinavian Peninsula.[3]

The most tangible testimonies to his power are the archaeological traces of a monumental construction programme of military roads, timber bridges and fortifications on the Danish islands. At his command, across a marshy area in Jelling, slaves built an almost 800-metre-long and more than five-metre-wide flat bridge on a foundation of posts, which they erected using advanced surveying techniques. The bridge consisted of more than 4,000 oak trees, and was probably part of a larger road network intended for moving soldiers.

Four large ring castles—Fyrkat and Aggersborg on Jutland, Nonnebakken on Funen and Trelleborg on Zealand—were constructed simultaneously in the early 980s with staggering geometrical perfection.[4] Huge turf walls and timber from thousands of trees were arranged in perfect circles behind deep moats, all with four gates and four large, equally sized quarters of boat-shaped longhouses behind the walls, some of them probably soldiers' barracks. Another ring-shaped castle also known as Trelleborg was situated at the southern tip of Scania, in modern Sweden, and was part of the same system. There may well have been more.

The largest castle, Aggersborg, was 240 metres in diameter and contained forty-eight buildings. The exact purpose and function of the ring castles has been much discussed, but these military bases show that the people in Harald Bluetooth's service had advanced engineering skills, along with the ability to plan, organize and co-ordinate large military construction projects that are impressive even when viewed in a European context.

One would think that anyone who had fought, suffered and risked their life to build this kingdom would be happy to lead a calm and peaceful existence once the conquest was complete; to reap the benefits of what they had sown. But this was not how the logic of expansion worked. Harald Bluetooth's enormous kingdom must not be mistaken for anything resembling a modern state. The realm was a network of personal alliances and oaths of allegiance arranged in a hierarchy with the Danish king at the top, and which was established through the extensive use of mercenaries. Warriors from near and far had flocked to Harald Bluetooth's banners to participate in his raids and conquests. And while peace may have settled over the kingdom when Harald, at an advanced age, laid down his sword and concentrated on building and consolidating his power, among those for whom war was their livelihood the discontentment increased.

In 987 a faction of the king's men staged a rebellion, and old Harald Bluetooth was struck by an arrow during a skirmish. Seriously injured, he fled south to his old Slavic allies from the war against the German emperor, and it was in one of their villages or forts that he died on 1st November 987. He was not the first successful ruler of the Viking Age to become caught up in a vicious cycle of expansion, raiding and war, only to fall victim to the very forces he had used to build his kingdom. Nor would he be the last.

The leader of the rebellion was none other than the king's own son, whose name was Sweyn. He was said to have cut his moustache so that it hung down on either side of his mouth, like the pointed tines of a two-pronged pitchfork, and therefore became known as Sweyn *Tjugeskjegg* or *Toskjegg*—"Sweyn Forkbeard". After a period of chaos, he succeeded in driving out his enemies and rivals and established himself as his father's successor as king and leader of the Danes.

Rather than repeating his father's mistake of resting on his laurels, Sweyn was quick to resume the type of leadership that had made his father so prosperous—waging constant war to satisfy his warriors' hunger for pillaging and plunder. He set his sights west, across the North Sea.

When the great Danish fleet arrived in England in the summer of 991 and crushed the Anglo-Saxon army at the Battle of Maldon, five years had passed since Harald Bluetooth's death. And the next summer, the fleet returned. Æthelred, now around twenty-five years old, gathered all his warships in the Thames to meet his enemy, even though his fleet was far inferior to that of the Danes. The Danish warlords avoided direct confrontation, but raided and looted areas all along the English coast before returning to Denmark.

The fleet came back the following summer, too, in 993, sailing up and down the east coast. Æthelred gathered together an army from among the peasants in the area, which followed the Danish fleet along the shore on foot. But when the Danes landed their army the Anglo-Saxon leaders fled, with the result that the army of peasants disbanded. The Dane warriors ravaged the coast unchallenged before returning to their homeland.

The Danish king was renowned all across England, and deeply feared and hated for his belligerent politics. "With him were always associated his three companions—plunder, burning and killing," wrote an English chronicler. The contemporaneous German bishop Thietmar of Merseburg summarized Sweyn's reputation in Europe as follows: "I have often heard that the Angles […] endured unspeakable suffering at the hands of Sven, the son of Harald, […] this filthy dog, not a ruler, but a destroyer." Sweyn's warriors, always on the hunt for silver, were described by the bishop as a flock of ravenous magpies.

While Sweyn Forkbeard was a major driving force behind England's second Viking Age, he did not cause it alone. Several warlords from Harald Bluetooth's kingdom, all with significant resources, decided to collaborate and joined forces. A central commander in the ever-returning Danish fleet was Olaf Tryggvason, who in the later Norwegian and Icelandic narrative tradition would become the fabled king of Christianization. The Anglo-Saxons knew him as "Anlaf". He is an obscure historical figure, transformed into the stuff of fairy tales after his death, but said to have been the son of a petty king from Eastern Norway who grew up under Harald Bluetooth's hegemony. According to preserved skaldic poems, he made his career as a Viking raider in Eastern Europe before joining Sweyn's wars of plunder in England. He was probably regarded as Sweyn's equal and partner, rather than his subordinate.

Sweyn and Olaf were both aboard the Danish fleet, now consisting of ninety-four ships, when it returned to England for a fourth consecutive year in the summer of 994. Having raided and burned villages along the coast, the Danes shocked the Anglo-Saxons by sailing up the Thames and stopping just before they reached London—the biggest, richest and best-defended city in all of Æthelred's kingdom. The city was besieged for an extended period before the Danish fleet gave up and sailed on to other, easier targets along the coast.

In the rapidly escalating crisis, Æthelred and his advisors made use of a proven old tactic from the days of Æthelred's forefather, Alfred. They attempted to split the Danish leaders, to get them to turn on each other by appealing to and using against them their foremost motivation and driving force—greed.

Independently of Sweyn Forkbeard, Æthelred negotiated with Olaf Tryggvason using bishops as middlemen, and made the Viking king an offer that was simply too good to refuse. After concluding the siege of London, Olaf Tryggvason left his army and ships at a camp on the coast and, surrounded only by his innermost circle of men, rode into the country he had so zealously raided.

In the little town of Andover in north Hampshire, Æthelred and his people awaited Olaf's arrival. There, through a formal ceremony, they entered into a pact. Olaf promised to leave England and never to return with hostile intentions; in exchange, he was given what must have been a significant share of the 16,000 pounds of silver—more than 5.5 tonnes—that Æthelred paid to Viking leaders that year.

Like Sweyn and many other Norse leaders at this time, Olaf Tryggvason was Christian, having been baptized in his homeland or in Denmark. Still, the pact with Æthelred was concluded with both Olaf and his closest men being re-baptized in one of Andover's churches with the Archbishop of Canterbury leading the ceremony, which probably took the form of a so-called "confirmation baptism". Æthelred stood as Olaf's godfather, which made the occasion into something approaching a feudal vassal ceremony or "commendation ceremony", through which Olaf became Æthelred's man.

The Viking king accepted Anglo-Saxon priests into his retinue; some historians have also pondered whether Æthelred might have provided him with ships, crew members and weapons. Now filthy rich and mortally dangerous, Olaf led his fleet east across the sea to challenge Sweyn's dominion over Scandinavia.

The power struggle between Sweyn and Olaf on the other side of the sea gave England a few years' respite from the attacks. But three years later, in 997, another large Danish fleet came to England, led either by Sweyn himself or by one of his deputies. This army ravaged the coasts of Devon, Cornwall and Wales for the entire summer. Then, instead of sailing east again when the autumn arrived, the Danes built a fortified camp on an island off the mainland. The ships were moored here while the army overwintered.

When the spring of 998 arrived, the army continued to terrorize the mainland. With their fast ships, the Danes attacked again and again at unexpected locations along the coast. They plundered villages before burning them to the ground; by the time Æthelred's soldiers arrived on the scene the Danes had always already withdrawn, taking captives, goods and supplies with them. They would then rest and make plans before attacking again elsewhere.

The Danes remained at the camp for the next winter, too. They executed a number of attacks in the summer of 999, before they finally decided to leave and sailed away.

Sweyn's armies were led by highly specialized and goal-oriented men, who knew exactly what they wanted and how they were going to get it. They acted in accordance with the age-old logic of pre-modern warfare, as practised by ancient kings and Roman emperors before them: they gave their enemies a simple ultimatum. The Anglo-Saxons could submit, giving the Danes what they wanted, and they would be treated well. Or they could fight, and risk the consequences of a defeat. These consequences might involve losing everything—estates, towns, property, provisions, livestock and churches, the lives of one's family members, or ultimately one's own life. Æthelred was a strong king, but he was unable to prevent local leaders and the heads of villages from striking deals with and paying tribute to the Danes without his permission in order to save their properties and their lives. His authority within his own realm was therefore slowly undermined.

Just as Æthelred had extended an olive branch to Olaf Tryggvason, Sweyn Forkbeard attempted to lure prominent men in England over on to his side, particularly in the eastern and northern parts of the kingdom, where many people were of Norse descent. The Anglo-Saxon sources tell of powerful English noblemen having illegal contact with the Danes. One such man, known as Æthelric, from Bocking in Essex, just north of London, was for example found to have been planning to "receive Sweyn", and consequently punished.

There is also much that indicates the Danes more or less took control of the Anglo-Saxon wool trade with the continent. Norse seamen had long played a dominant role in almost all trade by sea in Northern Europe, but during the 990s the warlords who worked for Sweyn Forkbeard, whether directly or indirectly, achieved practically complete dominance over the seas around England—it became impossible for Anglo-Saxon and Frankish merchants to do business without collaborating with them. The Danes either demanded protection money from the travelling merchants, or simply took over the trading activities themselves, transporting the wool products across the Channel in their own ships and then selling them on.

The constantly returning war fleets reflect an enormous expenditure of resources within Sweyn Forkbeard's realm in terms of time and labour, wood and iron; in terms of the sheep's wool and linen used to make the ships' sails; in terms of materials for rigging, ropes and tar; in terms of the production of weapons.

But it paid off, because Sweyn and the thousands of warriors attached to his growing war machine were rewarded thrice over for their efforts. First by taking control of the seaborne trade that brought silver into the Anglo-Saxon kingdom. Then through the raiding of Æthelred's subjects for food and plunder. And lastly by demanding great sums in tribute from King Æthelred to ensure their departure.

As Europe entered a new millennium, ever-larger Danish armies continued to return to England. Æthelred forged ties with a prominent Norse warlord by the name of Pallig, who was likely married to one of Sweyn Forkbeard's sisters. But "regardless of the extreme generosity of the [English] king in giving him manors, gold, and silver", Pallig participated in a large military expedition for Sweyn in 1001, when the Danish fleet burned and ravaged villages in Sussex, Dorset, Somerset and Devon. Reading the *Anglo-Saxon Chronicle* and other English accounts that describe the events of this period, one can't help but notice how these texts begin to take on an ever-darker, more pessimistic tone. They sombrely depict a kingdom in decline and chaos; one that is transformed into a maelstrom of burning villages and fleeing peasants over and over again.

This dark mood is also reflected in religious texts of the period. In the destructive Danes, Anglo-Saxon monks and churchmen saw God's punishment—even if Sweyn Forkbeard himself and many of his people were Christians. Around the turn of the millennium, the comet that had appeared above England in 975 seemed to be a watershed moment: the turning point at which the country's peaceful glory days slipped into darkness and chaos, and God showed his wrath at the Anglo-Saxons' sinful ways and insufficient piety. After the comet appeared, "the vengeance of the Lord was widely evident", a monk wrote in an annal.

A number of clergymen even saw the chaos around them as a warning that the end time was near—the notion of an impending Armageddon was widespread among the pious and learned around the turn of the millennium. Although nobody knew when the end days would come, those who served God believed that all creation was approaching the end of its existence, because just as God had created the world in seven days, world history was also divided into seven ages. The Church's scholars had calculated that they were living in the sixth age, and that the seventh was Armageddon, "the great world fire". The ancient prophecies of the Bible stated that the end time would begin with a series of catastrophes.

In one of the first years that followed the dawn of the new millennium, the most senior figure in the Anglo-Saxon Church, Archbishop Wulfstan of York, wrote an unparalleled fire-and-brimstone sermon in which he stated that:

> It is written and was long ago prophesied, "after a thousand years will Satan be unbound". A thousand years and more is now gone since Christ was among men in a human family, and Satan's bonds are now indeed slipped, and Antichrist's time is now close at hand [...] And people will contend and dispute among themselves. There will also break out far and wide dispute and damage, envy and enmity and rapine of robbers, hostility and hunger, burning and bloodshed and distressing disturbances, disease and death, and many misfortunes.

King Æthelred was now in his late thirties, and war and violence had overshadowed every aspect of his reign. Under increasing pressure, he attempted to enter into an alliance with the Duke of Normandy in order to prevent the Danes from receiving his help and support. In 1002 Æthelred's English-born queen died, possibly during childbirth, and so he asked for the hand of the Duke of Normandy's sister, Emma. She was very young, but was transported across the Channel to war-torn England. She fell pregnant almost immediately.

At the same time, Æthelred countered the terror and violence to which his people were being subjected with his own brutality, thereby adding momentum to the spiral of violence devastating the country. The increasing pressure he was under was obviously turning him into a somewhat paranoid ruler. As previously mentioned, his kingdom contained thousands of people of Norse origin, descendants of the great wave of immigration from the east that had begun almost two centuries earlier. They had lived mostly in peace in England for generations, even if the social and cultural bonds that linked them to the countries from which their ancestors hailed were strong. In the war-ravaged Anglo-Saxon kingdom at the start of the 1000s, these people's Norse roots gave rise to mistrust and suspicion. In the autumn of 1002 Æthelred heard rumours of a conspiracy against him among his "Danish" subjects, and became convinced that one of them was plotting to kill him. On 13th November 1002, therefore, he ordered that "all the Danish men who were in England" should be killed.

The massacres have left behind both written and archaeological traces that bear witness to ethnic cleansing. An Anglo-Saxon letter from 1004, only two years after the killings, tells of a group of Danes who were chased by an angry mob in the city of Oxford. In an attempt to save their lives, they sought refuge in one of the city's churches. But the mob set the church ablaze, and burned the Danes and the church's valuable books and adornments along with the building itself, says the letter writer, before explaining why: "Danes [have] sprung up in this island, sprouting like cockle among wheat, [and so they] were to be destroyed by a most just extermination." Around ninety years later, the English chronicler

Henry of Huntingdon wrote: "In my childhood I heard very old men say that the king had sent secret letters to every city, according to which the English either maimed all the unsuspecting Danes on the same day and hour with their swords, or, suddenly, at the same moment, captured them and destroyed them by fire."

In recent years, mass graves have been discovered in England that are thought to stem from this period of ethnic cleansing. The bodies of thirty-five men, most of them in their twenties and thirties, had been thrown into a pit in Oxford after being executed by blows to the head or neck. Their injuries indicate that the men were killed from behind, while on their knees. Some of the corpses appear to have been burned before being thrown into the mass grave.

In Dorset in Wessex another grave has been discovered, containing the bodies of fifty-four men of Scandinavian origin, all executed by beheading, apparently from the front.

These purges probably targeted men of Scandinavian descent of fighting age who lived in England. But over the years, recollections of what had happened mushroomed into a cloud of ghastly exaggerations. In the 1060s, the Norman monk and chronicler William of Jumièges wrote that Æthelred took England's chastity through a vile series of offences that shocked even the heathens:

For in a single day he had murdered, in a sudden fury and without charging them with any crime, the Danes who lived peacefully and quite harmoniously throughout the kingdom and who did not at all fear for their lives. He ordered women to be buried up to their waists and the nipples to be torn from their breasts by ferocious mastiffs set upon them. He also gave orders to crush little children against doorposts.

Æthelred's posthumous reputation would be a confused and paradoxical one. On the one hand, the chroniclers of the Middle Ages describe him as yielding and hesitant, indecisive, easy to influence and the weaker party in the battle against the strong Danes; on the other, they paint a brutal picture of him as a ruler with tyrannical, quick-tempered and despotic traits. Both characterizations are probably true.

One account claims that Sweyn Forkbeard's sister was a victim of the massacre; another states that one of those killed was Sweyn's brother. Another text provides an imaginative description of how a group of young Danes managed to flee down the Thames by boat before crossing the sea to Denmark, where they gave an account of what had happened to Sweyn and his warlords, who immediately began to muster their army—"the Danes were inflamed with justifiable anger, like a fire which someone had tried to extinguish with fat".

It is not improbable that people close to Sweyn Forkbeard were killed during the purges, but the Danish king was in no need of further motivation to attack Æthelred's realm. In the years that followed the massacre, he continued to send armies across the sea, and they continued to increase in size. England was attacked in 1002, 1003, 1004 and 1005.

Æthelred commanded that a major armament project be initiated, and announced new laws to reform his military apparatus. Deserters from the armies of conscripted peasants were executed. Archaeological surveys have shown that defences around cities and market towns all across the kingdom were repaired and reinforced at this time; the mints were moved from the coasts to fortresses atop hills further inland. To finance these construction projects and pay his workers and soldiers, Æthelred demanded supplies and great sums of money from the monasteries and churches; the landed property of nobles was confiscated and sold. This undermined Æthelred's popularity among his people, but was imperative in defending his country and regime.

In the autumn of 1005, while the war raged in England, large areas of Northern Europe were hit by either drought or heavy rain, which meant that the crops failed. In the wake of this followed a disaster that for the average man, woman and child posed a far greater threat than any Viking army—famine. A lack of food, hunger and death are documented in the annals in many places across Europe that year. "In this year was the great famine throughout the English nation," states the *Anglo-Saxon Chronicle*.

The difficulty in obtaining provisions forced the Danes to return to their homeland. And as hunger ravaged the towns and villages, England experienced its first autumn free of Viking raids, looting and burning villages in nine years.

In 1006, in the spring that followed the crop failures, when the kingdom's population and the Crown's resources were still reeling from the effects of the famine, a group of noblemen and their servants gathered somewhere in England; exactly where remains unknown. They feasted and drank and, as was the custom of such prominent men, they went on a hunt together on horseback through the forest. During this hunt, one of the most powerful men in Æthelred's regime was murdered.

The murder victim was an ealdorman, Ælfhelm of York. He was from a powerful noble family in the north of England whose members had been important supporters of Æthelred's forefathers for generations.

The person responsible for the murder was a man from far more humble beginnings, the son of a thane from the Welsh borderlands who, despite his low birth, had worked his way up to a position among Æthelred's inner circle of trusted advisors. His name was Eadric, and he would come to be known throughout history by the nickname applied to him after his death—Eadric Streona, "the Acquisitive" or "the Grasper". The murder of Ælfhelm of York was Eadric's first major step in a long and winding political career that would make him the most influential man in Æthelred's kingdom—and one of the most notorious figures in English medieval history.

For many years, Æthelred's court had been characterized by rivalries, conflicts and ruthless competition for the king's favour, and the murder of the ealdorman from York brought about a sudden reshuffling among the kingdom's most senior leaders that was reminiscent of a palace coup. The murdered ealdorman's two adult sons were arrested "for treason", and both had their eyes stuck out—if not on Æthelred's personal orders, then undoubtedly with his blessing. As the rumours swirled they retreated, blind and humiliated, to their home towns in the north of England, along with their supporters.

In the time that followed, many of the members of Æthelred's permanent council of aristocratic advisors were replaced with new men. Eadric Streona was appointed Ealdorman of Mercia, the large and densely populated midlands region that had formerly been a separate kingdom and which made up almost a quarter of Æthelred's England. Eadric was now regarded as the second most important man in the regime after Æthelred himself. In the years that followed, he likely became the kingdom's greatest landowner under the king, with properties in both the country-side and cities all across the country from north to south. He would later marry one of Æthelred's young daughters. Eadric's supporters, including his brothers, were given important positions within the court.

In the midst of this upheaval of power, Sweyn Forkbeard's army returned to England—and this time it was larger than ever before.

Æthelred gathered his new council, and in Wessex and Mercia called up a significant proportion of the male population fit for combat in order to defend the kingdom. Nevertheless, the Danish army's experienced warriors ravaged Southern England, causing destruction on an unprecedented scale. Some of Æthelred's troops were outfought on the battlefield; others were outmanoeuvred and circumvented. The Danish warriors stole horses and moved further into the country than they ever had before.

One day, the shocked inhabitants of Winchester stood powerless as they watched "an arrogant and confident host passing their gates on its way to the coast, bringing provisions and treasures from a distance of more than fifty miles inland". The Danes "lighted their war-beacons as they went", states the *Anglo-Saxon Chronicle* in a poetic paraphrasing of the sight of burning villages. The flames could be seen from great distances at night; columns of smoke during the day. By Christmas, the Danish army had spread such chaos that "no man could think or discover how they could be driven out of the land, or this land maintained against them; for they had every shire in Wessex sadly marked, by burning and by plundering".

Humiliated, King Æthelred was evacuated from his heartland in the south of England to the northern shore of the River Thames, and from there safely escorted north-westwards. Along with his court, he celebrated Christmas at a royal estate in Shropshire on the western outskirts of his kingdom, as far from the war-torn east and south coasts as he could get. He had no choice but to negotiate with the Danish messengers.

These negotiations were a new low in Æthelred's reign as Anglo-Saxon king. To save his subjects and regime, he agreed to pay Sweyn's army the unprecedented sum of 36,000 pounds of silver in tribute—more than 12.5 tonnes. It was a staggering amount. Had it been paid exclusively in coinage, it would have consisted of around 8.5 million silver coins. A portion of the tribute was likely paid in silver bullion, but that did not affect its staggering value.[5]

How the silver was collected is unknown, but the tribute was paid somewhere on the coast, where the Danes' winter camp was located, early in 1007. In addition to the silver, which must have been transported in a procession of carts drawn by horses and oxen, the Danes were provided with huge volumes of supplies in the form of corn and livestock, which must somehow have been procured in the famine-stricken country. The entire Danish army would have food to last them through both the winter and spring.

Payment of this tribute bought Æthelred two years of peace; when these two years were up, Sweyn's army would return. And there was every indication that the next wave of raids would be on an even greater scale.

At this time, Æthelred and the members of his council were painfully aware that the entire kingdom was in danger of collapsing under a new attack. Faced with this existential threat, the king managed to unite his circle of leaders in a series of frantic joint efforts, both military and financial. Early in 1008 he gave the most ambitious orders of his life: over the course of a single year, his people would equip an army and build a fleet of warships that were stronger than the Danes'.

Æthelred's machinery of power set in motion what in all likelihood was the most intense mobilization of armed forces to be seen in England since the days of the Romans; these co-ordinated efforts are an impressive testimony to the authority and organizational skill of the Anglo-Saxon Crown. Under the supervision of ealdormen and bishops, thousands of subjects all across England—men, women and children, the free and enslaved, peasants and merchants—were set to work. Fellers cut down and de-limbed thousands of trees in England's forests; men and animals transported the logs to the coast, where the shipbuilders constructed a number of new, large warships and smaller cutters in great haste. The Crown's old ships were repaired; women spun thread, which the sailmakers used to make sails. Farmers cultivated hemp, which the ropemakers used to make rope; the oar makers hacked and cut out oars. Blacksmiths forged nails and parts for all kinds of equipment, including swords, shield bosses, spearheads, arrowheads, axe heads, helmets and breastplates. In a kingdom still shaken from the famine of just a few years earlier, great volumes of butter, grain, bread and dried and salted fish and meat were collected and stored.

In the spring or early summer of 1009, Æthelred boarded his royal ship in London, surrounded by his household of servants and men. He was in his early forties, and by this point had been at war with Sweyn Forkbeard for almost twenty years. As the wars had raged on, his first and second queens had borne him a total of seven legitimate sons and five legitimate daughters who were still living; he also had a number of children with mistresses. Some of his daughters were sent to convents, but most of them were married to men in his inner circle of aristocratic advisors. They were child brides who bound Æthelred's government with his blood—and now the entire lineage's future was at stake.

The kingdom's leading men, many of them close relatives of the king, boarded other warships along with their own servants and sworn warriors; the ships sailed down the Thames and continued south along the coast. The mustering point where the fleet assembled was the small port town of Sandwich, situated on a long, pale, sandy beach between white chalk cliffs in Kent, in a wide bay just south of the Thames Estuary. Sandwich in itself was an unimportant town—a simple cluster of thatch-roofed, timber houses behind wattle fences and gardens, and perhaps home to

200 people. But its position at the mouth of a river that created a deep, natural harbour made it a suitable place to gather many ships at once. The Danish armies had landed there previously, and they were expected to show up there again soon. "In this year the ships […] were ready, and there were more of them […] than there had ever been before in England in the days of any king. They were all brought together off Sandwich, to be stationed there to protect this realm against every invading host," one chronicler wrote.

In the Middle Ages, there was no clearer manifestation of a king's power than the gathering of a fleet of warships. Those who saw Æthelred's armada assembling witnessed an event that must have seemed like a strange natural phenomenon, like migrating whales gathering at the same location, seemingly bound and controlled by a singular, invisible will. The ships glided into the bay, individually and in groups, some from the north and others from the south, in ever-increasing numbers. They sat there, swaying, beside each other, slightly out of step with the rhythm of the waves as the fleet grew in size over days, perhaps weeks, dwarfing the little town onshore. Flags and banners waved from the mastheads. The sound of commands, of shouts and fragments of conversation and song, were carried across the water and could be heard from far away. When all the ships were finally gathered, the fleet consisted of around 200 warships manned by around 9,000 men, most of whom were equipped with newly forged breastplates and helmets. This was equivalent to the population of a large Northern European city.

As the fleet lay assembled, waiting for the enemy's sails to appear on the horizon, Æthelred also gathered his leaders around him. At this meeting, the *Anglo-Saxon Chronicle* tells us, two ealdormen began to argue in Æthelred's presence. One of the men, named Beortric, was Eadric Streona's brother; the other was named Wulfnoth. We are not told what the conflict was about, only that Beortric accused Wulfnoth of a crime and demanded that King Æthelred punish him. The argument ended with Wulfnoth storming out of the meeting, gathering his men, and leading the twenty ships under his command away from the main fleet. They set their course for the south, making their way past the white cliffs of Dover, and disappeared.

The main fleet soon received reports that Wulfnoth had led his crew ashore, where he had begun to ravage and burn the coastal villages of the very country he was meant to be defending. The area he attacked was likely Beortric's ancestral seat. Æthelred gave Beortric his blessing to pursue Wulfnoth, to put a stop to the destruction and bring the accused man back in chains. Taking eighty ships with him—almost half the fleet—Beortric sailed off after Wulfnoth.

But foul weather was brewing as the eighty ships sailed south, and in the often fickle English Channel they ended up at the centre of a terrible storm. Some of Beortric's ships blew over and sank, taking all those aboard down with them; others tried to make their way ashore. In scattered groups, the sailors and soldiers managed to save the ships by dragging them up on to a beach.

The men Beortric's crews were chasing had also put ashore close by, where they lay in ambush behind the beach, awaiting the arrival of their pursuers. As the wind and the sea raged and roared, Beortric's men were unable to muster. They were massacred. Those who were not struck down or stabbed to death ran for their lives, and were scattered in the storm. When the storm passed, the victors burned Beortric's ships on the beach.

When sporadic messages containing word of the fate of the men and the ships reached the main fleet, which was still anchored just off the coast at Sandwich, a chaotic and panicked confusion arose among the ranks of nervous soldiers and seamen. As Æthelred's warlords fought to assert their authority and hold the fleet together, the solidarity among the uppermost ranks also began to crumble. Seemingly in fear for his own safety, King Æthelred left the fleet in great haste and sailed back to London with his guards. Many of the members of his war council followed their leader's example, and turned home to protect their own. "The king went his way home, and the ealdormen and the nobility, and thus lightly left the ships," relates the *Anglo-Saxon Chronicle*, "and they let the whole nation's toil thus lightly pass away; and no better was that victory on which the whole English nation had fixed their hopes." Part of the fleet remained for a short while, manned by conscripted peasants and their local leaders, but then it dissolved. A number of ships sailed down the Thames to London; the rest scattered.

All that remained were the cliffs and the pale, sandy beaches, naked and undefended.

And then they came.

NOTES

[1] There were silver mines in England too, but the silver extracted from them comprised only a tiny fraction of the country's total volume. Most of it came from German mines and found its way to England as payment for wool.

[2] In this context, a bullion is an unhammered coin not used in ordinary trade, but which has a value equivalent to its metal value, in this case silver.

[3] Towards the end of his life, Harald Bluetooth had a rune master carve a tribute to his parents and himself on a memorial stone beside his parents' grave. In Denmark, it is regarded as a kind of birth certificate for the Danish nation, and also contains one of the first references to Norway—*nuruiak*: "*Haraltr kunukr bath kaurua kubl thausi aft kurm fathur sin auk aft thaurui muthur sina. Sa haraltr ias sar*

uan tanmaurk ala auk nuruiak auk tani karthi kristna." "King Harald ordered this monument made in memory of Gormr, his father, and in memory of Thyrvé, his mother; that Haraldr who won for himself all of Denmark and Norway and made the Danes Christian."

[4] Timber from all four castles has been dendrochronologically dated as being from the year 981.

[5] The payment was made in pennies, the only denomination of coin; 240 pennies were equivalent to one pound; 36,000 pounds is 8,640,000 coins. An Anglo-Saxon pound was equivalent to around 350g. The weight is therefore 12.6 tonnes.

THE WARRIOR'S GOOD LIFE

THE LONG-AWAITED DANISH ARMY was organized into several large fleets, each of which sailed separately. From Denmark, they followed the coast westwards and approached England from the south. The first group of ships glided watchfully past the beaches and cliffs of Kent, past the inlet where Æthelred's fleet had been anchored and on to the Isle of Thanet, which lay just beyond Sandwich. Here they went ashore.

The island was the Danish armies' agreed mustering point. It was close enough to the mainland for the Danes to keep the coast under observation with the naked eye, without needing to worry about being ambushed or falling victim to unexpected attacks. The island's inhabitants were few, and most of them lived in a small village beside an old monastery. Perhaps they had fled the island. In any event, the first Danish warriors encountered no resistance when they anchored their ships, put ashore and set up their temporary camp.

The other groups of ships then followed. The fleets consisted of various types of vessels: some were short and wide, perhaps fifteen or twenty metres long, and manned only by around twenty rowing warriors. Others were far larger—narrow and fast longships propelled by around sixty men or more, all rowing in rhythm. The biggest ships had their own smaller boats in tow, or carried them upturned over the cargo. There were also substantial, wider transport vessels with smaller crews. The various parts of the fleet came together, just as Æthelred's fleet had done on the other side of the bay only days or weeks before. When the entire fleet was assembled, it was bigger than any Danish army that had come to England over the past 100 years. The Anglo-Saxon chroniclers gave it many names: "a new and enormous Danish army", "the enormous plundering army", "that immense hostile host".

On one of the first days of August 1009, the Danes left their camp on the Isle of Thanet and rowed across the narrow strait that separated them from the mainland. The large ships were anchored out in the bay; the smaller, lighter vessels were dragged all the way up on to the undefended sandy beaches. Thousands of men with long spears and big, round shields painted in bright colours waded ashore, group after group of them, until around 10,000 soldiers filled the beach and the tiny village that lay beside it, whose inhabitants had undoubtedly fled. Banners, weapons, tents, tools and all manner of equipment were carried ashore. The Danes had no horses or wagons; they carried their equipment on their backs and over their shoulders.

The soldiers were lined up by their leaders in divisions consisting of men from the same ship. Scouts moved inland, on the lookout for the enemy. This was a strictly led and highly efficient force, able to fight with discipline, build camps, distribute food to its soldiers and move as one over great distances on both water and land, with a speed that astonished its opponents.

Sweyn Forkbeard was the only king in the Nordic region—and perhaps the only king in all of Northern Europe—with the power to pull together such a force and control it at will. But he clearly didn't deem it necessary to lead his army in person. As on several previous campaigns, he remained back home in Denmark, where he reaped the benefits of his people's violence. This says much about his position.

The army's overall leader and Sweyn Forkbeard's entrusted deputy was a man the Anglo-Saxons knew as Thorkell. His Norse skalds called him Þorkell inn hávi—Thorkell the High, or Thorkell the Tall, a nickname that testifies to a dominating physical and social presence. He is said to have been from a jarl dynasty that ruled over Scania, and a younger brother of one of Harald Bluetooth's most prominent warlords—and consequently among the most powerful men in the Nordic region. Thorkell was a headstrong and ambitious man who already had extensive experience of war, and who would come to play a key role in the political power play that would unfold in both England and Scandinavia over many years to come.

We also know the names of several of the warlords who followed Thorkell, the leaders of the various divisions of the army. Under Thorkell was his younger brother, a man whose name the Anglo-Saxons recorded as Hemming. Another was known as Eglaf. Also present was a chieftain from the areas surrounding Uppland in modern Sweden by the name of Ulv—a veteran from an earlier raid on England. When he later died back home in Sweden, he was buried in a mound above which his descendants raised a memorial stone with an inscription stating that he was paid by Thorkell in England.

The final warlord we know of by name was a young king from the northern regions of Sweyn Forkbeard's kingdom. His Norse name was Óláfr Haraldsson—Olaf, son of Harald. His own people, at least later in his life, called him Óláfr inn digri—Olaf "the Big", "the Fat" or "the Stout". Like Thorkell's, this is a nickname that speaks of a strong, thickset physique, and probably also to a corresponding personality and leadership style.

*

He came from a dark world. Not because the sun didn't shine in his homeland, or because it was more primitive than other countries, but because Scandinavia in the early 1000s was a society without books. And a society without books is, in a way, a society without a history. The images and descriptions we have of Olaf's age were not created by people who experienced it, but belong to later ages' memories and depictions of it.

This is especially true in Olaf's case. Olaf, like several Anglo-Saxon kings, was canonized and venerated as a saint after his death, and his story was written down long after this had occurred. Recollections of him were therefore distorted and enhanced to create a figure that served the needs of posterity, rather than reflecting who Olaf really was. As if buried beneath his own legend, the historical man behind the hero of myth is a mysterious and shadowy figure. Despite the rich array of colourful stories that later grew up and blossomed around his memory, our knowledge of who Olaf was in reality is limited to just a few tangible details.

He came from a mighty family. His father was a king by the name of Harald of Grenland in modern Norway's Telemark, who after his death would be remembered as Harald Grenske. His mother's name was Asta. She was the daughter of a prominent man named Gudbrand Kule who lived in the ancient Norwegian Uplands, probably somewhere in the region surrounding Lake Mjøsa.

Harald and Asta were subjects of the King of Denmark, Harald Bluetooth. Harald Grenske had sworn allegiance to the great king in the south and was his petty king, or perhaps one of several beneath him, in *Vík*, the contemporary name for the areas around the Oslo Fjord and Skagerrak. The vast agricultural and forest-covered landscapes in Vik had for many generations been controlled by petty kings who operated in the more powerful Danish kings' shadow. In legends and poems that were already several centuries old in the 1000s, Olaf's seat is described as part of a communal southern Scandinavian environment with the area that corresponds to modern Denmark at its centre.

We do not know where Olaf was born; nor do we have a precise year for his birth. He was probably born sometime in the early 990s, a few years after Harald Bluetooth's death, around the time at which Sweyn Forkbeard set out on his first raids against England.

Olaf never knew his father. Harald Grenske died either just before or just after his son was born—during a Viking raid in Eastern Europe, according to later accounts. Asta was still a young woman, and she quickly remarried. Her new husband was another prominent man from Vik by the name of Sigurd, and he too is said to have called himself a king. In the later sagas he is referred to with the strange nickname *sýr*—"sow" or "swine". Olaf probably grew up in his mother and stepfather's household, surrounded by relatives, workers and slaves.

Olaf Haraldsson was born into the upmost elite in a society that was extremely hierarchical and stratified, where the weak submitted to the strong and the strong submitted to the even stronger. At the very bottom of the social ladder were the unfree slaves. The Norse societies were slave economies, and slaves comprised a significant part of the population, up to a quarter. Slave status was inherited; native slaves were valued more highly than those who were captured on raids abroad, and who were probably bought and sold in the market towns like cattle. Like livestock, a slave was his master's property, and could be sold or even killed by his owner. The system was built on force and violence. Male slaves performed the most demanding physical labour, such as chopping down trees and working the soil. Female slaves prepared food, worked in the houses, and probably spun the enormous volumes of wool required to make the Viking ships' sails. If they were beautiful, they also often functioned as their male owners' concubines.

Above the slaves was a large and varied group of free men and their wives, who formed the backbone of Norse society: farmers who owned or rented land, specialists in various handicrafts, travelling merchants and soldiers. The vast majority of them were born and died on peaceful farms, where they lived exhausting, repetitive lives that revolved around cultivating the earth and keeping cattle and sheep, just as their ancestors had done since time immemorial before them, and as their descendants would do for the distant, unforeseeable future.

Like others in Europe, Norse farming society was dominated by a landowning warrior nobility, the members of which lived anything but peaceful lives. For as long as anyone could remember, the free men had been subordinate to a ruling class whose status and power came from its military resources, and which was inherited. The restless and ever-shifting relations between such families were the framework upon which society was built.

From birth, Olaf was part of a far-reaching network of kings, jarls and chieftains. His father must have held great authority over all of Vik, and Olaf was his heir. Olaf's skalds referred to him later in his life using phrases such as "a young descendant of princes" and "a ruler's descendant"; he was Harald Grenske's "descendant and successor", and the farming districts in Vik and the Uplands were his "broad ancestral lands". He seems to have borne the royal name from a young age.[1]

Leading families from Hålogaland in the far north, Danish kings from the south and Swedish chieftains from the east all cultivated close connections with one another. The members of Olaf's societal class held banquets for each other in their timber halls, where they talked politics in magnificent surroundings while gorging themselves on food and drink, exchanged valuable gifts, and told stories and recited epic poems about their forefathers' achievements. They planned joint war expeditions, resolved conflicts and entered into alliances that were cemented through the swearing of oaths and by marrying each other's sisters and daughters.

Vik's farming villages were scattered across an undulating landscape of deep pine and spruce forests, where people lived in small, dark timber houses, among plots of cultivated land, pastures and vegetable gardens behind wattle fences. But Vik was not an isolated part of the world. The Nordic region's almost explosive expansion of people, produce and violence that characterized the Viking Age had already been under way for 200 years by Olaf's time. Since the early 800s, Viking ships had enabled Norse seafarers to travel further and faster than anyone else in Europe. By Olaf's time, they had long since learnt to set sail for other regions and return home on the prevailing winds, and had explored Europe's waterways in detail during times of both war and peace.

Olaf belonged to a stratum of society whose members possessed excellent knowledge of and maintained extensive contact with the world around them. To travel was an honourable pursuit. "He knows alone who has wandered wide, and far has fared on the way, what manner of mind a man doth own who is wise of head and heart," states the poem *Hávamál*. "He hath need of his wits who wanders wide, aught simple will serve at home." A person who had never travelled anywhere was called a *heimskr maðr*, or "unworldly man". Groups of young men—men close to Olaf undoubtedly among them—went to war in England, or on Viking raids elsewhere. Trading voyages and raids were often combined; while the men were away, their land was tilled by slaves under the leadership of women. Some never returned home; others returned home extremely wealthy.

People, animals, goods and news arrived in Vik from the east, south and west by ship. The small market town that would in time become the city of Oslo, and which was possibly founded by Harald Bluetooth, was one of many ports of call along the coast, which featured timber wharfs, boathouses, storehouses and buildings. From here, the seamen sailed to and from the large trading and power centres of the Danish kingdom—Jelling, Viborg, Hedeby and Roskilde, the latter being where Sweyn Forkbeard had established his most important court and where Harald Bluetooth was buried in a little wooden church. A few days' sail west was the important and century-old market town of Skiringssal in Vestfold, a link to the ancient Norwegian kingdom west of the mountains where Harald Fairhair and his sons had ruled in earlier times, as well as to the port markets of York, Lincoln, Fécamp and Rouen in the south-west—all of which could be reached in just a few days under ideal wind conditions. Merchandise and news were disseminated through a network of fixed trading posts, where Norse merchants sold furs, down and other exclusive goods from the north.

Like all peoples throughout all ages, the Norse communities lived at the centre of their own world view. They divided the outside world into *austr* and *vestr*—east and west. Sailing the eastern route brought one to Gardarike, or "the cities", an umbrella term for the multi-ethnic trading and craft centres located along the Russian rivers. In *Hólmgarðr* (Novgorod) and *Kænugarðr* (Kiev), the descendants of Norse warlords ruled as princes. In *Miklagarðr* (Constantinople, now Istanbul), Norse warriors served as bodyguards for the Byzantine emperors. Travelling even further east, you reached Baghdad.

On the western route, you would reach the land of the Frisians (along the coast of the modern Netherlands and Germany), the land of the Saxons (Northern Germany), the land of the *Valkerar* (the Dutch island of Walcheren), the land of the Flemish (Flanders), and so on. In the 700s, 800s and 900s, Norse seamen had established settlements on the Shetland Islands, Orkney

Islands, Faroe Islands and Iceland. From Iceland, they discovered Greenland in the 980s; Olaf was still a child when Leif Erikson headed his expedition from Greenland to Vinland (Canada) in around the year 1000.

The traders and Vikings who set out on voyages to the east and west not only returned home with slaves and exotic goods from foreign countries—they also brought with them new knowledge, new ideas and a new faith in God. Olaf was born in the middle of a great shift in religious belief, as the old was giving way to the new.

Like all Germanic religions, pre-Christian Nordic worship centred around war, fertility and the making of sacrifices to powerful spirits—along with an entire pantheon of gods. Above all, it was Odin, Thor and Freyr who were worshipped across Scandinavia. The people who practised the ancient religion left behind no proclamation; no tablet inscribed with commandments, no religious book. The depictions of their faith and rituals were written down by Christian and Muslim observers who regarded them as lost souls in need of saving, or as frightening and exotic barbarians. The lavish and intricate universe of gods and monsters born of fire and frost in the resounding depths of Ginnungagap, which goes up in flames in the war inferno of Ragnarök, has primarily been handed down to us through the Eddas, poems that were first written down in the 1200s: in the anonymous *Poetic Edda* and in *Snorri Sturluson's Edda*, his tribute to skaldic poetry and inherited knowledge of the ancient forefathers' mythological narratives. And despite both works' strikingly detailed accounts, both Snorri and the author of the *Poetic Edda* viewed their ancestors' stories from a great distance—from their own thoroughly Christianized age, with a stranger's wonderment and fascination. Just as we do today.

Some ancient worship was undertaken independently of the chieftains. People gathered and performed a range of religious acts and rituals at home on their simple farms and outdoors, in fields devoted to the gods or in meadows and groves with holy trees. But, as in the Christian world, religion in the Norse societies was also inextricably interwoven with the political power structure. Just as Frankish and Anglo-Saxon kings obtained their legitimacy through being crowned and anointed by their clergy, Norse kings and jarls had for centuries obtained their authority from their gods. They ruled by virtue of being their gods' descendants and were mediators between their subjects and the gods, responsible for ensuring that the gods made them successful in war and blessed the people with rich grain harvests; with breeding cattle and flocks of sheep.

The larger farms were used as temples. There are contemporary descriptions and archaeological traces of what were probably large houses of worship, similar to the stave churches that survive in Norway today, in the pagan chieftains' power centres. The chieftains themselves, or religious specialists in their service, led sacrificial ceremonies in which offerings were made of grain and fish, as well as wild and domestic animals. The sacrificed animals were sometimes eaten in ritual communal meals.

A generation after Harald Bluetooth's conversion, these traditions were rapidly dying out in Olaf's home region. *Hvitekrist*—Christ, the Almighty God worshipped among people everywhere in the west, who had mystically turned himself into his own son and allowed him to be sacrificed on a cross—was already known to the Norse societies, and had long since begun to make his mark on them. Around the year 1000, he was slowly starting to drive out the old gods.

Geographically, the new religion crept into the ancient Norse societies from the coasts that were closest to the Christian world. Socially, it trickled down through the various social strata from the elite.

A steady stream of German and Anglo-Saxon missionaries had been spreading the new faith to the inhabitants of the north for generations, and merchants often returned home having been converted in foreign ports. But above all, the new religion was spread by Norse kings and the warlords in their service. They allowed themselves to be baptized by European rulers with whom they had entered into pacts, and required the same of their sworn men. They observed Christian kings who enjoyed a prestige and authority unheard of in the ancient Nordic societies, and attempted to govern their homelands in the same way.

Olaf Tryggvason was one such Christian king. Olaf Haraldsson was just a young child when, having made peace with Æthelred, the king returned from England in the year 994 or 995. He landed on the island of Moster in Sunnhordland, Norway, with a great army, and quickly conquered the regions of Western Norway and Trøndelag. He built churches, and demanded that those who served him be baptized. The skald Hallfreðr vandræðaskáld was among a group of men who entered into the Christian king's service, and was baptized in a ceremony with the king as his godfather. He composed a poem, which 1,000 years later remains a personal testimony from the great shift in faith: "It is now the king's decree that sacrifice is prohibited; we must shun the Norns' old creeds in which we have previously believed. All people now reject Odin's kin. I, too, am forced away from Njord's descendants to pray to Christ."

In little Olaf Haraldsson's home, the upheaval of power in the north and west must at first have seemed no more than a faint, distant rumbling on the horizon. But then Olaf Tryggvason led his army east of the mountains in order to challenge Sweyn Forkbeard's supremacy in Vik, as he had elsewhere. He became the first king to incorporate Vik into a Norwegian kingdom along with Western Norway and Trøndelag; he may also have been responsible for the construction of the first known church in Eastern Norway, St Clement's Church in Oslo. Olaf Tryggvason travelled around Vik's rural districts with his company of warriors, demanding that the local leaders submit to him. The later sagas state that on one such journey, he visited King Sigurd and Asta's estate in Ringerike; while there is no way of knowing whether this story is true, it is by no means improbable. Just as he himself had been baptized by King Æthelred's archbishop in Andover in England a few years earlier, Olaf Tryggvason now had his own priests baptize Sigurd Syr, Asta and little Olaf Haraldsson, in what in reality must have been a subjugation ceremony.[2]

True infant baptism was not actually practised in the Nordic region at this time, and so little Olaf was probably blessed through the simplified baptism ritual known as *primsigning*, in which one of the king's priests breathed on his face, marked his forehead with the sign of the cross, and placed a grain of corn consecrated with salt in his mouth. *Primsigning* was a ritual that was not binding in the same way as a real baptism—the intention was that the individual would be baptized properly at a later date. In the meantime, they would be regarded as Christian enough to be able to do business with Christian merchants in Christian market towns, and to participate in the Christian community in other ways. Many therefore submitted to this simplified baptism for practical reasons and delayed the full baptism as long as possible, until they were old or dying.

But life under Olaf Tryggvason's dominion didn't last long. Sweyn Forkbeard was not the kind of ruler to sit idly by and watch as a rival ripped the majority of his ancestral lands right out from under him. Of how the conflict between the two rivals escalated we have only superficial knowledge, but Olaf Tryggvason's attempts to establish himself in Vik brought him into a direct confrontation with King Sweyn. In the year 999 or 1000, Olaf Tryggvason sailed west with his fleet. At a place called Svolder, now unknown to us but somewhere in the Øresund region, possibly near the German island of Rügen, he encountered Sweyn's fleet—which was far larger.

During the sea battle that would be inflated to mythical proportions in the medieval sagas, Olaf's army was defeated. Olaf himself was killed, along with many of his warriors, but his posthumous reputation would live on in the form of fairy-tale narratives. An urban legend that later found its way into the saga literature asserted that Olaf had swum ashore and started to wander around in secret, hidden beneath a wide cloak, not unlike the mystical god-king Odin; another story that flourished stated that he lived on as a monk in the Holy Land. At the Danish court, just two generations after his death, he was remembered as a great sorcerer who could decipher the language of birds.

After the battle at Svolder, Sweyn took direct control of Vik; those who had sworn allegiance to Olaf Tryggvason, whether voluntarily or under pressure, now submitted to the Danish king. Although it is not mentioned explicitly, there can be little doubt that Olaf's stepfather, Petty King Sigurd, and all those belonging to his household also submitted to King Sweyn's supremacy.

In other words, our Olaf—the son of Harald and Asta—grew up to be the Danish king's man.

Olaf Haraldsson steps into history's spotlight seven or eight years after the battle at Svolder. In the year 1007, he is said to have left his home town and, like many others of his standing, embarked on an honourable career of violence, robbery and destruction. When the sagas of the kings were written 200 years later, tradition had established that Olaf was just a boy of twelve when he set out on his first Viking raid. In reality, he was probably older.

But he may well have been closer to a boy than he was to being a grown man.[3]

Children worked on the farms as a matter of course as soon as they were old enough to perform simple tasks, and were regarded as adults as soon as they reached sexual maturity. Girls were married off at the age of twelve, thirteen or fourteen, and it was not unusual for them to become pregnant a short time afterwards. Europe's population was young, and many of the leaders making the decisions were therefore also young. The sons of Norse and European kings did not live protected and isolated lives, but participated in their fathers' political and military activities long before their voices had finished breaking. Surrounded by older advisors who told them what to say, they spoke before large gatherings in their high-pitched boy's voices. Protected by armed cortèges, they travelled both within and beyond the lands they would inherit, and so learnt about the world.

Like other Norse leaders of a certain rank and status, later in life Olaf had skalds in his service who were tasked with honouring him and paying homage to his achievements. They specify no age, but commend his youth when he voyaged out into the world.

Battle-bold king, you launched your ship when young. […]
King, your journey from the north became most successful;
I heard clearly about this, that you travelled; now you are
powerful on account of such boldness.

Young Olaf Haraldsson went to war at the head of a fleet consisting of an unknown number of ships and warriors, probably a mixture of men from Vik and other fortune hunters and adventurers of the kind that flocked to all Norse warlords due to the prospects of wealth and honour they offered. The skalds tell of a Viking raid, or a series of voyages, "east on the salt sea". Filtered through their belligerent and heroic language we can catch fleeting glimpses of isolated scraps of memory, fragments of longer narratives: men fighting for their lives on the archipelago of the land of the Swedes; landing on the island of Gotland, where cowed farmers surrender their property so as not to see their houses burn; stories of tributes paid by farm leaders on a beach or plain on the great island of Saaremaa just off modern mainland Estonia; local men arriving at a tribute ceremony with weapons and the subsequent battle; later, another raid further north, a hard, overland journey in Finland, where many of Olaf's men are killed; a storm that whips up the sea and blows the ships away from the coast and out into open water.

What kind of person was this young king who spent his formative years surrounded by warriors on long sea voyages to remote beaches?

Olaf was a Norse king in a society where, above all else, a king's role was to lead his men to victory with his sword in his hand and to distribute the spoils of war among them. To a king and his warriors, war was not an exceptional condition, but rather a kind of natural state, a completely commonplace part of the world and people's lives. Something that came and went, like the weather and the seasons.

Frankish and Anglo-Saxon rulers also systematically plundered nearby lands and lined their pockets with their neighbours' wealth, but the scale and scope of this in the Nordic countries was something else entirely. Over the past 200 years, returning successful Viking leaders had changed the power dynamics in the Nordic region in radical ways. Viking kings were not dependent on the old agricultural society's structures in order to be able to dominate it, because their power rested on the movable wealth obtained from raids and the payment of tributes; they used gold and silver to pay ever-larger groups of loyal warriors. This power dynamic resulted in the development of a political system in which waging war—in foreign countries or internally within Scandinavia—was not only profitable, but also absolutely necessary for obtaining and maintaining power and influence. The number of men for whom war was a vocation was far greater than before the Viking Age; the honour, fame and wealth that came from successful plundering raids caused them to flock to the leaders who led the best and paid the most. Any leader who significantly advanced his position attracted more and more men, who could contribute to ever more glorious and lucrative raids. The honour belonged to everyone, from the king down to the humblest warrior—it provided social capital, renown and connections with others. Kings and jarls were judged by their skill in battle and their ability to reap its rewards. For them, what mattered most was to make sure the men of war fought *for* them, not against them—because fighting was something they were bound to do regardless.

Like every other king, Olaf was surrounded by a retinue of men who had sworn their allegiance to him—prominent men and advisors, relatives and friends, whose names history has forgotten. They all had their own networks of family and associates; their success and advancement depended on Olaf's success and advancement. Olaf was the external face and representative of an organization with branches in the north, south, east and west. There were no nuclear families, no nation. Belonging and community were found in collectives that centred around lords, in which household warriors, slaves and servants were almost regarded as the lord's children.

The bands of warriors that surrounded the Norse kings took the form of tightly interwoven brotherhoods and small, introverted communities, and were based on a simple but strong mutual bond between the lord and his men. The men swore an oath on a sword, promising that they would fight for their lord—to the death, if necessary—and avenge him should he be killed. In return, their lord would reward them with "gifts"—that is, he would distribute among them their plundered goods in the form of money, objets d'art, valuable clothing, weapons, horses, ships, slaves, domestic animals and gold and silver rings. In skaldic poetry, Viking leaders are often referred to as "ring givers".

The warriors did not refer to themselves as Vikings—this is a Norse term of unclear origin, which at Olaf's time seems to have primarily been used to mean "opponent" or "enemy", regardless of whether these adversaries were Norse, Frankish, Anglo-Saxon or otherwise. They used other words to describe themselves—they were *liðsmenn*, "army men" and *skiparar*, "crewmen on ships". Young men who went to war together under the same lord were referred to by a dedicated term, *drengir*. The inner circle of fanatically loyal and carefully chosen warriors closest to the lord—many of them probably relatives who had grown up with him—were termed *húskarlar*, men who slept in the same house as their lord. Some memorial stones raised over the graves of Vikings who returned home to Sweden refer to those who went to war on the same ship by another term that remains recognizable to us: *bróðir*, or "brothers".

Among them, there must have been people who were responsible for rations, food supplies and cooking, musicians who played lyre harps and flutes, specialists who could manoeuvre the ships in open waters, veterans from previous voyages who knew how long it would take to sail to certain places and cross the land to others, people who could speak foreign languages, advisors who knew when it was wise to stand and fight—and when it was best to retreat to fight another day.

The feeling of belonging and sense of loyalty could be extremely strong. The men lived together in confined and intimate communities aboard the ships for months and years at a time, eating and sleeping together, like big families. The community was celebrated and strengthened with excessive drinking and tremendous feasts, for which the lord would foot the bill. Complex rules dictated how the booty would be fairly distributed, and betraying the group would result in merciless collective punishment.

The Danish *Vederloven*, or "Code", which was written down towards the end of the 1100s but is thought to stem from Olaf's time, states for example that anyone who stole from or struck any of his fellow shipmates would be set in a rowing boat with supplies and put out to sea. The rest of the crew had to wait until he was out of sight, and then they would sail after him in order to beat him to death. Should the guilty party choose to run into the forest instead of row, he was free to do so. Again, his former comrades would have to wait until he was out of sight before setting out after him. Exhibiting cowardice and fleeing the heat of battle was punishable by death. And in this culture, the most shameful act anyone could commit was to kill a fellow comrade-in-arms.

Since warfare was a Norse king's most important role and function, the entire culture also revolved around war. The closest we have to contemporary depictions of Olaf are the tributary poems composed by his own skalds a few years after his first Viking raids. These poems paint a very different picture of him from the saintly figure into which he would eventually be transformed in later Norwegian tradition. According to the skalds, Olaf was his men's "strong guardian of the troop" and "valiant prince"; he was an "ember-breaker of battle", "a warrior from a young age" who "enjoyed the warrior's good life". The Olaf described by the skalds paints his enemies' hair red with blood; he snaps their spears, crushes their shields and splits their helmets so that blood runs out.

These odes are an expression of the Norse warrior culture's conventions, and of course tell us more about how Olaf wished to be perceived in life and be remembered after his death than what he was like in reality. The Norse warrior culture legitimized the raids and ruthless acts committed against people who refused to submit, but it also went much further than this. In poetry, art and rituals, war was celebrated and glorified—not just for the heroism and bravery it could elicit in the warriors themselves, but in all its bloody chaos. The pre-Christian religion, as practised by those who waged war, cultivated aggressiveness and conflict. The Valkyries were the pre-Christian Vikings' war demons, and depictions of them continued to live on long into the Christian age. They were formidable beings, female personifications of violence and death who loved slaughter and blood and guts; who revelled in hacked-off limbs and heads. To look at them was like staring into flames. At the god of war Odin's command, they chose which of the warriors would live and who would die. Using decapitated heads as weights and swords as spindles, they spun the threads of fate with men's entrails.

> Let us wind,
> let us wind,
> the web of war

In Olaf's time, the Valkyries were sometimes depicted as female warriors who rode across the sky above the battlefield.[4] In the poems they bear names such as *Herja*, "Devastator"; *Þrima*, "Fight"; *Þǫgn*, "Silence"; *Randgríðr*, "Shield-scraper"; *Róta*, "Disorder"; *Hrist*, "Shaker"; *Hjǫrþrimul*, "Sword-sound"; *Goll*, "Battle"; *Hjalmþhrimul*, "Helmet-clatter"; and *Tanngniðr*, "Teeth-grinder".

Norse armies were renowned for their distinctive banners, which they called "ravens", possibly because the banners were painted or embroidered with motifs of ravens, or because the banners themselves were shaped like them. The raven, the eagle and the wolf were the three mythical beasts of war. These three creatures also appear in Anglo-Saxon war poetry, but only as grim reminders of the horror of war, to conjure up terrible images of battlefields full of corpses and carrion birds. But in the Norse tradition, the animals were used to glorify and celebrate the victorious warrior, who quenches the wolf's thirst for blood and sates the raven and eagle's hunger for the flesh of corpses. The skalds wrote of Olaf, for example, that he ensured that "the eagle drank its fill of blood, and the she-wolf fed upon the corpses", and "reddened the tooth of the she-wolf with blood".

Throughout all ages, soldiers have freed themselves of responsibility by dehumanizing their enemy through comparing him with animals. But the Norse warrior culture is among the few known examples of the opposite—of cultures that have dehumanized themselves; that have devoted themselves to the bestial side of their nature by making themselves into predators and their enemies into prey.

Traces also remain of Norse warriors who went even further in their search for inspiration from the animal world. Norse poetry describes warriors imitating raging wild animals, biting their shields and giving baying war cries. Contemporary Byzantine eyewitness accounts contain similar images. Norse warriors fighting on the empire's northern borders are said to have howled like animals, frightening the Byzantine soldiers. Norse mercenaries serving in the emperor's bodyguard, the so-called Varangian Guard, also made an impression at court, where they performed aggressive, ritualistic war dances wearing masks, shields and spears. Such descriptions have been likened to those made of Aztec jaguar and eagle warriors and Cheyenne Dog Soldiers by Europeans. The later "berserkers", so enshrouded in myths, were probably hand-picked warriors who imitated animals either by fighting without armour, in "bare shirts", or wearing shirts made of bear hides, "bear shirts". So-called *ulvhedner*—wolf warriors—were men who fought with ecstatic energy wearing wolf skins.

The cultivation of martial skills naturally went hand in hand with an equally strong admiration for sporting and intellectual abilities. "I am master of eight skills," states a poem that summarizes the classical virtues of the ancient Norse world. "I can forge words into rhymes; I can travel quickly on horseback; I have often swum races; I can glide well on skis; I shoot and row well; I value harp music and poetry." The culture was also a vain one. Bodily cleanliness was held in extremely high regard, and one could exhibit one's wealth with attractive items of clothing—cloaks sewn from exclusive fabrics and resplendent with silver jewellery. A generation before Olaf was born, an Arab traveller to Hedeby on the southern tip of Jutland reported that both women and men painted themselves around the eyes.

Having the gift of the gab, along with the ability to make a good speech with a voice that carried at gatherings and a talent for publicly reciting poetry, were all skills expected of a man of honour. Training in how to write poetry in verse was regarded as a necessary part of the education of kings and prominent men. Poems composed by a long line of Norse kings and jarls have been preserved, among them a few that were later said to have been composed by Olaf Haraldsson himself.

It is impossible to confirm whether these poems are authentic—they may have been created as court entertainment by others at a later date—but they *may* have been composed by Olaf, and are regardless representative of the culture to which he belonged. They tell of sea voyages and battles, of drinking and conquests of women, with sexual undertones. A solitary fragmentary verse, later said to have been composed by Olaf in his youth, in the time before he set out on his Viking raids, states the following—we do not know the context, but he is ridiculing a man from Sogn who has fallen off his horse:

> Fill the horn, woman;
> Rannveig's son fell from his horse where the fine fellows
>   were riding.
> The Sygnir do not know how to travel very well on saddle-
>   beasts;
> bring [it] to me and to you.

A well-dressed and well-spoken assailant, then, who was never alone, but throughout his entire adult life surrounded by and part of a close-knit community of male warriors. Of Olaf's personality we know only this: that he was a self-confident and ambitious leader, held in high esteem by those who followed him; that he was determined and competent, willing to take significant chances and to walk over corpses in order to succeed in his aims. He must have been this way—otherwise he would never have managed any of the things he achieved in his life. From a young age, he guided his men on long journeys and through great danger, at a time when a king had to lead by example. A king had to dominate his surroundings with his character in order to earn respect; be charismatic and witty, strong and merciless. Contemporary descriptions of successful kings paint a picture of unpredictable and frightening men who kept the people around them on their toes; warm and gentle in one moment, quick-tempered and furious the next. The king gave, and the king took away.

After Olaf's death, his foremost skald remembered him as follows:

> I was with the lord, who gave gold to his loyal men
> and carrion to the ravens.

In the spring or summer of the year 1009, two years after the first Viking raid in the east, Olaf was in Denmark with his fleet. He was probably there because his lord, Sweyn Forkbeard, had summoned him. The Danish king was in the process of mustering what the Anglo-Saxons called a "vast hostile army" in order to send it to England, under Thorkell the Tall's command. Like the previous armies Sweyn had assembled, this one also consisted of a range of more or less closed bands of warriors who came from far and wide across Scandinavia and the Baltic coast, led by warlords keen to participate in the systematic plundering of the country in the west. One of these groups was Olaf's *lið*.

Olaf's first Viking expeditions in the east have left no traces other than the cryptic poems composed by his skalds, for the simple reason that the Norse, Slavic and Finno-Ugric peoples against whom he waged war had no book culture—just like his own. But when the groups of ships that together comprised Sweyn's war machine sailed west, they moved into the part of the world in which learned scribes and churchmen wrote annals and letters, which means we are able to see tiny glimpses of the course of these events through their eyes. Some of them describe the same events that Olaf's skalds tell us about, as seen from the perspective of his victims and opponents.

One of Olaf's skalds recounts how, as the ships followed the coast westwards towards England, a violent storm gathered out at sea and "beat against the prows of the ships".[5] This may well be the same storm as that described in the *Anglo-Saxon Chronicle*, which raged further west and destroyed many of Æthelred's ships in the English Channel. The skald states that Olaf's fleet put ashore during the storm, at a place the Norse seamen knew as

Kinnlimasiða. There, the young warrior king led his men in battle against the people who lived in the land.

Kinnlimasiða is probably synonymous with the coastal district of Kennemerland in today's Netherlands, but which 1,000 years ago was part of the kingdom of Lotharingia. And it is apparently from Lotharingia that the oldest traces of Olaf have survived in a written source, in what seems to be a description of the great Danish fleet written by a Lotharingian monk a few years later. His name was Alpert of Metz, and he was a Benedictine monk at the Abbey of St Symphorien in the Moselle Valley, where he wrote a work about the history of his homeland. Among stories of Jews and merchants, famine and monastic life, and the intrigues of noble men and women playing out in the shadow of the German Roman emperor, we find a long and for its time extraordinarily detailed passage that must have been based on eyewitness accounts, about a large, foreign war fleet with *normanni*, Norsemen, which suddenly came in from the sea in precisely this summer in 1009.

The fleet sailed into the country down the river systems south of Utrecht. Back then, this flat and low-lying part of Europe was swampy and boggy, and little suited to agriculture, but the many rivers that run through the area were important busy traffic arteries that connected the interior to the sea. Along the riverbanks, people lived in stilt houses built on piles. Brother Alpert describes how the coastal populations sent warnings inland to alert people of the fleet's arrival, but the foreign ships moved at such speed that both the people along the rivers and the local rulers were taken by surprise. The local population fled their homes and property, but the foreign ships sailed straight past them without stopping, further and further inland. The local count was an old man, so decrepit and weak that when word of the approaching fleet reached him he only just managed to mount his horse to lead his army of subjects. However, he was unable to prevent his men from fleeing.

Only when the warships reached the small town of Tiel, which was situated at the mouth of a smaller tributary many kilometres from the coast, did they lower their sails. Tiel was a rich town, a lively hub of busy wharfs and narrow streets, home to merchants who made a living trading English wool. The town's inhabitants fled as the ships approached, and watched from a distance as the warriors came ashore at their docks; they looked on as the foreigners ducked into buildings and storehouses and emerged carrying anything of value they found. The Danes moved systematically through the entire merchant quarter, where the town's richest citizens lived. Then they set the buildings alight, and the entire district burned down. They also plundered the town's monastery, taking relics and precious treasures, but left its church undamaged. When darkness fell, many of them settled down to sleep on the wharfs.

Over the course of the evening and night, the decrepit old count finally received reinforcements from the neighbouring districts. Another earl arrived, a younger man who had served the emperor in his battles in Italy and who was renowned for his skill in the art of war. He took over as head of the army.

At the crack of dawn the next day, the young count led his own soldiers and the local peasants in a counter-attack on the foreign warriors who still lay sleeping on the wharfs beside the charred remains of the merchant quarter. Caught off guard, the Norsemen ran aboard their ships, loosening the moorings with such speed that for a while it seemed they were fleeing in panic. But as soon as the ships were out on the river, they recovered their composure and discipline. As large bands of local men and their reinforcements followed them along both banks, the Norse warriors rowed calmly down the river.

When it was light, the Danes went ashore in several places in small groups, looking for booty in the buildings that lay along the banks of the river. Small skirmishes arose at the water's edge when the local population attempted to protect their houses, and men on both sides were injured and killed. Alpert of Metz concludes his account as follows:

> The enemy burned all of the settlements that they were able to reach along the banks of the river. Then, at noon, they all disembarked from their ships and formed a phalanx, offering our men an opportunity to fight. Our men then gathered at this place. However, because many of them had come together after being summoned from the fields, they were less experienced than the enemy in the conduct of battle. [...] Consequently, they did not dare to commit themselves to battle. When the barbarians saw that no one was advancing to fight, they decided that they had made a sufficient demonstration of their own bravery and returned to their ships. They then withdrew without any opposition.[6]

Not long afterwards, the ships crossed the English Channel and sailed along the coast of King Æthelred's England to join the rest of the Danish army on the Isle of Thanet. From there, the fleet sailed across the strait to Sandwich. The *Anglo-Saxon Chronicle* relates that Thorkell the Tall led his entire army ashore immediately after landing. Thorkell's first target was the city of Canterbury with its churches and castle, just a short distance from the coast and easily reached on foot.

It isn't hard to imagine the long, meandering procession of men, weapons and flags, not marching in step but trudging with an uneven rhythm, singing perhaps, down a winding country road through the rolling and burgeoning green summer landscape of Kent; through small forests and past deserted fields, empty pastures and houses made of logs, clay, straw and sticks, abandoned by the local population in great haste.

The Danish army was much like its Anglo-Saxon, Norman and Frankish counterparts. The warriors dressed in the same simple, sack-like tunics as other Northern Europeans, in grey, green, yellow or red and fastened with buckles, clips and belts over stockings and light leather shoes. They wore the same round or conical helmets as other soldiers at this time, some featuring protection for the nose, others that left the face fully exposed. Most had simple armour that covered the torso, made of thick layers of fabric or small iron plates. On the men's shoulders rested long spears, with greyish-black iron heads. Their round, painted shields they carried around their necks on straps; from many of their belts hung simple axes that functioned as both weapons and tools.

The leaders could be easily identified by their exclusive, expensive equipment, and used this to distinguish themselves in the same way as other elite noble warriors all across Europe. Like continental knights, they wore coats of mail made of thousands of tiny iron rings that hung from their shoulders to their knees, featuring long sleeves that extended all the way to the wrists. Unlike the majority of the men in the army they carried swords, costly status symbols that were often made of blades imported from France, and forged with patterns and inscriptions on them. The skalds composed odes that paid homage to these swords, which were given names such as "Golden-Hilt" and "Mail-Biter". They hung in decorated scabbards made of wood, leather and wool, which were affixed to the shoulders using straps. Even the spears and axes belonging to the most prominent men were works of art, adorned with magical inscriptions. Their shields might be painted with motifs from stories about gods and heroes.

After a short march, the Danes arrived in Canterbury. With its roughly 6,000 inhabitants, the city was one of the biggest in England—and an impressive sight for Scandinavian men. It lay at the centre of a sweeping landscape of cultivated fields that spread out in all directions, criss-crossed by small roads and cattle tracks and dotted with small clusters of houses, a market where cattle and horses were traded, and an abbey. The city's Roman origins were evident in its high and strong stone walls, which were built upon 700-year-old Roman foundations and enveloped the town on all sides. Many of the ancient Roman gate towers in the city walls had been converted into churches, and behind the walls the towers of the city's cathedral pointed proudly towards the sky. Nothing in foreign lands made a greater impression on the Norse travellers than such large, fortified cities—a fact reflected in the poetry of the skalds, in which the city walls were sometimes poetically portrayed as the city's "arms". One of Olaf Haraldsson's skalds called the city *Breiðr Kantaraborg*—"Broad Canterbury"– to emphasize just how magnificent it was to behold.

Canterbury was regarded as the cradle of Christianity in England, and was among the most important centres of the Anglo-Saxon Church. Around 1,000 of the city's inhabitants were religious workers, and the archbishop was among the kingdom's most influential and richest men. The city's many churches and monasteries meant that huge volumes of gold and silver were gathered behind its walls, making it a natural target.

The Danes prepared to attack the city, says the *Anglo-Saxon Chronicle*, which presumably means that they began to establish camps, cut down trees, knock together ladders and possibly set up catapults. We know from other sources that Norse armies at this time used catapults and created battering rams to smash open barricaded city gates. But it soon became apparent that it was neither necessary to storm the city nor begin the siege, because just after the Danish army's arrival a group of men came out through the city gates with the authority to negotiate on the city and the archbishop's behalf. Thorkell received them, and they negotiated the city's fate.

A short time later, 3,000 pounds of silver was transported out of the city and surrendered to Thorkell's men—this was the price that had to be paid to spare the city, its inhabitants and its surroundings. The money was likely immediately distributed among Thorkell and the rest of the Danish army's leaders—Olaf Haraldsson among them—who in turn used their new-found wealth to pay their men. This was just a foretaste of the enormous riches that would end up in the hands of Olaf and the Danish army over the coming years.

NOTES

[1] In Snorri's saga about Olaf (and other sagas), Olaf is the successor and heir to Harald Fairhair, who in the sagas and early Norwegian historical tradition united Norway as a single kingdom in the early 900s. In the sagas, Norway is depicted as having previously been a natural unit which Olaf reunites, and which regardless of internal conflicts and shifting regimes remains a unit over the subsequent period.

Today, this image is regarded as the saga writers' construction. The sagas' portrayal of Harald Fairhair's unification of the kingdom is probably highly exaggerated. In reality, his royal power was likely limited to an area in Western Norway and symbolic supremacy over parts of Trøndelag.

The kinship between Olaf Haraldsson and Harald Fairhair also lacks support in sources from Olaf's own time. When Olaf's skalds referred to him as Harald's successor and heir, they were probably not referring to Harald Fairhair, but to his father, Harald Grenske, as Klaus Krag has pointed out.

[2] Even in the Middle Ages there was confusion regarding whether Olaf Haraldsson had been baptized as a child by Olaf Tryggvason. The Norwegian monk Theodoricus, who wrote a historical work at the end of the 1100s, states that in his time there was a widespread belief among the people that this was the case, but that he himself did not know what was true, because he had read in the history of the Normans that Olaf Haraldsson was baptized many years later in Rouen. However, it is not improbable, as the Norwegian philologist Egil Kraggerud has argued, that Olaf was baptized twice. There are many examples of people who were baptized as children confirming their Christian affiliation as adults through confirmation baptisms—such as Olaf Tryggvason, for example. See Kraggerud 2012.

[3] That great heroes achieved impressive feats or were given command over their own armies at the age of twelve was a common motif in the Norse narrative culture, a kind of genre cliché. See for example Jesch 2001 and Krag 1999.

[4] This is the image of them that has remained through Romanticism.

[5] Olaf's skald, Sigvat Tordarson, also mentions a battle outside Sudervik on the west coast of Jutland, where Olaf is said to have fought against an unknown rival band of warriors and won.

[6] Alpert of Metz does not tell us the year in which the attack on Tiel took place. In the first modern edition of Alpert's text, Pertz's translation from 1826, the translator guesses that it took place in 1006, a date that is repeated in the newest edition, Bachrach's translation from 2006. The determination of the date is not explained further, but I would guess that it is due to the fact that in the text Alpert refers to a famine in the year before the attack, and that the only known famine to have taken place in the period was in 1005. However, I find it highly probable that the Viking attack described by Alpert took place in 1009, and that this must be the same Viking army that attacked England that same year, as others including O.A. Johnsen have argued. Indeed, the Viking attack at Tiel is emphatically dated to 1009 in another primary source, the chronicle of Sigebert of Gembloux: *"1009. Nortmanni Fresiam infestantes, Thilae oppidum incedent. 1010. Nort-*

manni Fresiam repetunt, et, multis caesis, Vultrajectum oppidum incensum est." Furthermore, Alpert's description accurately corresponds to the description of Olaf's fifth battle in Sigvat's *Vikingavisur*. The famine to which Alpert refers may have been due to local crop failures in 1008, which are not mentioned in other chronicles. Another Viking attack also followed in the same area the following year, in 1010.

FIRE AND SMOKE

TODAY, THE AGE IN WHICH Olaf Haraldsson lived is regarded as a hugely significant turning point in Europe's history. The time around the year 1000 appears to be a kind of ground zero, an era during which centuries of stagnation were gradually giving way to a dawning growth and development in Western civilization. The Vikings in the north were becoming Christians. The expanding Moors in the south no longer set out on plundering raids through the Pyrenees. The Magyars, the nomadic Hungarian horse people who had wrought chaos in Eastern Europe, had settled down and become farmers.

Relieved of the foreign invasions that since late antiquity had disturbed and reversed societal developments, over the centuries that followed Europe's population would increase, generation by generation. Cities would flourish. With the exception of a few significant interruptions and setbacks this growth continued, and Europe eventually became the world's richest continent, home to the world's most prominent and powerful leaders—the centre of the world.

For the people who lived in Olaf's time, however, it was almost impossible to perceive the signs of change. At the start of the 1000s, large areas of the European continent were covered by forest and wilderness. Europe's population was little more than a tenth of what it is today, and significantly smaller than it had been 1,000 years earlier.

Compared with Byzantium or Córdoba, the Western Christendom ruthlessly exploited by Olaf and his people appeared meagre, rustic and rather primitive. It was a world of rich monasteries and poor peasants, of thin women and men who hacked and shovelled, lifted and carried; of oxen pulling heavy loads down winding roads, wandering shepherds and flocks of sheep. The occasional settlement, a church or a castle of stone surrounded by patches of land, small gardens and thorny hedgerows; a few dozen huts that housed weavers, blacksmiths, craftsmen and slaves.

The remnants of the bygone but not forgotten Roman Empire were visible in stone structures that had been converted into churches and fortresses; a forge in an old archway here, shepherds dwelling under the ruins of a bridge there. The empire's ancient power lines could still be glimpsed in the overgrown remains of paved roads that linked the cities together, and its infrastructure lived on in Europe's most far-reaching and sophisticated organization—the Catholic Church's network of episcopal residences that linked Western Christendom with its Latin scholars and religious ceremonies. The ruins of the magnificent Roman structures confirmed the Church's teaching that history's pinnacle was past, and that creation was moving towards its end.

The population consisted almost exclusively of peasants, who toiled in an existence that, viewed from our present time, looks hard and bleak. Their ploughs were primitive wooden contraptions drawn by emaciated oxen, able to scrape only shallow furrows in the earth's hard surface, so that when sowing a grain of wheat no one could count on it becoming any more than two or three new ears of corn—a tiny fraction of what seed corn yields today. The fields often had to lie fallow for two, three or four years or more, to permit the soil to rest and regain its natural fertility.

Crop failures were the medieval population's greatest fear because a deadly wave of hunger always followed in their wake, dragging both young and old with it so they fell like corn to the scythe. Practically all chroniclers of the age described such instances of famine—and not without a certain macabre satisfaction: "People pursued one another in order to eat each other up, and many cut the throats of their fellow men so as to feed on human flesh, just like wolves." Bede the Venerable, an English monk and historian who lived during the 600s, wrote of Anglo-Saxon peasants in former times who entered into suicide pacts in order to avoid dying of hunger. "Frequently forty or fifty emaciated and starving people would go to a cliff, or to the edge of the sea, where they would join hands and leap over, to die by the fall or by drowning."

Although many years usually passed between outbreaks of famine of the kind that occurred in 1005, hunger was never far away. Having enough to eat throughout the entire year was an incredible privilege, and the preserve of the rich. The agricultural year, if a good one, produced food until around Easter. After that, most people had to assume they would have to make do with less: herbs, roots, the makeshift food that could be gathered from riverbanks and the forest floor. Anglo-Saxon and continental accounts describe peasants grinding pine cones and bark for lack of flour, and others eating grass while performing the summer's heavy work on half-empty stomachs, drained of strength as they waited for the grain harvest.

In England, the corn was ready to be harvested in late July and early August. A large portion of the population—men, women and children all across the kingdom—would then be intensely occupied with reaping the corn using scythes, binding it into sheaves, and transporting it in carts and wagons to the country's many thousands of windmills, where it would be ground into flour and used to bake hard, round, flat loaves of bread.

On 1st August each year the Anglo-Saxons celebrated *hlafmaesse*— "loaf-mass", or Lammas Day, to celebrate the harvesting of the long-anticipated corn—and it was no accident that Thorkell's army arrived in England at precisely this time. As the *Anglo-Saxon Chronicle* specifies, "then came, soon after Lammas, the vast hostile army, which we have called Thorkell's army, to Sandwich".

In the Middle Ages, no army could support itself over an extended period of time with the provisions the men brought with them, and living off the enemy's land was a natural and necessary part of the art of waging war. Right from the start, the campaign in which Olaf Haraldsson and his men participated therefore took the form of a constant hunt for the huge amounts of food required to keep the many thousands of men well fed and strong, week after week. In addition to the food the warriors needed to survive during the campaign, the stores that would feed the army through the coming winter also had to be stolen, robbed or extorted from the Anglo-Saxon peasants.

After Canterbury submitted in August 1009, the procession of men and weapons marched back to Sandwich and boarded the waiting ships. The entire army sailed south around the coast, into the English Channel and to the lush Isle of Wight. Here, Thorkell led his army ashore and set up camp at an old site where Sweyn's armies had spent the winter in previous years. He sent out plundering expeditions, which systematically began to burn, loot and gather food in Sussex, Hampshire and Berkshire, while Thorkell and his army's other leaders planned the further raiding of King Æthelred's kingdom.

What in retrospect might appear barbaric and arbitrary ravaging and burning had since antiquity been the most rational and effective method of waging war. By plundering the enemy's supplies one not only obtained provisions of the utmost necessity for one's own people, but also made it difficult for the enemy to feed their own army.[1]

In order to procure enough food for their campaign of 1009, the Danish army was forced to disperse and venture far deeper into the country, away from their ships and the possibility of retreat they represented.

For the Danish warriors, life during a campaign was neither particularly heroic nor lucrative. They spent most of it trekking through coastal regions on foot in small groups, surrounded on all sides by an alien, terrified and furious local population who would be merciless should they ever get the upper hand. The warriors rowed and waded ashore, where they trudged through forests and crossed rolling plains and grass-covered hills and fields. They set up camp, packed up and moved on, made fires and prepared food over their open flames, slept under the open sky, kept watch, traipsed onwards, repaired their equipment, ate some more, withdrew. They spied on their enemies and ambushed them; they walked into farmyards and small, scattered villages, no more than skeletons of the Roman cities they had once been, their streets invaded by weeds, and threatened their inhabitants, forcing local leaders to hand over grain, bread, beer, sheep, cattle and hens; they ducked into low buildings in broad daylight and came out carrying all they had found of food and valuables; they raped local women, set their torches to dry thatched roofs and burned down the homes of those who refused to give them what they wanted. They carried their booty in their hands and took live animals with them to be slaughtered later.

This was how war was for everyone, everywhere—not only during the Viking Age but also before and after. For all ordinary people who lived in Europe more than 300 or 400 years ago, armies on the move were to be deeply feared—regardless of who they were fighting for—and soldiers were by definition hated figures.

As the rural communities in the south burned, thousands of Anglo-Saxon peasant soldiers from all across the kingdom trudged along the country roads to London, in small groups under their local leaders. The *fyrd*—the traditional Anglo-Saxon militia that consisted of free men subject to compulsory service—mustered outside the city walls. Such poorly equipped peasant soldiers are given little attention in the *Anglo-Saxon Chronicle*, which instead focuses on famous nobles and individual heroic deeds, but they made up the main part of King Æthelred's forces. Æthelred, his council and his hard core of Anglo-Saxon warrior nobles waited in the city. The remnants of the king's fleet of warships, which still constituted a significant force, were on the Thames.

As late summer became autumn, King Æthelred led his main army's columns of men, horses and wagons south under waving war banners, and so began a new round in what seems almost a repetitive ritual dance, where after nearly twenty years of warfare both the Anglo-Saxons and the Danes knew each other's tactics all too well. Neither Æthelred nor Thorkell wished to enter into open battle, which would be a highly risky enterprise for both sides. Instead, the Anglo-Saxon army attempted to defend the population and prevent the Danes from moving freely through the country, while the Danes attacked in new and unexpected places their opponents were unable to reach quickly enough to defend. As one English chronicler described it, the Danes played their usual game, moving their fleet around from place to place, while bands of soldiers followed each other up and down the coast, along roads and trails, through forests and across marshes, heaths and cultivated land.

One of the commissioned officers on Æthelred's side was Eadric Streona, the Ealdorman of Mercia who had been behind the palace coup that took place at Æthelred's court three years previously. After Æthelred himself, he was now regarded as the most important man in England. Eadric headed a large division of the army, which at one point succeeded in cutting off and surrounding a group of Danish warriors who were on their way back to their ships with their booty. But there would be no confrontation. To the great frustration of and condemnation from the Anglo-Saxon chroniclers who later wrote about these events—and who loathed Eadric Streona—Eadric chose to negotiate with his enemies. According to the chroniclers, he accepted payment, a pure bribe, and let the Danes slip past the Anglo-Saxon lines. The Danes reached their ships and sailed away.

As villages and rural communities in the south burned and refugees streamed towards the heart of the country, the prevailing anxiety and atmosphere of doom spread through England with renewed force. Early in the autumn, the Anglo-Saxon Church initiated a national prayer programme of a scope that has astounded modern historians. On the Church's behalf, Archbishop Wulfstan of York composed a detailed decree to all Æthelred's subjects, which described how they should celebrate that year's harvest festival, Michaelmas, on 29th September. Many copies of the announcement were written out and sent across the kingdom with messengers. When the festival arrived, thousands upon thousands of people in cities and the countryside across the kingdom fasted for three days, consuming only bread, herbs and water. Similar fasts had been held in response to previous Viking raids, but this year they also walked barefoot to the churches with relics in long processions as they "called on Christ eagerly from their inmost hearts". Even slaves were released from their work so that they could walk with their owners, and alms were distributed to the poor. Every pastor in England was ordered to sing Mass and lead prayers of intercession for King Æthelred and his subjects. In the churches, parishioners praised the Lord by singing Psalm 3, about David fleeing his enemies:

> O Lord, how many are my foes! Many are rising against me
> [...]
> But you, O Lord, are a shield about me,
> my glory, and the lifter of my head.
> I cried aloud to the Lord,
> and he answered me from his holy hill.

The archbishop concluded the instructions that were sent out across the kingdom with the words: "God help us all. Amen."

In early November, the Danes packed up their camp on the Isle of Wight. The army had plundered the south coast of England for almost two months, without experiencing any great clashes with Æthelred's forces. Thorkell and his circle of leaders had set themselves a new target. They would attempt to do what King Sweyn and many of his commanders had never before managed—that is, to conquer London.

The fleet sailed north once again, past the cliffs and sandy beaches of Kent, through the strait between Sandwich and the Isle of Thanet, on into the Thames Estuary and up the wide river. Close to the sea, the landscape along the banks of the river consisted of wetlands and uninhabitable marshes, but further inland agricultural areas opened up, with meadows, cultivated fields and houses. More and more people and livestock could be seen as they sailed up the river. Large timber cairns were set alight along the riverbanks as the Danes approached, the smoke acting as an alarm system that warned London's defenders and inhabitants of the Danes' imminent arrival. As the Danish fleet sailed and rowed, Æthelred led his army north overland at great haste. He reached the city first, and awaited the attack behind the city walls.

The men on the fleet of ships encountered an impressive sight as they approached the most important and by far the largest city in the Anglo-Saxon kingdom. London had been the capital of the Roman province of Britannia. The city, which the Romans had called Londinium, the Anglo-Saxons called *Lundenwick* and the Norsemen *Lundúna*, was situated on the north side of the Thames. With its roughly 20,000 inhabitants, it was one of Northern Europe's largest cities, consisting of row upon row of wooden buildings and storehouses, dotted here and there with small churches of timber or stone, divided into eighteen districts and protected by high defensive walls that towered above the surrounding cultivated fields, which were wide and flat.

Around the walls were steep mounds and deep moats, so that the city was "surrounded on all sides by a river, which is in a sense equal to the sea". St Paul's Cathedral, the city's main church, could be seen from far outside the city. Wide roads for horses and carts stretched across the landscape, continuing over bridges and into the city through gates that could be locked from the inside and which were protected by towers, from which guards could shoot arrows, catapult and throw stones, and pour boiling water and oil on to anyone who might attempt to break down the doors. The city's male inhabitants were organized into a militia that was divided into divisions, each responsible for defending their part of the wall. In the city's north-western corner, built into the old Roman fortifications, was Æthelred's palace.

A bridge built of logs on strong poles, around 250 metres in length, stretched across the Thames, blocking the river to hostile ships; the bridge could be occupied by soldiers and effectively defended. Safe behind the bridge were the remains of Æthelred's once-proud fleet, along with the armada of barges and small rowboats that belonged to London's inhabitants, moored to the city's wharfs.

London had been besieged time and again in previous years, but it had never fallen. The Danes had attempted to set the city ablaze, to starve out the population and to storm the city—all without success. Nowhere else in England had they lost so many men. "And oft they fought against the city of London: but praise be to God that it yet stands sound, and they there ever met with ill fare," wrote a chronicler who recorded the Danes' former attempts to take the city. Both the Danes and the Anglo-Saxons regarded London as being practically impregnable.

But Thorkell made another attempt regardless. His army put ashore on the south bank; at the southern end of London Bridge was Southwark—or *Sudervirke*, as the Danes called it—a market town from the days of Alfred the Great, which had developed into a kind of small suburb of the great city on the other side of the river. Small buildings and storehouses formed a little town centre around a crossroads in front of the bridge. Southwark was fortified with its own walls and moats, but it was quickly surrendered by its defenders or taken by Thorkell's forces. The town provided a good, defendable camp for the coming winter and siege, and Thorkell seems to have made the location his new headquarters.

Olaf Haraldsson did likewise. "Some of the troop had huts in Southwark," relates one of his skalds.

The Danes had extensive experience of building such camps—which they always established beside their fleets of ships—often by making use of existing buildings such as churches, monasteries or farming complexes with facilities for storing and keeping food supplies. Around the camps, they constructed defensive mounds with gates that could be closed. Some of the large camps established by their forefathers in the 800s, which housed not only the warriors but also the women and children who accompanied them across the sea, have been excavated by archaeologists. In camps in York and Ireland dating from the 800s, along with large numbers of coins myriad objects have been discovered that tell the silent history of everyday life behind camp walls: weights, needles, bowls, knives, jewellery, cooking equipment and board-game pieces.

With the main access route to London from the south bank of the river blocked, Thorkell dispatched plundering expeditions in all directions to pillage more food for the coming winter. Groups of men rowed along the river to ransack large areas along both banks.

In the run-up to Christmas, the Danes attempted to storm the city. It is likely that they shot large stones and burning projectiles over the city walls using so-called catapults or *blíða*—ballistas— from their ships or the south bank of the river, the aim being to set the city's buildings ablaze. These simple but effective catapults, whose design had remained unchanged since antiquity, were used all over Europe. They consisted of a tilting arm that was tensioned with a rope held in place by a hook, and were able to throw projectiles over large distances. The Danish warriors rowed across to the north side of the river and tried to climb over the walls and break down the gates using battering rams, but the city's defenders showered them with arrows and stones.

One assault was led by Olaf Haraldsson himself. Using violent imagery, one of his skalds describes how he fought at the head of his army of men in a storm of violence and death and biting swords against the men who defended the moat. The skald recounts how Olaf attempted to take London's *bryggjar*, which Snorri Sturluson interpreted as the bridge that crossed the river but was more likely the wharfs that lay beside the bridge, and which were defended by mounds.

The skald probably wasn't exaggerating when he depicted Olaf at the centre of the fray on the front lines. We must imagine him, perhaps around twenty years old at this time, not as a general standing on a hill behind the battlefield and looking down on his men as they advanced against enemy lines, but as a warlord who, with his sword in his hand, participated fully in the battles as they played out: dirty and bloody, in crowded, chaotic and intensely personal hand-to-hand combat. The Norse leaders led by example—they had to show great personal courage in order to earn the respect and loyalty of their men. Surrounded by specially chosen and fanatically loyal warriors who protected their lord with their shields and bodies, they fought at the head of the army below the standard—the banner carried by a hand-picked *merkesmann*—which showed both friends and enemies the king's exact position among the throng of bodies, shields and weapons. "We followed the leader," several skaldic poems explicitly state. Norse kings were regularly killed in battle.

Olaf's attack failed—as did many others launched by Thorkell against the city. The *Anglo-Saxon Chronicle* states that in the run-up to Christmas, the city's defenders repelled a number of attacks that cost the Danes many lives. Weeks passed. Still the city didn't fall. Christmas came. Æthelred sat behind the city walls along with his besieged court, the Danes behind their own walls in Southwark. Early in the winter of 1010, Thorkell abandoned his attempt to conquer London.

Instead, he divided his army into several large groups and sent them out looting again. In midwinter, the main part of his army, probably led by Thorkell himself, set out on foot along the Thames, heading upriver, deeper into the country. A short distance from London they crossed the river using small boats, and on the north side walked up through the Chilterns to *Oxenaforda*—the city of Oxford. It was a young city, and small, located beside a ford where people had led oxen across the River Cherwell since time immemorial—the border between Mercia and Wessex. Thorkell's soldiers set fire to the city and let it burn to the ground. Afterwards, they made their way back to the camp in Southwark in two groups, one on each side of the river. The group that marched along the north bank nearly walked into an ambush set by London's defenders, but the Dane scouts discovered it, and everyone managed to cross the river and returned to Southwark unscathed.

The situation remained deadlocked throughout all of January and February of the year 1010. Spring came, the winter slowly loosening its grasp on the people and landscape. The spring equinox on 21st March was a magical day in the Anglo-Saxon calendar, on which there would be exactly equal amounts of daylight and darkness. Around this time, London's defending forces on the city walls could see that the Danes were carrying out repairs and maintenance on their ships in the Thames. After Easter, the Danes began to dismantle the winter camp at Southwark, and one day, leaving their dead behind, they rowed away down the river. They followed the Thames to the sea and continued northwards along the coast for a time, before they once again came ashore at the little village of Ipswich in East Anglia.

When the siege of London was broken off, Æthelred ordered his main army to march once more. The man to whom Æthelred now entrusted command of the Anglo-Saxon army was known as Ulfcytel. He was the Ealdorman of East Anglia, and in all probability the king's son-in-law. He was an experienced leader who had fought valiantly against the Danes in previous campaigns— and who was also renowned among them. They knew him by the nickname *Snillingr*—"the Brave"—and called East Anglia

"Ulfcytel's land". Their respect for him as an opponent is evident in preserved skaldic poems and later sagas.

Ulfcytel led thousands of Anglo-Saxon soldiers east along the north side of the river towards the Danish army. He was accompanied by a long line of prominent Anglo-Saxon nobles, many of them Æthelred's kin. A decisive confrontation became imminent. According to the *Anglo-Saxon Chronicle*, both Thorkell and Ulfcytel had now decided that the time for battle had come. Thorkell's spies kept a close eye on the Anglo-Saxon army's movements, and at the beginning of May the Danish army marched to meet the Anglo-Saxons in order to force them to fight. Instead of retreating, Ulfcytel chose to stand his ground.

On 5th May 1010, having dodged and evaded each other for ten months, the armies finally faced one another on a large plain close to Ipswich which was surrounded by hills on both sides. The place was known as *Ringmarheia*—Ringmere.[2]

There stood the two great armies, each of them consisting of thousands of men, surrounded by the colours of spring. Neither the Anglo-Saxons nor the Scandinavians used cavalry on the battlefield, but fought exclusively on foot. Both sides used the same basic tactics as Greek hoplites and Roman legionaries: they lined up in dense formations that would be difficult for the enemy to break through, and which also made it hard for their own people to flee.

Both the armies were organized in divisions around their noble leaders and their chainmail-wearing *hird*, or retinue. The soldiers were placed beside men they knew and cared about—the Anglo-Saxons with men from the same village, area or town, the Danes with men from the same ship. They assembled in long lines, often three or four men deep. With their shields before them, the armies could look like a vast wall or barrier of shields, which both Norse and Anglo-Saxon poets described in their war poetry.

Both sides used bowmen, and so lined up their men out of range of the enemy's arrows. One of Olaf's skalds describes how the Anglo-Saxons spread out before the Danish army on *Ringmarheia* so that they "occupied the entire field".

Like Christian armies on the continent, the Anglo-Saxons practised the custom of bringing relics to the battlefield. Holy books or ornamented reliquaries of gold and silver, containing body parts and hair from the Anglo-Saxon Church's martyrs, were carried before the army by monks so that their power would radiate out over both friends and enemies, and ensure that God's people were victorious.

Before any battle commenced negotiations would usually be held, in which the army leaders met one another in a courteous and ritualistic manner between the lined-up armies and discussed their terms. The army leaders made speeches to their own men, which were later often recounted using poetic turns of phrase in skaldic verse. They attempted to boost their men's morale by praising them and ridiculing their enemies—and reminded them that fleeing was not an option.

Thorkell's army consisted almost exclusively of brutalized men for whom war and battle were a way of life—who had crossed the sea to achieve wealth and honour, or die trying. And the Danish leaders were all experienced men of war. The core of the Anglo-Saxon army also consisted of such men—warrior nobles and the men in their service—but around them stood many peasant soldiers of the *fyrd*. Men who were not used to fighting.

The nervous tension during the preparations could be unbearable—this is something never disclosed in the heroic skaldic poems, but which shines through in the more down-to-earth Anglo-Saxon sources. In the tense and oppressive atmosphere before battle, the men found an outlet for their anxiety through aggressive and obscene shouting. Wild battle cries and primitive howling could be heard across the plain as the men on both sides shook their quivers and raised their spears to the sky. The *Anglo-Saxon Chronicle* tells of an ealdorman who had led an army in a previous fight against the Danes, who was so nervous before the battle that he began to vomit in front of his men. His people consequently refused to fight, and the army then disbanded.

The start of the battle was signalled by a fanfare of horns—and it was Thorkell's army who attacked. The Danes probably advanced in columns, as they usually did, in the formation that the Norse skalds and later saga scribes referred to as the *svinfylking*—the "swine array" or "boar snout". These columns were easier to hold together than lines as the men moved forwards. The best warriors were placed at the front, with more in the following rows, so that they could penetrate the enemy lines and break up their formation. According to the later Danish historian Saxo Grammaticus, the Danish army had learnt this formation from Odin himself, but it was not exclusive to the Norse warriors. Almost 1,000 years earlier the term "boar's face" had been used as military slang among the Roman legionaries to describe a column on the march.

The Danish formations slowly began to advance towards the enemy before them, and as the distance between the two armies narrowed arrows began to fly in both directions. When the armies were around thirty metres apart, both sides began to cast spears at each other: simple, cheap and unembellished projectiles. The men held their wooden shields before their faces and chests to protect themselves, well away from their bodies because the spears could pierce right through them. As the Danes' forwards movement continued, the men at the front of the columns were pushed towards the enemy by those behind. They didn't run, but walked calmly in order to hold their formation. And so—in as controlled a manner as possible—they clashed with their opponents.

Archaeological surveys of other medieval battlefields have uncovered mass graves containing skeletons of men with signs of strange damage to their teeth. The damage appears to have occurred just before death, and is thought to be the result of the men gritting their teeth with great force in the moments leading up to this clash of shield walls.

The killing happened face to face. The spears, with blades up to half a metre long, were thrust in among the enemy's shields from both sides, into unprotected faces, arms, feet, hands, shoulders, stomachs, thighs and necks. Men who fell were trampled on. The Norse warriors used the simple, light axes many of them carried in their belts to strike over and under the shields. There are also descriptions of individual warriors who moved out of the formations carrying huge axes, which they swung through great arcs around them using both hands. The leading figures on both sides, and the elite warriors who surrounded them, struck and pierced their opponents with their valuable swords. These most prestigious of killing tools were a little less than a metre long, and forged with so-called "blood gutters" or "blood grooves", which made the blades flexible and allowed the blood to flow from the wounds when the weapons were thrust into and pulled out of human flesh.

In describing the fantastically bloody theatre of war, the skalds revelled in almost pornographic images of violence. Rows of shields move like living walls across the battlefield. Banners swing and swell in the wind above the men's heads, like birds of prey eagerly awaiting the blood that will soon flow below them; the gilded posts to which they are attached shine and flash in the sun. As the banners and posts shiver and shake above the men's heads they are spattered with blood; beneath them, the swords sing with their cold tongues. They strike holes in shields. They split helmets in two, the grey iron turning red with the blood of the men it was meant to protect.

In the sheer terror of the battle, some of the Anglo-Saxon peasant soldiers were gripped by panic. A weak point in the English battle line buckled under the immense force of the clash with the Danes. The *Anglo-Saxon Chronicle* tells of the men of the *fyrd* from East Anglia who turned their backs on the enemy and began to run, even though the men of Cambridgeshire, who fought beside them, held their lines. From this point onwards, the Battle of Ringmere descended into a military catastrophe for the Anglo-Saxons; after the initial collapse their army suffered the same fate as any that broke formation in the medieval era. The panic was infectious, and quickly spread from line to line. More and more fled. Those who stood their ground found that the enemy streamed past them, only to appear at their backs. Over the course of a few moments, what had at first appeared to be an equally matched fight became a massacre as the Anglo-Saxon army's formation collapsed and the fleeing troops were cut down from behind.

In the panic and chaos that followed the breakdown of their order of battle, a large number of prominent Anglo-Saxon men were killed. Among the dead, the *Anglo-Saxon Chronicle* lists a number of Æthelred's own family members: "There was slain Athelstan the king's son-in-law, and Oswy and his son, and Wulfric, Leofwin's son, and Eadwy, Efy's brother, and many other good thanes, and numberless of the people." When the fray was over, piles of corpses remained on the battlefield.

A few years later, a skald stood in a hall somewhere in Norway and recited a poem for Olaf Haraldsson and the members of his court in remembrance of this battle:

> King, I have heard that your men cast bodies in great
> heaps,
> far from the ships they turned Ringmere Heath red with
> blood.

> The people threw themselves at your feet, and many fled
> before it was over.

The bloody battle would be remembered in narratives and poems
on both sides of the North Sea. It marked the great turning point
in the war, and in the time that followed those of Æthelred's
forces who had not participated in the fighting also gradually
began to dissolve. The Anglo-Saxon *fyrd* of peasant soldiers had
never before been called up for such a long period, and after the
defeat at Ringmere the farmers returned home to save their crops.
There was nobody left to prevent the Danish army from moving
through the country, raiding and plundering wherever its members
so wished. Æthelred held a series of crisis meetings of his *witan*
in London, but it would be impossible to raise another army. The
battle signified the end of all organized resistance.

Gloomy passages of the *Anglo-Saxon Chronicle* describe the
Norse warriors' determination and ferocity, in biting contrast to
the king and the other Anglo-Saxon leaders' inability to act:

> But although something might be then counselled, it did
> not stand even one month: at last there was no chief who
> would assemble forces, but each fled as he best might; nor,
> at the last, would even one shire assist another.

No longer at risk of being outmanoeuvred and ambushed by
Æthelred's forces, Thorkell's army began a terrible and violent
series of raids on Eastern England, which developed into a three-
month-long orgy of burning, killing and plundering. "The land
[they] three months ravaged and burned; and they even went
into the wild fens, and they destroyed men and cattle," states the
Anglo-Saxon Chronicle. The consequences were catastrophic for
those who lived in the areas visited by the Danes. Things got so

bad that the Danes had problems obtaining enough provisions—simply because there was no longer anything left to steal. They were forced to send groups of looters into the almost uninhabited and marshy Fens in search of food.

Soon, Thorkell and his army marched south. His soldiers burned the towns of Thetford and Cambridge along the way; they stole an enormous number of horses, which entire divisions of the army used to traverse the English road network more efficiently than ever. They quickly made their way deeper into the country on horseback—to Oxfordshire and from there to Buckinghamshire, along the River Ouse to the town of Bedford and on to Tempsford, "ever burning as they went". Huge volumes of goods and live animals were transported back to the ships on the coast.

Somewhere in the midst of all the chaos, Olaf was leading his division of the army. One of his skalds later paid tribute to him as follows:

> Widely renowned lord, men of English lineage could not stand against you when you took their treasure, showing no mercy.

> I have heard that people often gave gold to the worthy king, they went to the beach in great flocks.

An English chronicler tells the same story in a rather more sober tone, from the perspective of the victims: "They did not desist from making incursions in straggling bodies throughout the provinces wherever they chose, laying waste towns, spoiling some wretched people of their property and slaying others."

At the end of October in the year 1010, Thorkell's main army arrived in the town of Northampton and here, too, burned everything to the ground. Having thoroughly looted the town's environs and the neighbouring districts, the army crossed the Thames and took themselves into Wessex, on through the swamps towards All Cannings in Wiltshire. According to the *Anglo-Saxon Chronicle*, they burned almost everything they passed.

By Christmas 1010, when the Danish army had once again returned to their ships, they had over the course of a period of eighteen months caused greater destruction in England than any other Viking army before them. In the words of the *Anglo-Saxon Chronicle*, they had

> ... over-run, 1st, East-Anglia, and 2d, Essex, and 3d, Middlesex, and 4th, Oxfordshire, and 5th, Cambridgeshire, and 6th, Hertfordshire, and 7th, Buckinghamshire, and 8th, Bedfordshire, and 9th, half of Huntingdonshire, and 10th, much of Northamptonshire; and south of Thames, all Kent, and Sussex, and Hastings, and Surry, and Berkshire, and Hampshire, and much of Wiltshire.

England had been brought to its knees. Early in the winter of 1010, Æthelred gave up trying to defend his kingdom. Envoys rode to the Danes' main camp, somewhere on the banks of the Thames, and expressed their ruler's wish to begin negotiations. Thorkell met with them. Perhaps Olaf did, too. Æthelred's negotiators promised to produce a greater tribute than any Danish army had ever received before. Thorkell ordered his people to stop their plundering and wait.

Over the period that followed, an uncertain and nervous peace settled between the two parties. Indeed, it was sporadically broken by small groups of Danes who went around plundering villages without their leaders' permission, but for the most part the Danish army remained in the camp by their ships, where they lived on provisions supplied by Æthelred. Weeks and months passed. Winter turned to spring. Spring became summer. Summer passed into autumn.

Then war broke out again. By early in the autumn of 1011, the Danish army had still seen nothing of the promised tribute, probably because the tribute Thorkell had demanded was so great that Æthelred was unable to obtain enough coins. In early September the Danish army therefore made its way deeper into the country once again, in long columns of armed men. They marched through the forests and flatlands of Kent until they reached Canterbury. Over two years had passed since the army last stood before the cathedral city's walls, immediately after it had arrived in England. On 8th September 1011 the city was surrounded, and a siege began.

This time, no negotiations led to peace. Responsible for the city's defence was Ælfheah, the Archbishop of Canterbury—incidentally the same man who, seventeen years earlier, had ridden with King Æthelred to Andover to meet Olaf Tryggvason, and who had led the ritual of baptism in which the Norse king had knelt before Æthelred before heading back across the sea to conquer his homeland. Ælfheah was now an ageing man, almost sixty years old. He was obstinate and proud. With the Danish army camped outside the city walls he refused to surrender, instead waiting determinedly for his people to come to his aid. No help came.

For two weeks, Ælfheah and the city's population held their ground. But then the Danes made their move. Exactly what caused the city's fall is unclear, but several Anglo-Saxon sources briefly describe how the city was betrayed by an abbot, who managed to make some sort of deal that ensured he would be spared, perhaps along with his monks and abbey. Maybe he opened the gates. In any event, the city fell on 29th September 1011, the day on which the Anglo-Saxons usually celebrated the harvest festival.

Among warriors there was an ancient, unwritten rule that cities which surrendered voluntarily would be spared from being plundered and burned. But with any city that fell after resisting, the victor was free to do whatever he wished. What happened in Canterbury would for generations be remembered as the most horrifying expression of the Danes' brutality in England in all the almost thirty years for which the war had raged.

> … a part of the city was burnt, and, the army effecting an entrance, the city was taken. Some were slaughtered with the sword, some destroyed by the flames. […] The women were dragged by their hair through the streets of the city, and then, being thrown into the flames, were thus put to death.

> You would have seen a terrible sight: the whole of the ancient and beautiful city reduced to ashes, corpses of the citizens lying packed together in the streets, the ground and the river blackened with blood, the lamenting and wailing of women and children being led away into captivity.

Whether or not such depictions are exaggerated is hard to say. The fate that befell Anglo-Saxon Christendom's most important city—where a significant proportion of the inhabitants were monks and nuns—was a huge shock, and the memory of the city's fall would over the following centuries grow into a dark cloud of horror stories—exaggerated tales of sadism and martyrdom. These tales describe, for example, how a great number of men were strung up by their testicles; how women had their breasts cut off and infants were pierced through with spears, cut up into pieces and crushed to death under the wheels of carts and wagons.

But the fact that the city was burnt and its inhabitants met a grim fate is confirmed by the Norse skaldic poems. Indeed, one of the warlords who led the forces that stormed the city was Olaf Haraldsson. His skalds relate directly, as in an homage, how he burned the city's buildings and went after the blood of the city's people:

> ... the town reeves were not able to hold Olaf from their city, Canterbury; much sorrow and destruction was caused there.

> King, you reddened broad Canterbury in the morning. Fire and smoke played mightily against the houses as you gained victory; I heard that you harmed the lives of the people, bringing them great sorrow.

The Danes took a number of prisoners from among the city's inhabitants who survived the first wave of spontaneous violence, including many of the up to 1,000 monks, nuns, priests and sextons who lived in the city. Most of them were quickly set free, say the Anglo-Saxon sources, including all the women and children. A number of men were retained to be sold back to their families; others likely ended up on the slave market. Prisoners of high birth who held important positions in the Church or in King Æthelred's machinery of power were particularly valuable to the Danes.

Among those who were set free, we are told, was the abbot who had helped the Danes enter the city. But Archbishop Ælfheah himself was not so lucky. Together with King Æthelred's ombudsman in the city, an abbot, a bishop and countless other captives, the old clergyman was led out of Canterbury's smoking ruins in chains. He was taken on a long march down country roads to Thorkell's main camp, where he was imprisoned in a cage. He remained there for a long time.

One of Olaf's skalds states that Olaf fought in yet another battle after the fall of Canterbury, at an unidentified location known in

Old Norse as *Nýjamóða*, where "the young, not unwilling king made the hair of the English red; dark-red blood again ran along the swords".

This is the last battle of the war that is described by Olaf's skalds. After it, a kind of peace settled over the country once more as Thorkell and his circle of leaders again negotiated with Æthelred and his people regarding the redeeming of prisoners and the outstanding payment of tribute. Things dragged out. Autumn turned to winter. Winter became spring. Half a year passed.

At the start of Easter in April of the year 1012, Eadric Streona came to London to lead Æthelred's *witan*. Æthelred himself stayed away while Eadric conducted the final negotiations and arranged payment of the tribute. Wagon after wagon rolled down bumpy roads to the city, carrying silver from the kingdom's other towns.

The Danes' most prestigious prisoner was Archbishop Ælfheah. They hoped to obtain a significant sum for him, and tried to get him to assist them in their negotiations regarding the purchasing of his freedom with Æthelred's *witan*, but he refused to help them. This would cost him dearly.

On Easter Eve, the Danes held a victory celebration at their camp. During the war they had looted great quantities of wine, and this was consumed with much enthusiasm by the warriors. The festivities deteriorated into a drunken orgy—at some point someone brought the archbishop out of his cage, where he seems to have been kept for months, and hauled him across to the feast hall. He was set before a group of men who were sitting there drinking; they began to throw stones, bones and animal skulls at him.

Thorkell himself was present, and according to what was later said in England attempted to intervene and prevent the valuable hostage from being harmed, but he no longer had control over his drunk and angry men. In the escalating wine-fuelled melee, the old archbishop was hit hard on the head with the butt of an axe, which cracked his skull. The man who beat him to death appears to have been named Thrum. As one of the Anglo-Saxon chroniclers poetically expressed it: "So the man of God fell, sprinkling the earth with his holy blood, and his blessed soul adorned the temples of heaven."

And so peace finally came to England. London's inhabitants collected the archbishop's dead body and carried him into the city, where he was ceremoniously buried in St Paul's Cathedral. At the same time, Eadric Streona handed over the extraordinary sum of 48,000 pounds of silver to Thorkell the Tall in a tribute ceremony. This was by far the greatest amount any Viking army had ever received in England, and represented a not insignificant part of all the coinage in circulation throughout the Anglo-Saxon kingdom.

The Danish army's leaders shared the wealth between them in accordance with the detailed agreements they had entered into, before in turn distributing parts of the booty among their men. Some of it was probably also sent across the sea to King Sweyn in Denmark.

At this time, Olaf Haraldsson was only in his early twenties. He was already an extremely rich man—but his military career had only just begun.

NOTES

[1] This was just as true in the 1000s as when the late Roman historian Vegetius wrote in his theoretical treatise on the art of war in the late 300s, "The main and principal point in war is to secure plenty of provisions for oneself and to destroy the enemy by famine. Famine is more terrible than the sword."

² Traditionally, it has been assumed that Ringmarheia (which the Anglo-Saxons called *Hringmere-hūō* and Olaf's skalds *Hringmaraheio*) is the modern Ringmer, which is in Sussex near England's south coast, but the place is probably modern Rymer in Suffolk, near Thetford. This fits in with the Vikings' route, as it is described in the primary sources, which went via Ipswich.

india ma qua sunt gentes ulime · modi
monti au
fenes
hic

leone

euilath
modia
arabia
deserta

armenia
sina
cadamon
monti sina

mesopotamia
chaldea
fluuis

saule flura
maabre
monti sarge
emorica

hiberia
manly
doricha
mons
mianaia
rabas
phili
sina

conmagna
cesaria phily
anteatos

israhel
tribu dan
effinni
galilea
iurichio
assur
ebron

mahia
aribul rabu
tori

nobe sabulon
neptalim

ihursaler

mons
eluneai
thario cilicia

alia enor
cappadocia

napha
nappolim

naptha
melina
syria

galgetia
ria obi en
grecia

iunonum
pannonie
iolana

libra unpallis

bethleel
fluuis
acha

macedonia

mauritania

affrica magna

britannia
gallecia
tana
tana
mauricania
annat melos

ispania

spania

MIDGARD

AFTER THE PEACE SETTLEMENT, the Danish army disbanded. The Danish king's formidable war machine quite simply split into its individual component parts, and the many smaller groups of which it consisted each went their own way. "When the tribute was paid, and oaths of peace were sworn, then the army separated widely, in like manner as before it had been gathered together," reports the *Anglo-Saxon Chronicle*.

Æthelred had saved his kingdom, but it was a painfully costly peace. The collection of the silver had been difficult and distressing. Churches were emptied of valuable objects, and high-ranking Church leaders and nobles had been pressured to sell their properties by their king. Æthelred himself had to sell off property that belonged to the Crown's ancestral lands in exchange for silver bullion. Large quantities of Anglo-Saxon coins imprinted with Æthelred's image have been found buried at various locations across Scandinavia.

The king's prestige had been dealt a fierce blow. Discontent and bitterness at the tribute's ruinous economic consequences caused new cracks to appear in the already split Anglo-Saxon nobility. After years of war in their home country, Æthelred's military forces were exhausted; his grip on power was beginning to slip. His subjects were unable to trust in his ability to defend them. He would be unable to withstand another attack of this kind.

In the summer of 1012, old hostilities were therefore renegotiated and new alliances forged in now-devastated England. In a manoeuvre that must have caused quite a stir among both Anglo-Saxons and Danes, Æthelred joined forces with the only man in England able to protect his position—Thorkell the Tall himself. The man who had led the Danish army for the past three years, and who had done his utmost to destroy Æthelred's country, to murder and ransack his subjects and to fleece the king for money. Thorkell had naturally become a widely renowned and deeply feared figure in England—perhaps even as renowned and feared as the man for whom he had worked, Sweyn Forkbeard.

Switching sides in this way seems stranger today than it did in Æthelred's time. In the 1000s, a man's loyalty to his lord was regarded as the highest of virtues, but at the same time the age's political and military realities made its power dynamics chronically volatile. The foundations upon which all of Europe's political system rested were alliances—loyal allegiances and agreements between individuals—including in Scandinavia. Men swore oaths and took pride in and established their reputations by keeping their word—the Vikings were known for ceremoniously swearing on rings and swords. But these alliances were often temporary, and when a man had fulfilled his obligations he was free. Anyone who wanted to survive and be successful in the world had to be opportunistic, headstrong and adaptable, and within certain limits there was significant cultural acceptance for reshuffling one's friends and enemies as dictated by changes in the political situation. Mortal enemies might make peace, kiss each other's cheeks and collaborate in order to defeat a common foe, only to become mortal enemies again soon afterwards. It made the age's battles for power and resources endless, and the lives of society's leaders incredibly unpredictable.

Instead of going back to his home in Scania, or to his lord Sweyn Forkbeard's court in Roskilde, after the peace settlement Thorkell entered straight into Æthelred's service. With him he brought his forty-five warships and their Norse crews of around 3,000 men—loyal men who had sworn an oath directly to Thorkell himself. Through a ceremony, Thorkell swore an oath to Æthelred in which he promised to defend the very same kingdom he had spent the past three years destroying.

For his part, Æthelred promised to keep Thorkell's soldiers clothed and fed, and to pay them—with even more jangling coins. In order to finance his new army of foreign warriors, the king imposed on his subjects a new annual land tax known as the *here-geld*. To pay Thorkell personally, Æthelred gave him direct control over large areas of land in Southern England. Thorkell thereby assumed a position that made him one of the most influential men in Æthelred's kingdom, alongside Eadric Streona and other prominent ealdormen in the king's *witan*.

Olaf Haraldsson chose another way forwards. Five years had now passed since he had led his men out into the world to live the "warrior's good life". He was not only rich, but undoubtedly also a hardened young man. The war in which he had fought for the past three years was the most intense this part of the world had seen for many generations. The men in his service were experienced war veterans—and there were great opportunities for men like them in the Europe of the 1000s.

As peace came to England, a ship from the continent also came to the war-ravaged island; on board was a group of delegates who served the Duke of Normandy. Their mission was to find willing mercenaries among the scores of experienced and newly out-of-work warriors. The aforementioned Norman monk and historian William of Jumièges says that these envoys sought out two Norse kings, each of whom led a large band of warriors. One of them was called Lacman, and he was probably a king from the Hebrides. We otherwise know very little about him, but according to the Norman chronicler he had been a success-ful commander during the war in England. The other was Olaf Haraldsson.

William of Jumièges describes how the two kings courteously and obligingly received the Norman delegates, before sending them back to Duke Richard with many gifts and the promise that they too would soon follow.

Gold, silver and other booty was then carried aboard the two fleets of ships, along with fresh and preserved provisions, drink, bedding, tents, warm clothes, woollen cloaks, rowing gloves, cooking vessels, bailers, drinking cups, buckets, flints for making fires, coils of rope, furs and skins, ladders, knives, swords, unstrung bows, bowstrings, quivers and arrows, axes, spears, shields, hel-mets, coats of mail and all the other myriad items carried by a Viking army on the move. The fleets, which together constituted a significant fighting force, left the coast of England and "sailed over the foaming sea", as William writes, as they made their way south towards France.

*

The kingdom of the Franks covered most of the territory of modern France. The neighbouring Holy Roman Empire stretched across vast areas from Northern Germany to Southern Italy. Both realms were the heirs of Charlemagne's enormous domain, which had covered almost all of continental Western Europe north of the Alps and the Pyrenees, before it was broken up in the mid-800s. Both were also built on the dream of Roman greatness and unity, but in reality the Holy Roman Emperor in the east and King of the Franks in the west were nowhere near the almighty personages suggested by their titles. Their realms were first and foremost theoretical and symbolic constructions, completely lacking in the institutions necessary to enforce any credible form of centralized power.

The King of the Franks, Robert II of the Capetian dynasty, controlled only a small area around Paris. The rest of the kingdom was divided into vassal territories, led by a handful of enormously rich and fiercely feuding princes—in name subject to the king, but in practice men who did more or less as they pleased. Swathed in colourful fabrics and covered in jewels, they could be seen along the country roads, on horseback and surrounded by their escorts as they passed their working subjects, en route to their fortified residences. They continually disturbed the peace by sending their men into each other's domains to plunder and steal, into border feuds and minor battles, where rather than attacking their rival's castles and knights they often chose to strike him by plundering and beating to death his peasants.

Olaf's new employer was one of these princes. Richard II, Duke of Normandy, was forty-nine years old and had been the Normans' ruler for sixteen of these. He was among the most prominent political figures in the Frankish kingdom, an obstinate feudal lord who maintained wide-reaching connections with other princes and their kin all across Europe. He had marked himself out among the Frankish princes by declaring his loyalty to Paris. He had also repeatedly supported the king in his disagreements with unruly vassals by dispatching soldiers and knights to his aid, including to areas as far away as Burgundy.

But he was also a sly political fox, experienced and volatile, who knew how to manoeuvre through a rapidly changing landscape.

For years he had wavered between both sides in the conflict between the Anglo-Saxons and the Danes, and collaborated with both parties depending on what best served his own interests at any given moment.

Formally, Richard was Æthelred's ally. As previously mentioned, for the past ten years Æthelred's queen had been Richard's own sister, Emma of Normandy. Richard was her elder brother, and he had entered into the marriage pact on her behalf.

But over the past decade, Richard had also repeatedly given Sweyn Forkbeard's war fleets access to his ports. The Danes sailed injured warriors across the English Channel so that they could receive treatment, and sold their loot in the Norman port markets. The Danes likely also sold slaves in Normandy, a lucrative business that was a natural and integrated part of the Danish culture of war and plunder. In Rouen, Normandy's most important city and the duke's main seat, there was an active slave market.[1]

Among the Christian princes in Western Europe, the Duke of Normandy had a unique relationship with the Danes, and he made a tidy profit by collaborating with his Norse friends. This gave rise to suspicion and head-shaking from Normandy's Frankish neighbours—and to rage from the Anglo-Saxons on the other side of the Channel.

The duke's enemies would have claimed that he was simply co-operating with his own kind—he was, after all, of Norse descent. Richard was the great-grandson of the mythical Viking who in Frankish descriptions is given the name *Roso*, *Rodo* or *Rollo*, and who in the later Icelandic saga tradition is known as *Gange-Rolv*. This Viking chieftain, whose origins are unknown, led an army up the Seine in the early 900s, where he ruthlessly exploited peasants and defenceless monks before making a deal with the then Frankish king. He stopped his plundering, renounced his heathenism, was baptized, swore allegiance to the king, promised to defend his land against other Vikings and took the Frankish name Robert. In exchange, he was given control of the lands he had plundered—with a Frankish earldom thrown into the bargain.

A hundred years later, the country was known as Normannia, or Normandy—the land of the Northmen—and was a Frankish dukedom with proud churches and monasteries. The descendants of Rollo's Vikings were woven into the local Frankish ruling class through marriage, and looked much like their Angevin, Parisian and Picardian neighbours. They spoke French, and often gave their children French names.

Scandinavians were regarded with a mixture of suspicion, fear and condescension in the Frankish kingdom, which had been afflicted by Viking attacks for 200 years. And the Normans themselves had an ambivalent relationship to their Norse origins. On the one hand, they strove to present themselves as civilized Franks, while on the other they were openly proud of their roots, which were glorified by their historians. Our chronicle-writing monk, the aforementioned William of Jumièges, for example, wrote in his works that he felt the Norse peoples were more noble than other barbarians. After all, their roots led all the way back to Greek antiquity—they were the descendants of heroic Trojan warriors, who after the fall of Troy had travelled north in search of a new home, finally settling down in Scandinavia.

The Norman ruling class also maintained close connections with Scandinavia. Duke Richard and his sister Emma's own mother, Gunnor, was the daughter of a prominent Dane. She was said to have had an incredible memory, and to have taught her children about the Danish family from which she came.[2]

Richard's greatest rival in the Frankish kingdom was Odo II, Count of Blois, Chartres, Châteaudun, Beauvais and Tours, whose lands encircled Normandy to the west and south. Count Odo was a formidable and aggressive feudal lord who continuously waged war on his neighbours and by various means attempted to appropriate their territories. Richard and Odo had once been allies—like King Æthelred, Odo had been married to one of Richard's many sisters—but the relationship between the two families had soured when Odo's wife had died childless and Richard demanded the return of the lands Odo had received as her dowry. The two princes had been playing a prolonged and devious diplomatic game of cat and mouse ever since, and regularly fought each other on the battlefield. For years they had looted each other's lands and beaten each other's peasants to death. Castles had been conquered and reconquered.

This long-standing conflict was the reason why Richard II sent delegates to England to recruit mercenaries—in the words of William of Jumièges, to "punish Count Odo's disobedience".

Olaf and Lacman did not take their fleets to Rouen, but instead sailed directly to the coast of Brittany, further west. This was where Dol Castle, one of Odo's fortresses, was located, and the duke had probably tasked Olaf and Lacman with destroying it. Sometime during the summer of 1012 the two Norse fleets arrived in a shallow bay on the Cotentin Peninsula in Brittany, where the rich and famous Benedictine abbey of Mont-Saint-Michel lay on an island out in the bay—just as it does today—surrounded by water at high tide and by endless sandbanks at its ebb due to Europe's strongest turning tide. Olaf's skald called the bay "the beautiful Hringsfjǫrðr".

The Norman chronicles describe how Olaf and Lacman led their armies ashore and immediately began to plunder the people who lived along the coast. They caused great destruction. Then they led their main forces further inland, and walked to a flat plain. While their scouts kept watch for enemies the soldiers dug deep and narrow trenches in front of their lines, and then camouflaged them with branches and earth.

It was a cunning trap, an old tactic used by Vikings to defend themselves against attacks from mounted men—descriptions of which are also found in older continental chronicles from the 800s. Because unlike the Anglo-Saxons—who fought on foot as the Danes did—the Frankish princes commanded organized cavalry. Foot soldiers had little chance of emerging unscathed from an encounter with mounted men on open ground, which may be part of the reason why the Vikings often preferred to attack England, rather than France.

Soon, a Breton army on horseback turned up. Covered in chainmail from head to toe and protected by long, almond-shaped shields, Frankish mounted knights were the age's most effective and feared weapon. The knights tended to attack in tight formations and at a gallop, accelerating towards their enemies so that the ground thundered beneath them. They stood in their stirrups and lowered their long spears, which, propelled by the power of the horses, were able to pierce shields, chainmail and human bodies.

Olaf and Lacman lined up their men behind the hidden trenches. The Norman chronicle states that the knights attacked in a group, blindly and boldly, but that the attack came to an abrupt halt when they rode straight into the hidden ditches. Men were thrown from their saddles; many of the horses broke their legs. Lying dazed and injured on the ground with no battle formation whatsoever, the Bretons were immediately subjected to an attack so violent that few managed to flee from the bloodbath.

Olaf and Lacman then led their men to Count Odo's boundary castle, Dol. The castle was situated at the innermost end of the bay beside a small town, between the Norman Cotentin Peninsula and Brittany. Like most castles at the time, Dol was of the motte-and-bailey type; wooden towers and buildings were constructed atop a raised area of earth and stone, encircled by a palisade of perpendicular stakes. It was defended by Odo's man, a Frankish nobleman by the name of Solomon.

Olaf and Lacman's warriors surrounded the castle. Then, after a brief siege, they stormed it, clambering over the walls and overpowering the castle's defenders in hand-to-hand combat. The chronicle describes how Olaf and Lacman massacred everyone they found within the castle's walls, down to the very last man. Even the lord of the castle, Solomon himself, was struck down or stabbed to death. The Norse warriors then set the timber castle ablaze and it burned to the ground.

The army returned to the ships, raised anchor, rowed out into the bay, raised sails, and followed the coast east until they reached the mouth of the Seine. Then they continued to sail or row against the current up the wide river, past settlements, trading sites and Jumièges Abbey—which lay on a plain on the eastern bank—towards Rouen.

The Normans' most important city and Duke Richard's seat was just a short day's journey from the coast, located on the inside of a sharp bend on the eastern bank of the wide river. It was a small town, not especially wealthy, and surrounded by steep, green hills. Jetties stuck out into the river, and behind these rose a city wall. A visiting Norse skald describes how the ships were moored directly to the outside of the wall; on the inside was a packed city centre with low buildings, a market, mills, stone churches and the duke's palace. Rouen was an ancient Roman administration centre, and several of the buildings from that time were still standing, having been either converted or repaired. A large church that would become the city's cathedral was under construction.

Duke Richard received Olaf and Lacman personally. He is said to have "very gladly received them with honour befitting kings", continues the chronicle. But Richard had to leave his guests not long after they had arrived, because the news that Vikings had burned and ravaged the coast had spread rapidly throughout France and reached Paris and the Frankish king, Robert II. The fact that the king's vassal had used Norse mercenary troops against one of his other vassals in the kingdom was scandalous. Worried about what further destruction they might cause, King Robert took immediate action and sent out messengers—not only to Duke Richard and Count Odo, but to all his vassals all across his extensive kingdom. He called them to a gathering.

While Olaf and Lacman seem to have enjoyed some time spent resting in Rouen with their men at the duke's expense, Richard himself went to Chartres, where, under the king's supervision and with his peers as mediators, he negotiated peace terms with Count Odo. They reached a compromise. Richard would be permitted to keep the lands he had taken from his enemy, and in return Odo would be permitted to keep some of the lands he had received many years earlier as part of his wife's dowry when he had married Richard's sister.

Richard quickly returned to Rouen and his "two kings", as William of Jumièges calls Olaf and Lacman; he also rewarded them "with gifts fitting for kings". Before they journeyed onwards, the Norse leaders assured the duke that they would return should he ever need their help again in the future.

The assistance Duke Richard received from Olaf and Lacman in this internal Frankish conflict would cling to him always—the incident served to damage the already dubious reputation by which he and his kin were known in the Frankish kingdom. Ten or fifteen years later, Rodulfus the Bald, a monk and historian from Burgundy, wrote sourly that the Duke of Normandy's ability to call on help from the other side of the sea made him immune to attack. Richer of Reims, another chronicler, described Richard with contempt, dubbing him the "duke of the pirates".

In order to counter such perceptions and protect his reputation, Duke Richard later appointed his own literate monk, and assigned him the task of writing an official biography of the Norman dynasty that would quash all doubt regarding its legitimacy. This honourable assignment was given to the monk Dudo, who panegyrically set to work and wrote a beautiful history of Norman piety, in which he failed to mention that the Normans had come to the kingdom of the Franks to plunder and pillage, instead emphasizing how quickly they had set aside their heathenism and barbarity and become civilized.

*

Before the summer of 1012 was over, Olaf led his fleet westwards from Rouen, past the smoking remains of Dol, along the coast of Brittany and around the Finistère Peninsula, from where the fleet set its course south. We can follow him on his journey through the preserved poems composed by his skalds, and through sporadic mentions in various European chronicles. The destruction of Dol is just the first in a long line of raids and battles that were woven into verse by Olaf's skalds in the weeks and months that followed, and philologists and historians have long discussed the locations to which the Norse place names in the poems might refer.

Whether Lacman followed Olaf further, or whether the two kings parted ways, is unknown. But several Viking fleets of various size were recorded sailing north and south along the coast of France at this time. The mobilization of bands of warriors and mercenaries that had participated in the wars in England—from Scandinavia, from the settlements along the Baltic coast, from the Norse islands off Scotland and from Ireland—led to renewed Viking attacks on the continent, including in France. In the chronicles we read of attacks on many places during these years, after decades of peace. As in earlier times, Viking warlords temporarily banded together, seeking strength in numbers, before parting ways once more when the battle was over.

Having left Rouen, Olaf seems to have joined up with one or more bands of warriors from Ireland. Without mentioning any of the Viking leaders by name, an almost contemporary Aquitanian chronicle tells of "a terrible horde of Norsemen from Denmark and Ireland", which sailed into the country along the wide and heavily trafficked River Loire. A hundred years earlier, the rich and fertile Loire Valley had been visited by some of the biggest Viking fleets ever to have gathered, and was consequently one of the most heavily fortified areas in Europe—castles and timber forts lined the banks of the river, and bridges with towers and parapets blocked many of its tributaries. Nevertheless, states the chronicle, the fleet sailed into the country. Its crew came ashore and established a camp, and "ravaged, destroyed and burned". They made it all the way to the heavily fortified city of Poitiers.

Poitiers was the main seat of another leading figure in France, namely William V, Duke of Aquitaine and Count of Poitiers. The next act of war mentioned by Olaf's skalds after Brittany is a battle outside "the town of Viljálmr".[3]

The Aquitanian chronicle describes how Duke William, who was a middle-aged man, gathered a great army of knights and foot soldiers, which he personally led. He set up camp close to his enemies. Early one morning, the duke's army lined up and prepared to attack; a contingent of heavily armed knights led the charge. What followed only strengthens the suspicion that the duke's opponent was Olaf. The cavalry spurred on their warhorses and galloped confidently towards their enemies, lances aimed and ready.

The knights galloped straight into camouflaged trenches in front of the Viking camp, dug by their enemies during the night. The chronicle relates that the Norse soldiers succeeded in taking around thirty men prisoner in the chaos. They used them as hostages, threatening to kill them should they be attacked again—which they were not. The following night they sailed away with their captives, and later, closer to the coast, set them free in exchange for silver and gold. Then they sailed out to sea and disappeared.

Taking prisoners and demanding a ransom was not peculiar to the Vikings. It was a natural and accepted part of the way in which war was waged all across Europe, and often an important source of income for European noblemen at this time. But the Vikings had taken the practice one step further, and specialized in making money from captives on a greater scale than anyone else in this part of the world. Frankish monastery annals and chronicles are full of accounts of people along France's coasts and rivers who simply found themselves in the wrong place at the wrong time when the Vikings attacked, and so ended up being taken prisoner. Rich and famous individuals were sold back to their families for sky-high sums, but ordinary people were also abducted. These individuals were not sold back to their relatives, however, but taken away by ship and sold as slaves.

There were many markets for slaves in Europe. Most Western European rulers enforced the Church's prohibition on the trading of Christian slaves, but along Europe's outer fringes the practice of human trafficking flourished. The biggest market in Western Europe was in Dublin, where Irish traffickers of Norse origin conducted the buying and selling of slaves, including Europeans and Africans, on a vast scale. Strong young men and beautiful young women were most sought after. They ended up in Normandy, in Ireland, in England, in Scandinavia and in Iceland. Even in the Anglo-Saxon kingdom with its pious clergy, slaves made up a significant portion of the population, if not as great a portion as in the Norse countries. An Arab diplomat from Baghdad who encountered Norse Vikings in Russia, and who witnessed them burying their dead chieftain, wrote a dark depiction of their religious customs, describing how they ritually raped and murdered the women they owned. Slaves who died were not buried, but left out under the open sky, where the dogs and birds of prey would devour them.

Olaf having been one of the leaders in Sweyn Forkbeard and Thorkell's long-term war in England—a war in which we know the Danes repeatedly took captives and hostages—it isn't hard to imagine that he might have ended up with many prisoners who could be sold. This might also explain why he continued to sail ever further away from Scandinavia, because from Aquitaine Olaf continued south, on a journey that became increasingly exotic. The ships sailed into the Bay of Biscay, shaving past the Basque kingdom of Navarre, where the Pyrenees meet the Atlantic Ocean. As days turned into weeks, they continued along the rugged coasts of the Northern Spanish county of Castile and the kingdom of León, towards the outer limits of Christian Europe. Further south was al-Andalus, the Muslim kingdom that covered over half of the Iberian Peninsula—and in al-Andalus was the biggest slave market in the known world.

*

Three hundred years had passed since the Islamic conquest of North Africa reached the boundaries of Christendom. In the year 711, a Berber army under Arab leadership crossed the Strait of Gibraltar and began the conquest of the Visigothic kingdom that had reigned over the Iberian Peninsula since the dissolution of the Roman Empire. With the exception of a narrow strip of land in mountainous Northern Spain, where Christian princes still clung on for dear life, Muslim armies quickly captured the entire territory that comprises today's Portugal and Spain. They founded a realm that would exist in various forms and constellations for over eight centuries.

In Olaf's time, al-Andalus was a caliphate centred around Córdoba and managed by the Umayyad dynasty, a branch of the Prophet Muhammad's later descendants. By most standards, the caliphate of Córdoba was Europe's most advanced and sophisticated society, challenged only by the Byzantine Empire on Europe's south-eastern fringes. From their palaces and residences in the fertile Ebro and Guadalquivir river valleys, the Arab warrior nobility dominated a diverse and multicultural population that consisted of Christians, Jews, Visigothic converts to Islam, Arab immigrants from today's Syria and Iraq, and Berber nomads from the merciless desert plains of North Africa.

In Córdoba, the caliphate's seat, lived around 100,000 people—a population roughly the same as Constantinople's, and many times more than that of any other city in Europe. Here, a strictly hierarchical, centralized and professional bureaucracy worked in the caliphate's service, consisting of ministers, judges and tax masters, who organized the minting of coins and collection of taxes and co-ordinated the provincial governors' local administrations. It was a system the Arabs had continued from the Roman Empire's administration of its eastern regions in late antiquity and brought with them to Egypt, Damascus, Baghdad and Spain.

Despite the fact that Christians broadly regarded al-Andalus as Christendom's arch-enemy, the vast kingdom in the south was also famed for its knowledge—its libraries with collections of Persian and Arabic books, its mathematicians and astronomers. It was also known for its exotic textiles and gilded and engraved goatskin products; for its musicians and poets and harems. For

spices imported from the Middle East, jewellery lined with mer-
cury from local mines, exclusive ointments and toothpaste.

Al-Andalus was also a brutal slave society, with a larger slave
economy than any other European realm. And just as Christians
were not meant to have other Christians as slaves, in the Muslim
world it was forbidden to keep other Muslims as slaves. This
made non-Muslim prisoners one of the most sought-after goods
in al-Andalus, and laid the foundations for a slave trade of vast
proportions.

One important route crossed the burning heat of the Sahara
from Sudan in the south; another travelled from Aquitaine in the
north, through Orleans, Poitiers and Bordeaux, and from there
through the Pyrenees to Pamplona. The most far-reaching and
well-organized route ran from Kiev in the east, via Prague and
Koblenz to Verdun—where the male slaves that would become
eunuchs were castrated by specialists using razor-sharp knives—
then down the Rhône to Arles on the southern coast of France,
from where the journey continued overland or by ship to Zaragoza
in al-Andalus.

A fourth route went by sea along the Iberian Atlantic coast—
this was the route operated by Norse and Irish Vikings—and the
trading went both ways. Norse slave traders brought Christian
prisoners to the south, and sailed north with Muslim captives and
Africans, whom they purchased from Muslim slave traders and
sold on the markets in Ireland.

On the slave markets in the al-Andalusian cities, Africans,
Franks, Northern Spaniards, Anglo-Saxons, Germans, Italians,
Norsemen and—the most numerous group—Slavs were bought
and sold on a huge scale.[4] Many were purchased by Jewish, Muslim
or Christian families, but the largest group were forced into the
caliphate's service, either as soldiers or as eunuchs who were set
to serve in the administration and bureaucracy. According to

Arab historians, tens of thousands of slaves in al-Andalus ended up as eunuchs.

Towards the end of the 900s, however, the importation of slaves from the north and east began to dwindle. The areas from which the eastern slaves came was in the process of being Christianized; in the north, Frankish princes began to tighten up the enforcement of the prohibition on selling Christians as slaves. But at the same time, the demand for slaves was increasing sharply in al-Andalus. A growing desperation in the slave-hungry caliphate caused Muslim pirates to begin to hunt for slaves along the Italian coast—not unlike the Vikings did along the coasts of France.

Around ten years before Olaf Haraldsson was born in the far north, the lack of slaves in al-Andalus triggered a series of military raids against the Northern Spanish kingdoms of León, Castile, Navarre (Pamplona), Aragon and Barcelona, which together made up a cramped and already hard-pressed galaxy of Christian princedoms along the caliphate's northern border. Armies consisting of tens of thousands of soldiers—mounted Arab warriors equipped with lances and saddle axes, turban-wearing tribal Berber warriors, slave soldiers and Christian mercenaries—spread death and destruction on a scale that made even the Danish attacks on England seem like no more than minor raids. Between 981 and 1002, Arab and Berber armies under the caliphate's banners are said to have executed no fewer than fifty-seven military expeditions against the Christian north—around three per year, season after season, in both summer and winter. Barcelona was plundered in 986; Santiago de Compostela in 997 after hired Christian scouts helped the caliphate's army to find the path through the mountains to the city. The famous cathedral's church bells were hauled down and taken south as booty. The heads of decapitated enemies were carried back in their thousands, and set on stakes along Córdoba's city walls.

The military expeditions were known as jihad, and Christian chroniclers described their opponents as Satan's helpers on earth, "the scourge of the Christians". But the Muslims' raids against their Christian neighbours were no more religiously motivated than was the Danes' waging of war in England. The objective was to obtain loot, tributes, noble hostages and—above all else—to acquire slaves.

The violent wars demonstrated the caliphate's military superiority over its neighbours, but at the same time they were also a symptom of a growing internal crisis within al-Andalus. As in Christian kingdoms north of the Pyrenees, true power did not always rest in the hands of the monarch. The man who initiated the military raids was not the caliph himself but his vizier, or minister—an Arab noble by the name of Almanzor, who had been responsible for advising and helping Caliph Hisham II in his childhood, thereby acquiring himself a position of power that he would hold for the rest of his life. The caliph was reduced to a symbolic figure in Córdoba, where he lived with his many wives—several of them daughters of Christian princes in the north, either taken prisoner or handed over by their fathers as tribute. In his place, it was Almanzor who led the honourable and prestigious military raids in the north.

In the year 1002, Almanzor died while on his journey home after a raid. "Our provider of slaves is no more," the inhabitants of Córdoba are said to have complained. The caliphate's next most prominent man was al-Malik, Almanzor's son, who, in order to consolidate his popularity and power, continued the great military expeditions. Catalonia was plundered in 1003, Castile in 1004, León in 1005, Aragon in 1006.

Then, in 1008, while Æthelred ordered the construction of his great war fleet in England and Olaf Haraldsson was on Viking raids in the east, al-Malik also died, and al-Andalus descended into a deep crisis.

Almanzor and his son had used the wealth obtained during war to build palaces and expand their already surging army. Thousands upon thousands of Berber mercenaries had been transported across the strait from North Africa in boats, to fight for the caliphate. They fought in their tribes, alongside people with the same language and culture, under their leaders from their homeland. They were consequently loyal not to the caliphate, but to their tribal leaders.

In the chaos and power vacuum that arose after Vizier al-Malik's death, and without any clear leadership to channel the violence outwards, the caliphate's war machine turned its full destructive force on its own lords. The Berber armies began to plunder the caliph's lands. The Umayyads—the caliphs' family—divided into various factions, all struggling for power. For a time, there were even two caliphs at once, both with tens of thousands of Berber warriors in their service. One of them, Muhammad, entered into an alliance with the Christian Count of Castile, who in 1009 led his knights in a military expedition south in the caliph's service, and who together with Berber and Arab warriors occupied Córdoba itself.

With command of Córdoba, Caliph Muhammad was on the verge of achieving a measure of control over the entire kingdom. But then he was assassinated—and the Berber armies that had fought for him again spun out of control, marching all across the until recently united caliphate as they squeezed money out of the cities, lived off the land, and plundered and ravaged at will.

This was the situation in the south when Olaf's fleet made its way down the coast of Galicia.

*

Olaf's skald tells of a raid at a place Olaf and his people called *Fetlafjǫrðr*. This is probably a Norse name for the estuary the

Romans in their time called Flavium Brigantium, today Ría de Betanzos, beside the Galician port of A Coruña and not far from Santiago de Compostela in the kingdom of León. We are given no concrete details of the battle or of who Olaf and his people fought against, simply that they fought, and that men lost their lives.

Olaf's fleet then continued south, passing the lonely Tower of Hercules—the Farum Brigantium lighthouse—a monumental and renowned construction built by the Romans nine centuries earlier and modelled on the famous Lighthouse of Alexandria. The tower marked the place the Romans had called *finis terrae*—the end of the earth—where to the north and west one could look out across the seemingly endless sea.

The voyage continued, along the jagged and crag-covered Iberian Atlantic coastline, through stormy and cold waters that were difficult to manoeuvre in due to the treacherous currents and many reefs. Today the area is known as the Costa da Morte—the Death Coast—due to its many shipwrecks. During antiquity and the Middle Ages, almost nobody sailed there, and there was therefore little contact between Northern Europe and the Mediterranean by sea.

Today, it can seem almost inconceivable that Olaf and his men were able to travel as far as they did. Their ships were open, without decks; seawater leaked in between the joins and planks of the ships' sides and the waves lapped in over them, so that the seamen were forced to continually bail out the water using buckets and pails. A ship was regarded as seaworthy if it sufficed to bail it out twice a day. The men wore clothing of wool and leather, along with caps and strong rowing gloves, but otherwise had no protection against the rain and wind.

Norse sailors of the 1000s possibly used so-called sun com-passes, simple devices taken from the Arab world which in direct sunlight showed the cardinal points by a shadow cast on a carved board. Other than that, they had no navigation instruments. They were dependent on the ability of experienced seamen to study the sun, moon and starry sky with their own eyes, and to read the sea. The pattern of the waves could reveal how deep the water was and the direction of the currents; the kinds of birds that flew above them and how they behaved indicated how far it was to land. At the aft end of the vessel, a steersman—who was typically the leader of the ship and the one who led the men in battle on land—set their course with a simple steering oar that was affixed to the starboard side. In order to avoid running aground, sounding lines or sticks were used to discern the water's depth.

The Norse ships were the result of the revolution in shipbuilding techniques that took place in Scandinavia around 300 years before Olaf's time. Over the course of just a few generations in the 600s and 700s, Norse shipbuilders improved upon the seagoing rowing ships that had brought Saxons, Angles and Jutes to England since the 400s by adding sails while retaining the oars. They experimented, and managed to make the ship's hull, mast and rigging function as a single unit in a way that nobody had ever achieved before.

The secret was to build a ship's hull that was extraordinarily strong and flexible by splitting out the planks from wet wood with razor-sharp axes, using a time-consuming method that demanded both patience and expertise, and always closely following the rings in the wood. Using this technique, they made many-metre-long planks that were no thicker than a finger but so strong that they could carry the weight of a grown man without snapping. The planks were set together using the clinker method, so that they overlapped and strengthened each other while also retaining their flexibility.

The result was a ship that was light and pliable, but still able to tolerate being tossed and turned in the waves. The keel was slightly curved underneath, so that air was pushed down under the ship to run along a cavity on its underside. The ship therefore rode on a wave of air that held it up, stabilizing it and increasing its speed. The ships could sail through both night and day, wind permitting, and be rowed if they were becalmed, in which case their masts could be taken down. Because the ships could be rowed, they could also travel up rivers, against the current. Smaller vessels could be pushed and hauled overland for short distances.

In the ancient world, forests, mountains and deserts were barriers that were exhausting and time-consuming to cross, especially with heavy loads. But with a ship it became possible to transport people and produce more quickly and over far greater distances. In the 1070s, the German monk and historian Adam of Bremen, who was familiar with conditions in the Nordic region, wrote that it took a month to travel from Scania to Sigtuna in Sweden if one travelled overland, but that the same journey could be completed in just five days if one instead sailed along the coast. All across Europe, society was therefore organized along sailing routes. Trading centres, small harbours and ports of call were strewn along the coasts. The rivers were teeming with various means of transport—simple flat-bottomed vessels, ferries, rowing boats of various kinds, rafts that were towed between the banks using ropes and which carried animals, people and goods. One could still see people in hollowed-out tree trunks of the type that had been in use since the invention of the first primitive boats.

The ships were built in countless shapes and sizes. The vessels Olaf and his people travelled in were probably of the type sometimes referred to in the sagas as seagoing ships. These differed from warships, which were constructed to be as fast and light as possible, and were instead heavier and wider vessels, built for long voyages and for the transportation of large loads. They were used as trading and supply ships during the wars in England. Such a ship could be thirty metres or more in length, with a crew of around twenty or thirty men. The biggest carried separate rowing boats, which the seamen used to row ashore when the ships dropped anchor. Out on the open sea, they were lifted into the ship and upturned over its cargo.

Along the centre of the ships ran an open aisle; the men sat on rowing benches along the ship's sides. They stored food and their personal effects under their seats, in small chests and in sacks made of leather, which they also used as bedding. Their oars either rested on carved oarlocks or protruded through holes in the sides of the ship. The holes could be covered using wooden flaps in bad weather, in order to prevent the ship from taking on water.

But the ships' primary driving force was the wind, and skilfully crafted sails could be so valuable that they were given as gifts between kings. The sails were large and trapezoid in shape, narrow at the top and wide at the bottom. Made of wool or linen, they could be grey or coloured, or sometimes striped—the skalds wrote poems about dark-blue, red and purple sails. The sails were always the first thing to be seen when the Vikings approached. An Arab poet who witnessed a Norse war fleet in the distance with his own eyes compared the sight to a flock of red birds.

The ships could cross open stretches of sea, but it was preferable to sail within sight of the coast, along known routes. If time wasn't an issue, and it was thought safe enough to do so, the Vikings would put ashore at night, anchoring their ships in a calm bay, and cook food over a fire. The provisions were simple: porridge, butter and hard bread; dried, salted and fresh fish. On long sea voyages to distant latitudes, they ate food that they stole or purchased along the way. The men slept on land or between the rowing benches of the ships, under an open sky or in tents; the sails could also be drawn over the ship and used as tent canvases. "We let the ships skulk with their awnings up out by an island," writes one of Olaf's skalds about another journey.

Ships and sea voyages were central to the Norse warrior class's culture and self-image. We find ships depicted on gravestones; their shapes in jewellery and children's toys. A significant proportion of the preserved skaldic poetry refers to ships. In the pre-Christian mythology, ships were the medium that bound the world of humans to that of the gods. The Danish kings' mystical forefather, Skjold, came to Denmark as a naked child on board a ship, and upon his death returned by ship to the world of the gods from which he came. The most important symbol of the god of fertility, Freyr, was the ship Skíðblaðnir, which always had wind in its sails. At Ragnarök, the end of the world, the dead would stand up and return to earth in the terrible ship *Naglfar*, which was made of the fingernails and toenails of the dead. Leading men and women were buried in great ships, which were either burned or set in burial mounds. Less prominent individuals were similarly buried in rowing boats.

The ships were often given animal names, like Olaf Tryggvason's famous ship *Ormr hinn langi—The Long Serpent*. Later in life, our Olaf built a ship called *The Bison,* another named *The Crane* and a third named *The Reindeer*. The animal names were part of a larger Norse and Anglo-Saxon tradition of imbuing ships with the souls of birds and other animals—falcons, swans, dogs, wolves or horses. The skalds described the ships swimming in the waves, and gave them heads and backs, foreheads, manes and dragon mouths.

> Over the waves, with the wind behind her
> and foam at her prow, she flew like a bird
> until her curved neck had covered the distance

> and on the following day, just when they hoped to,
> those seafarers sighted land,
> sunlit cliffs, sheer crags
> and looming headlands, the landfall they sought.

Other than the wild horrors of war, there is nothing that characterizes the Norse skaldic poetry more than a deep respect, wonder and reverence for the sea. Terrible forces hid beneath the waves; deep down at the bottom of the sea lived the enormous Midgard Serpent, which at Ragnarök would rise to the surface once more. The sea was beautiful and terrifying, a dangerous, mighty and wild force that had to be surmounted and tamed with skill, courage and the wise warrior's fortune.

> You were not afraid of the ocean; you travelled across a
> great sea.
> The mighty prince never ceased to battle against the sea.

The skalds described the sea using words like cold, strong and heavy. It is restless; it shivers. It rises and falls. It howls. It tears and pulls at the rowers' oars. It shakes carved heads at the ships' prows and icy sterns. Huge waves crash over kings at the helm.

The relief at having made it home unscathed could be great, as in the skaldic poem *Háttatal*, composed by Snorri.

> The prow becomes rime-covered at the stem; the ocean
> falls, and the ship glides powerfully forwards against the
> roar of the sea; the crew is deprived of rest

[...]

The wave strokes tall planks, keels split the breaker; the hideous sea wants to break the fair ship

[...]

When winter follows summer, the long ships take a rest after the journey. Ale wearies the host of men; the empty hall is again filled, and the full cup swings empty after the gift of gold.

More soberly, rune stones in modern Sweden tell of men who did not come home:

Sassurr raised this stone for his father Halvard; he drowned out at sea with all his crew.

Long voyages were life-threatening, and for this reason also provided proof of fearlessness, virility, strength and courage. But dying far from home was an honourable way to end one's life—on the memorial stones erected for those who did not return home, it is often referred to as "finding death". One Gudbjørn from Södermanland "stood bravely at the ship's prow, and now lies buried in the west". One Asgaut "voyaged to both east and west". A different Olaf from ours "ploughed his warship through the waves to the east, and died in the land of the Lombards". Just prior to the year 1050, a Harald who led a Viking raid was remembered as follows: "They journeyed bravely, far for gold, and in the east gave food to the eagle, and died in the south in Serkland."

Olaf was far from the first—or last—Viking to sail to the caliphate of Córdoba. The Muslim realm's fabled wealth had attracted Norse adventurers since the 800s, and they had established tried and tested travel routes. Most renowned is an enormous Viking fleet of several hundred ships, which in 844—that is, around 160 years before Olaf's journey took place—sailed past the Christian kingdoms in Northern Spain to Lisbon in al-Andalus, and from there to the coast of Morocco, before crossing the strait northwards again and entering al-Andalus along the River Guadalquivir. Among those aboard the ships were *westfaldingi*—men from Vestfold in Norway.

Arabic sources describe how the foreigners took people prisoner along the banks of the rivers and used interpreters who called from the ships in Arabic, informing people that if they kept their distance they would be permitted to pay a ransom for the return of their relatives. They made their way all the way to the great city of Seville, where they set the main mosque ablaze using a catapult that shot flaming projectiles. They plundered the city for seven days before they were finally defeated by the emir's army, which had marched south day and night from the borderlands in the north. A number of the Norse warriors were taken as slaves; the rest of the fleet sailed away. The story of the attack spread among Mediterranean seafarers, and was written down in Egypt, among other places.

The attack in 844 had interesting consequences the following year, when survivors from the Viking army returned to al-Andalus with peaceful intentions. The emir instructed an Arab court poet to accompany the Vikings back to their homeland, and his extraordinary account of the journey is among the earliest preserved descriptions of the Norse world. He says that after a long and dangerous sea voyage they reached the Viking's beautiful homeland, which consisted of several islands—he must have been in either Ireland or Denmark. He knelt before a king, and they exchanged gifts. Some people prayed to the Christian God, while others prayed to other gods. Through interpreters, he discussed a great number of things with the learned men at the king's court. The Vikings' queen was strikingly beautiful.

Some years later, another large Viking fleet sailed towards Seville, but it was driven back before it could reach its destination. After plundering the coast of Morocco it continued westwards into the Mediterranean. A few years later still, another Viking fleet sailed far into the Mediterranean, to Italy.

The Viking attacks caused the Arab rulers in al-Andalus to build significant defences along its vulnerable southern coast. Watchtowers, beacons and castles were constructed along the shoreline; walls were erected around cities that lay dangerously exposed. They built a fleet that eventually came to consist of several hundred ships. An Andalusian chronicle tells how in the 800s a division of their fleet came across three solitary Viking ships out at sea and boarded them. They found "silver, gold, prisoners and supplies".

Many more Norse expeditions followed throughout the 900s and the early 1000s. The vast majority were peaceful trading voyages, and it is likely that only a tiny fraction of them have left behind traces that we can observe today.[5] The Norse seamen earned good money for skins and furs, which were highly valued luxury products in al-Andalus. They also brought Frankish swords, another desirable item in the Arab world, as well as in the Nordic one.

The Nordic merchants returned home with textiles, precious metals, weapons, jewellery, glassware, ceramics, ivory and spices, in addition to enormous quantities of dirhams—the small silver coins that circulated as currency throughout the entire Arab world. In the Nordic region, more dirhams have been found than any other type of coin from this period, the vast majority of them minted in the Middle East, but some of them also from al-Andalus. In Arabic sources we find the Norse travellers referred to as *majus*, an Arabic-Islamic term for idolaters and heathens. Arabic texts express astonishment at the Norsemen's huge ships, which could be rowed both forwards and backwards.

In addition to the court poet mentioned above, several Andalusians are known to have journeyed north and visited Scandinavia. Just a few years before Olaf was born, the observant and curious geographer Ibrahim ibn Yaqub from al-Andalus visited Hedeby on the southern end of Jutland. He observed a small Christian community among the town's population, and described religious festivals and animal sacrifices among the non-Christians. He noted that people ate mostly fish, that both men and women used eye make-up, and that the women could divorce their men. During a festival or religious ceremony he witnessed the Danes' choral singing—to his refined ears a terrible racket which he compared to the sound of baying dogs.

The last great Viking fleet that has left its mark on Iberian sources did not attack al-Andalus, but the Christian kingdom of León in the north. In 968, forty-four years before Olaf's journey, a Norse king by the name of Gundered put ashore on the coast, just outside Santiago de Compostela, with his 100 ships. His army plundered the areas surrounding the city and killed the bishops there, before the Count of Castile, "in the name of the Lord and for Santiago's honour", fought them in a great battle. "With the help of God's mercy, [he] killed all these people along with their king, and burned their ships."

Since that time, many smaller groups of bandits and opportunists, and particularly many Irish Vikings of Norse descent, had operated in the area covering modern Portugal and Coimbra—a lawless no-man's-land at the border between the Christians in the north and Muslims in the south. From their camps on islands or by the mouths of rivers, these bandits traded, plundered and hired out their sword arms to the local rulers. Like Vikings elsewhere, they specialized in kidnapping people, who were then either sailed south and sold as slaves in al-Andalus or sold back to their kin for ransom.

In Northern Spanish accounts we can read about princes, counts, priests and aristocratic ladies who were kidnapped. Two years before Olaf's arrival, for example, a Castilian nobleman by the name of Arwevadus gave away property to people who were supposed to protect him and his wife, and pay their ransom should they be kidnapped. A few years later, a noblewoman by the name of Meitilli and her daughter were kidnapped by Norse bandits and released for a ransom of "a wolfskin fur, a fine sword, a shirt, three pieces of cloth, a cow, and three measures of fine salt".

What Olaf's skalds relate about his journey falls into this picture of opportunistic raids by Norse pirates along the coast. According to one skaldic poem, Olaf raided a place his people knew as *Seljupoller* while on a voyage south. This was probably the Norse seamen's term for the mouth of the River Minho, not far from today's border between Spain and Portugal.

Beside the River Minho at this time was a small town and a castle or fortified residence which was where the Castilian bishop of the diocese of Tui lived. The skald states that Olaf led his men ashore early one morning and that the "entire army" marched up to the castle as one. They stormed and took the castle and succeeded in taking its lord prisoner, whom the skald names as Geirfiðr. Later, it was said in Norway and Iceland, and eventually written down by Snorri, that Olaf demanded a ransom for Geirfiðr and that he received a significant sum of money for him—but Snorri provides no details of who he was or who paid. A Castilian chronicle, however, states that the episcopal castle was attacked, overrun and destroyed at this time. A diploma issued by Alfonso V of León describes how the bishop and several of his relatives were kidnapped and later ransomed.[6]

The journey continued southwards, all the way to the Iberian Atlantic coast—a voyage that must have taken weeks. Olaf's fleet sailed past the ancient Roman city of Lisbon, the Arabs' Lishbunah, a teeming al-Andalusian market town. Perhaps Olaf and his men went ashore there. They travelled past the cities of Silva and Huelva, the landscape changing the further south they went—dry and burnt beneath the sun but also strangely fertile and lush, with palm trees, fine sandy beaches and dark cliffs. They sailed along the coast towards Gibraltar, which the Spanish today call the Costa de la Luz—the Coast of Light—because the haze renders the sky in grey-blue and pastel shades and makes the sea glitter silver and gold.

The next place name we have from Olaf's journey is *Karlså*, said to be the city the Arabs called Qadiz, modern Cádiz, which was located on an island between the wide mouth of the River Guadalquivir in the west and the Strait of Gibraltar with its unpredictable winds in the east.[7] The ancient city had a deep natural harbour, and had for centuries been regarded as the Mediterranean civilization's westernmost outpost—the final stop on one's journey west before one reached the Atlantic Ocean. In 1012, the city appears to have been Olaf's last stop on his journey in the opposite direction. It had been home to Phoenicians, Greeks, Romans and Visigoths in centuries past. Almost 1,000 years before Olaf's visit the city had been renowned throughout the Roman Empire for its dancing women, but in Olaf's time it was nothing but a shadow of its former magnificence. It had been almost wiped out during the great Viking attacks 150 years earlier, and is hardly mentioned in Muslim sources. It was not an important place in al-Andalus.

How many people lived in Cádiz when Olaf's fleet arrived is not known, but archaeological surveys show that the port was in use. The ancient Roman city wall was still standing, along with a partially destroyed and overgrown aqueduct. The city's most famous ancient seamark was also standing strong—the so-called Pillars of Hercules, which were erected on a dedicated little island, probably by the ancient Phoenicians. Arabic texts state that they consisted of three limestone pillars on top of each other, the two at the bottom wide and rectangular, the uppermost round and narrow, and topped by a three-metre-high bronze statue. The statue depicted the figure of a man with a long beard, wearing a tunic. In one hand he held a staff, and used the other to point east, towards the Strait of Gibraltar and the Mediterranean Sea. According to Arabic sources, the figure's outstretched hand told seamen sailing towards the Atlantic Ocean to "turn back"—for the ancient Mediterranean civilizations, the Atlantic Ocean was the world's end. It was possibly this statue that caused the Norse skalds and later saga authors to call the island Karlså—"Man-island".[8]

It is likely that Olaf reached Cádiz in the autumn of the year 1012. Perhaps he overwintered here—some historians have wondered whether Cádiz was a common Norse overwintering port in Olaf's time. In any event, Olaf, his retinue and the fleet's crew members must have waited for spring somewhere in the south before they sailed north again, because it was almost impossible to sail along the Iberian Atlantic coast during the winter.

In the winter of 1012–13, during which Olaf and his army stayed in the area, the war between the various Andalusian factions on the mainland entered its most intense phase. Armies of Berber warriors marched back and forth across the land; a great number of villages were burned and the roads filled with their displaced and fleeing inhabitants. A Berber army even reached Córdoba and began to besiege the caliphate's most important—and Europe's most famous and fabled—city.

Perhaps Olaf sold his Frankish and Anglo-Saxon prisoners on the slave markets along the coast that winter. Maybe he sold merchandise and booty from the north for silver dinars and silks.

Might he also, in some way or another, have played a peripheral role in the war that was raging in the area? He had sailed there with a fleet and an army big and powerful enough to have come out on top in several major war campaigns further north, and which had also stormed and taken castles. It is not unthinkable that he sold his men's violence in al-Andalus, too.

When the spring came, Córdoba fell—the Berber soldiers' extensive looting marked the end of the city's glory days for all eternity. According to Andalusian sources, a significant portion of the city's population was slaughtered, along with displaced villagers who had sought refuge in the city and over sixty named scholars. The corpses lay rotting in the sun-baked streets for days and weeks without being buried, and plague broke out among the survivors, exacerbated by the spring flooding of the River Guadalquivir. The caliph's famous library was destroyed, its precious books scattered on the winds. And among those killed was the caliph himself.

By this time Olaf was probably on his way north again, leaving behind the caliphate whose crisis would continue to escalate over the coming years and decades. A number of caliphs without true power would rule like puppets under Berber warlords, until al-Andalus was split up into a number of smaller Muslim kingdoms, and in 1031 the caliphate of Córdoba finally ceased to exist.

NOTES

[1] The slave trade in Rouen is confirmed by a Norman clerk and poet by the name of Garnier of Rouen, who lived in Rouen in the early 1000s and wrote a book that has survived until our time. In it he describes his neighbour, an Irishman by the name of Moriuht, who with his wife had been taken prisoner by Vikings in his homeland. Each of them had been sold as slaves. Moriuht managed to buy his freedom and travelled to Rouen to find his wife, who had been sold

there. He found her working in a mill south of Rouen and purchased her freedom. They settled in Rouen together. See Musset 1954.

[2] The term *normanner* was used in the Latin-speaking world to describe both Vikings from Scandinavia and the Normans.

[3] It is the Frankish chronicler Ademar of Chabannes who tells of Duke William's battle against Vikings from Ireland and the Nordic region on the coast of Poitou. He dates the attack somewhat later, around 1018 or 1019, but his chronology is confused and his dating inaccurate. P.A. Munch, who was the first Norwegian historian to study the Frankish chronicles systematically, believed the Viking attack Ademar describes must be the same as that described by Olaf's skalds. The Norwegian medieval historian Oscar Albert Johnsen guessed that Grislupollar could be Castropol in Asturias, and that "William's town", *Viljamsbær*, is a distortion of the Spanish place name Villameia. Modern philologists who have analysed the place names in the skaldic poems have said they would put their money on Munch being right. See Jesch 2001 and Munch 1853.

[4] The number of Slavs bought and sold was so great that the word for slave came to refer to both an enslaved person and a person from Eastern Europe in English as well as Arabic (*saqaliba*).

[5] Radiocarbon studies of mouse bones found on Madeira indicate that Vikings also visited this area during the same period. The mice probably ran ashore from visiting Scandinavian ships sometime in the early 1000s.

[6] The *Chronicon Lusitanum* dates the attack on the episcopal castle to 1015 or 1016, but this does not preclude it from being the same incident since the chronicle's chronology is confused and inaccurate. Olaf's skald called the castle "old Gunnvaldsborg". Perhaps this is linked to the fact that a generation earlier, the castle may have been the residence of a Castilian bishop by the name of Gundisalvus, who in the early 970s waged war against the Vikings and drove them away. It is possible that Geirfiðr is a Norse distortion of Vermund, which is the castle's name in Spanish sources.

[7] Karlså is not mentioned in any preserved skaldic poems, but is both in Snorri's *Saga of St Olaf*, in *Fagrskinna* and the *Legendary Saga*, and must therefore have featured in the later lost "oldest saga", upon which all these sagas are based, and have been part of a very old tradition. The tradition probably stems from a skaldic poem which has been lost. Dozy was the first to suggest that Karlså is Cádiz, and this is the most reasonable explanation. Others have suggested Mino, Duero, Alcácer do Sal, Guadalquivir and Garonne.

[8] The Phoenician statue is said to have stood until 1145. This may be the reason for the Norse place name Karlså—"Man Island". It is also conceivable that it is stories about this statue that have been twisted into the saga tradition to become the dream scene in Snorri's saga about Olaf. Snorri states that Olaf was in port in Karlså, waiting for a fair wind on his way to *Norvasund*, Gibraltar, and that his plan was to travel on to *Jorsalaheim*, Jerusalem. But one night the figure of a man appeared to him and pointed north, and Olaf understood that this was a sign—his fate was to become King of Norway.

HVÍTI KRISTR

WHILE OLAF AND HIS MEN witnessed the death throes of the caliphate of Córdoba in the south, England was also inching closer to its fate in the north. In the winter of 1012–13, Sweyn Forkbeard and his advisors in Denmark began to plan a new attack on King Æthelred's realm.

More than twenty years of war, devastation and ruinous tribute payments had brought Æthelred and England to their knees—and now King Sweyn intended to lead the war into a new phase. This time, the aim was not to collect tributes but to conquer the kingdom itself. Sweyn planned to drive Æthelred from power and make himself King of England.

Perhaps the conquest of England had long been King Sweyn's ultimate goal. In many ways, it was a natural continuation of the martial politics Sweyn had been conducting against Æthelred ever since he himself had come to power in Denmark. There is much to indicate, however, that the decision was influenced by more pressing matters. According to later English accounts, King Sweyn was furious at his former commander Thorkell the Tall. The Danish king was simply unable to tolerate Thorkell's new career as Æthelred's man and defender.

Sweyn didn't necessarily regard Thorkell switching sides as treason, or as a breach of their agreement. But at Æthelred's side, with his experience of war and extensive resources, Thorkell made it difficult to send new bands of raiders to England—and if the Danish king's access to English silver was cut off, his authority within and control over his own Scandinavian empire would be threatened. Sweyn and his advisors may even have feared that the headstrong and ambitious Thorkell, who at this point must have been renowned and idolized all across the Nordic region for his accomplishments, would return to Scandinavia and challenge Sweyn's power on home turf with assistance from King Æthelred—just as Olaf Tryggvason had done in Norway almost two decades previously. This was a threat Sweyn could eliminate if he himself became England's king.

Sweyn's plan was to exploit the significant splits that existed within the Anglo-Saxon aristocracy, and late in 1012, or early in 1013, the Danish king's envoys sailed across the North Sea to the Northern English regions that had been part of the old Danelaw. Far from Wessex and London, the links and loyalty to King Æthelred and his circle of leaders were weaker than in the south. Sweyn's men travelled around, speaking with local noblemen in Northumbria and the areas around York, in order to pave the way for the invasion.

To a certain extent, parts of the population in the north of England still lived in accordance with Norse customs. But more important than ethnic and cultural affiliation was the bad blood between King Æthelred and the leading Northern families. Seven years had passed since the ealdorman Ælfhelm of York had been murdered and his sons blinded by Eadric Streona with King Æthelred's blessing. The surviving members of the family and their friends had since had little contact with the court in the south, but continued to be dominating figures in the Northern English region from which they came. They had withdrawn from political life, and were waiting for times to change in their favour. Sweyn's envoys now offered them an opportunity to avenge themselves and to win back their lost status.

While agreements were negotiated and entered into in Northern England, the people of Denmark once again set to building, toiling, forging, baking, brewing and spinning in preparation for war. William of Jumièges writes that the Danish king "sent couriers in all directions to invite soldiers greedy for wealth from other countries to take part in this expedition and to assemble".

In the spring of 1013, chieftains and bands of warriors again flocked to Sweyn's army, which swelled and grew as the war season approached. And this time, Sweyn meant to lead the fleet west himself.

Before departing, Sweyn made sure to put his affairs in order. He was in his early fifties, an ageing man, and there was no guarantee that he would return to Denmark. Like most kings, he had fathered many children with several different women; he had both sons and daughters—some of whom had died in early childhood, and some who were still living. With his Slavic queen, who in Denmark went by the name Gunnhild, he had two healthy sons. Sweyn had dissolved the marriage with their mother several years earlier, and sent her back to the Piast dynasty's kingdom in modern Poland, her family's homeland. But the boys were still in Denmark, and Sweyn regarded them as his true heirs. One of them was named Harald—he was probably the youngest, perhaps just a little boy. The other was named Cnut, and he is said to have been fourteen years old.

Together with his council, Sweyn drew up plans for his sons' futures. Harald would inherit Sweyn's sovereignty in Denmark should the king not return home. Sweyn established a dedicated council around the boy, which likely consisted of some of his most loyal and experienced advisors, and which was tasked with watching over Harald and protecting him.

But when it came to Cnut, Sweyn had other plans. He decided that Cnut would accompany him across the sea, and that his future would be in England. The king's son had his own *hird*, and the skalds composed poems about him as the youngest leader in his father's fleet: "you launched ships forward at no great age; no ruler younger than you, Cnut, went from home".

Sometime early in the summer of 1013, Sweyn and Cnut crossed the sea at the head of the biggest fleet the Danish king had ever assembled, which likely consisted of more than 200 warships. A tribute to Sweyn and the Danes that was written down a generation later contains a fantastic description of the immensely expensive royal ships, reportedly lavishly adorned with banners and flags shaped like fabled animals in order to convince the English of their new king's unrivalled status and power.

> On one side lions moulded in gold were to be seen on the ships, on the other birds on the tops of the masts indicated by their movement the winds as they blew, or dragons of various kinds poured fire from their nostrils. Here there were glittering men of solid gold or silver nearly comparable to live ones, there bulls with necks raised high and legs outstretched were fashioned leaping and roaring like live ones. One might see dolphins moulded in electrum, and centaurs in the same metal, recalling the ancient fable.

The extent to which such colourful depictions are rooted in reality has been much debated, but the description is not necessarily as exaggerated as it might sound. Gilded embellishments, shields on the sides of the ships and monstrous animal figures are reflected in other contemporary accounts and have been confirmed by archaeological findings. Norse kings placed enormous prestige and sunk vast sums of money into the decorating of their ships—and Sweyn was the richest of them all.

Like many of the preceding Danish armies, this one also came ashore at Sandwich by the mouth of the Thames. But unlike previous landings, when the Danish armies had immediately focused on plundering the rich areas of Southern England, the fleet made only a brief stop. After reboarding the ships, the army sailed quickly northwards along the coast, without burning or laying waste to the area's villages. It then continued across the mouth of the Thames, sailing north along the coast of East Anglia. Without stopping, the fleet continued on up into the Humber Estuary, moving deeper into the country along the River Trent, in the old Danelaw. The ships rowed up the river against the current until they reached the small town of Gainsborough, where the townspeople were expecting them.

Thousands of people had gathered to welcome the Danes. Sweyn and Cnut were received and bade welcome by local leaders from the north, under the leadership of the Ealdorman of Northumbria, Uhtred of Bamburgh. Soon after their arrival, Sweyn gave a speech before a large assembly of people, and announced his ambition to become England's king. In all likelihood he promised the members of his gathered audience better times, assuring them that although he had so far been nothing but a scourge on the English people he would now give them what the weak King Æthelred had not managed to provide—peace. Then representatives from towns and villages across the old Danelaw broke their oaths of allegiance to Æthelred and hailed and swore their allegiance to Sweyn as their king.

Sweyn showed off his young son and heir, Cnut, to his new subjects. To cement the new alliance, and perhaps as a part of his being hailed king, Sweyn held a wedding for his son and a young Northern English woman by the name of Ælfgifu of

Northampton. She was no less than the daughter of the murdered ealdorman Ælfhelm of York—the sister of the two young men whose eyes had been put out with Æthelred's blessing.

The marriage was undoubtedly agreed before Sweyn and Cnut's arrival. The wedding ensured Ælfgifu's family a place in Sweyn's inner circle in the England of the future, while simultaneously ensuring Sweyn and Cnut support from large parts of the population in Northern England.

William of Jumièges states that Sweyn also sought support from Normandy. From Northern England, Sweyn sailed south to Rouen with a small delegation and a few ships. He was received by the opportunist Duke Richard, who must have seen which way the wind was blowing and abandoned any allegiance to Æthelred, despite the fact that his own sister was Æthelred's crowned queen. In the duke's palace on the banks of the Seine, Sweyn and Richard swore solemn and ceremonious oaths to one another and entered into a formal dynastic alliance in which they vowed to help each other in any and all matters. The duke promised that Sweyn's people would receive assistance and shelter in Norman ports, where they would also be permitted to do business at the markets.

Sweyn then returned to Northern England, where he supplied his Anglo-Saxon allies with horses and provisions for the army, which now swelled even further with reinforcements of local men. He left Cnut in Gainsborough with his new wife and gave him responsibility for the ships, while Sweyn himself led the army south overland with the aim of systematically conquering the rest of Æthelred's kingdom. It was still summer when the columns of men and horses set out from Gainsborough for the city of Lincoln, where Sweyn's army generals established a kind of administrative headquarters and mustering point for the next stages of the invasion. Soon the army marched onwards, to the city of Peterborough and through Northamptonshire. From there, they crossed Watling Street, an ancient paved main thoroughfare from Roman times, which wound its way through England.

This road was an important cultural and psychological boundary, because it had also marked the border between the Norse-dominated Danelaw and the rest of the country. Having marched peacefully through the old north, when it crossed the ancient border the conduct of Sweyn's army suddenly changed. The *Anglo-Saxon Chronicle* describes how, on the south side, "they wrought the most evil that any army could do". Once again, black columns of smoke rose towards the sky from Anglo-Saxon farms and villages, while terrified refugees filled the roads and dead bodies lay in the wayside ditches.

But before long, Sweyn stopped his plundering and burning—it soon proved unnecessary, because he encountered hardly any resistance along his way. England's inhabitants were afraid, exhausted by war, and deeply disappointed in their leaders. In the summer of 1013, town after town opened its gates without a fight, and the population surrendered. In the regions through which Sweyn led his army, he called the local ealdormen to him. These prominent men led the area's nobility and free peasants in collective submission ceremonies, in which everyone hailed their new king.

Central to these ceremonies was the handing over of hostages. Everywhere Sweyn went, he demanded that hostages be provided by the local upper class. A large number of boys and young men, the sons of the nobility, were entrusted into Sweyn's custody by their fathers as insurance that their kin would not resist. As the victory procession slowly but surely made its way south, Sweyn sent the hostages north to Gainsborough, where the ships were moored, and where his newly married son and heir Cnut resided with his wife.

While Æthelred's subjects submitted, Æthelred himself hid behind London's mighty walls. His authority was running quickly through his fingers, and he was unable to organize any effective defence. The only force of any power that he could call on was Thorkell's army and its forty-five ships, which were anchored in the Thames outside London. But Thorkell did not march to fight his former lord.

Sweyn therefore marched into Æthelred's old family seat of Wessex unopposed. Winchester, Wessex's largest city, surrendered without a fight. When Sweyn's army finally approached London, as the summer was slowly giving way to autumn, Æthelred sent his family to safety. Escorted by the Bishop of Peterborough, Queen Emma sailed back to her original homeland of Normandy. In Rouen, her brother Duke Richard—who was now in cahoots with Sweyn—received her. Escorted by another bishop, the two sons she had with Æthelred followed her just a short time later.

Sweyn's army reached London and began to lay siege to the city. It was a fundamentally absurd situation—a Danish king besieging London, which was being defended by a Danish warlord who had himself besieged London just three years earlier.

The *Anglo-Saxon Chronicle* describes how Sweyn lost many men to drowning as they attempted to cross the Thames—they could not use the bridge, which was defended by Thorkell's ships, and so probably tried to cross upriver, in rafts or small vessels that capsized or sank. Sweyn called off the siege soon afterwards in order to concentrate on forcing the rest of Southern England into submission. He marched to the town of Wallingford, which gave itself up without resistance, and to Bath, which did the same. In Bath, the city in which Æthelred's brother had been crowned King of the Anglo-Saxons in his time, Sweyn's army set up camp. The prevailing ealdorman and the local nobility submitted and handed over a number of hostages, who were also sent north.

Having rested for a while in Bath, in the autumn the army was on the march once again, turning northwards to set a new course towards London. When the army approached this time, Æthelred and Thorkell gave up on defending the city. Æthelred and the remaining members of his court boarded the warships in Thorkell's fleet and, surrounded by rowing Danish warriors, they were transported down the Thames—probably taking what was left of Æthelred's royal treasury with them. The fleet lay anchored in the river, somewhere between London and the sea, when Sweyn reached the city.

With King Æthelred out of sight, the city that had withstood all former attempts at siege and storming finally surrendered. The heavy gates were lifted without protest and Sweyn rode in, triumphant. He spared the city's inhabitants, who followed the rest of the kingdom's example by providing hostages and submitting to their new king. King Sweyn of England commanded the city's terrified residents immediately to start gathering supplies for the army for the coming winter—an order they obeyed without hesitation.

For his part, Æthelred now found himself in the most tragic situation a king could face. While London's inhabitants worked for the new king, Æthelred and the remaining members of his royal household were still aboard Thorkell's ships, which were moored somewhere along the Thames. Thorkell demanded supplies for *his* army from the people who lived along the riverbanks between the city and the coast. The peasants gave up their food voluntarily, says the *Anglo-Saxon Chronicle*, but still the fleet made a number of landings in order to plunder the riverside villages. The fleet then sailed out into the North Sea, continuing south around the coast until it reached the Isle of Wight, which Thorkell and his men knew well. This was where they had established their head-quarters during the great plundering raids on Southern England three or four years earlier.

On the lush island, Æthelred and Thorkell spent what must have been a miserable Christmas for the fleeing Anglo-Saxon king. After Christmas, they again boarded the ships and set their course south, crossing the English Channel and sailing up the Seine to Rouen. Duke Richard received them—despite his alliance with Sweyn—and promised Æthelred safe conduct and shelter. And there, Æthelred was reunited with Queen Emma and his sons.

The last remaining representative of the old regime in England was now Archbishop Wulfstan of York. Of his life in occupied York nothing is known; perhaps he had fled the city. But wherever he was, at the time of Æthelred's flight he wrote his most indignant and doomsday-influenced sermon, the so-called "Sermon of the Wolf to the English", which was probably intended to be read aloud to the prominent Anglo-Saxon men who had left Æthelred's side. A brief excerpt leaves no doubt as to what the archbishop thought of this development:

Beloved men, know that which is true: this world is in haste and it nears the end. [...] The devil has now led this nation astray for very many years [...] Nothing has prospered now for a long time either at home or abroad, but there has been military devastation and hunger, burning and bloodshed in nearly every district time and again. And stealing and slaying, plague and pestilence, murrain and disease, malice and hate, and the robbery by robbers have injured us very terribly. And excessive taxes have afflicted us, and storms have very often caused failure of crops [...] Now very often a kinsman does not spare his kinsman any more than the foreigner, nor the father his children, nor sometimes the child his own father, nor one brother the other. [...] And it is the greatest of all betrayals of a lord in the world, that

a man betray his lord's soul. And a very great betrayal of
a lord it is also in the world, that a man betray his lord to
death, or drive him living from the land, […] and Æthelred
was driven out of his land.

With Æthelred out of the country, Sweyn sent messengers to all
four corners of his new kingdom. The envoys visited the ealdormen from Æthelred's old council, along with representatives for
cities and regions all across England, and called them to York,
where King Sweyn led his first *witenagemot*, or "meeting of wise
men"—the Anglo-Saxons' traditional national assembly. Through
solemn conventions and in accordance with ancient Anglo-Saxon
customs, Sweyn's subjects would ceremonially choose him as their
rightful king and formally confirm their loyalty. This was the final
stage in conquering the kingdom.

At the end of January 1014, scores of important people from
all across England were making their way to York in the winter
cold. Now around fifty-five years old, the shrewd warrior king left
his war camp in Gainsborough to lead his army to the very same
place, on the victory procession of his life.

He died on the way.

Exactly what happened is unclear. One chronicler attests that
Sweyn fell off his horse and died from his injuries; others insin-
uate that he had been ill for a while. There is speculation that he
may have suffered a stroke. A well-informed account written a
generation later states that he managed to cry out for his son Cnut
before death finally came and took him, and that on his deathbed
he appointed Cnut as his successor. He made his son promise to
transport his body back to Denmark and bury him in his homeland.

But no matter the circumstances, Sweyn was dead. And so—just
as the war's outcome seemed certain and the fate of Æthelred and

his sons decided for ever—the whole situation was thrown wide open again, and nothing was certain in the slightest.

York, or Jorvik, as the city was known in Old Norse, was the biggest city in England after London—and, with its roughly 10,000 inhabitants, actually one of the largest in Europe. It was a densely populated city of narrow streets, consisting of low wooden houses, small stone churches and timber wharfs and loading berths along the riverbank. Walls and palisades encircled the city, separating it from the surrounding fields and agricultural land. In the days that followed Sweyn's death, the freezing-cold city became even more crowded as it filled up with multitudes of churchmen, thanes, peasants' representatives, prominent nobles, Norse warlords, seamen and soldiers who had all come to hail the new king.

Upon arrival, they learnt that the conquering king before whom they had all gathered to bow was dead.

The sworn warriors and advisors that made up Sweyn's *hird* immediately gathered around their dead lord's young son. They swore oaths of allegiance to Cnut Sweynsson as his father's heir, and proclaimed him leader of the army and King of all England.

Cnut was now around fifteen years old. It must have been an incredibly intense situation for him—suddenly fatherless, he was expected to fill the shoes of the most dangerous warrior king Northern Europe had seen in generations, surrounded by his father's old veterans on one side and his young Anglo-Saxon queen's noble relatives on the other, in a country in which he had only just arrived and of which he had not the slightest knowledge but was now supposed to rule over as king, in a city where the country's entire elite had gathered—and which was therefore simmering with intrigues and conspiracies, both old and new.

Cnut had no control over the situation whatsoever. He was not feared like his father. The authority he had, he had only as his father's son—and it was limited to the hard core of the Danish army.

Parts of the Danish army seem to have disbanded immediately. Many warlords probably left Cnut and sailed away, taking their bands of warriors with them—the lord to whom they had sworn their oaths, and who had paid them, was dead. Among the Anglo-Saxon ealdormen who had gathered to pay homage to King Sweyn, there were many who had left Æthelred's side out of fear and with great reluctance. For them, an opportunity for a rematch had suddenly opened up. A sense of disquiet and agitation spread at once, and developed into a dawning insurrection against the Danish army. "From the south came word that King Sweyn is dead and his property destroyed; men are rarely spared by misfortune," said the Icelandic skald Tord Kolbeinsson just a short time afterwards.

Without Cnut and his advisors and the warlords who remained loyal to him managing to prevent it, many of the members of Æthelred's old *witan* came together, both secular nobles and members of the clergy. They dictated a letter to Æthelred, in which they promised to support him if he returned to England—but their support was not without certain conditions. They declared that "if he would treat them more humanely than previously, they would be happier to accept him as king than any other".

A group of envoys immediately sailed south with the letter, across the ice-cold Channel and up the Seine, before they moored their ships at the wharfs in Rouen.

In many ways, Rouen was in a similar situation to York in the north of England; it had become a temporary gathering place for powerful individuals of extremely different backgrounds, who had all ended up in the same location due to the war in England. In Rouen was Richard II, the duke who for years had

alternately supported Sweyn and Æthelred as it suited him, as
well as Æthelred—the king who had lost the power that had been
handed down through the unbroken line of his dynasty for 500
years. In Rouen were Emma, Richard's sister and Æthelred's queen,
and her sons, who had lost their future as Anglo-Saxon kings.
Thorkell the Tall was there, too—the jarl who had first broken
the back of King Æthelred's military power, but who was now the
same king's most important friend in the world—along with his
several-thousand-strong army of Norse soldiers and their ships,
which were moored at the docks. In Rouen were the Anglo-Saxon
bishops and prominent men who had fled along with Æthelred,
and their entourage of helpers and servants; there were French-
speaking Norman lords and ladies, knights and bishops, the high
lords who made up Richard's council and his great entourage of
servants and footmen.

To add to this complex tangle, it is also at Richard's court in
Rouen in the winter of 1014 that Olaf Haraldsson and his fleet
once again emerge from the shadows of history. They had finally
returned from their long journey in the south.

*

Olaf must have led his fleet north on their long voyage from
al-Andalus during the spring or summer of 1013, when the Iberian
Atlantic coast became sailable again after the winter. He was
probably at sea, making his way northwards, when Sweyn's army
arrived in England. He had been travelling for an entire year, and
likely knew nothing of what was going on further north.

He was obviously in no rush. The skalds describe how on his
way north along the Atlantic coast of France, Olaf once again
ventured down the River Loire and plundered "Tuskaland"—a
Norsification of Touraine—attacking the same regions he had

vandalized on the way south. He is said to have burned "Varrandi",
probably the French coastal town which is today known as
Guérande, which lies north of the mouth of the river.

Where Olaf led his fleet next is not known. Perhaps he sailed
to England or to Denmark; maybe he stopped by his home region
of Vik, or sailed directly to Normandy. In any event, in late 1013 or
early 1014 he returned to Duke Richard's winter court in Rouen.
Perhaps his warships were already long since moored beside the
wharfs when Thorkell's fleet arrived in the city after Christmas,
with Æthelred on board.

None of the preserved chronicles or skaldic poems tell us
anything about what transpired when Olaf and his people were
reunited with their old comrades-in-arms and opponents from the
war in England. But that winter, Rouen simmered and seethed
with renegotiations and the forging of new alliances. And among
those who found that they had common interests under this set
of new circumstances were Olaf Haraldsson and Æthelred.

It is highly probable that the two had met face to face previously, having fought each other for three long years. Like so many
other supposedly sworn enemies in this age, it seems their enmity
did not run deep enough to prevent them from redefining their
relationship now that it suited them to do so.

Olaf and his army entered Æthelred's service—that is, Olaf
did exactly as Thorkell had done a year earlier, and committed to
fight by Thorkell and Æthelred's side against his former Danish
lords and employers. The motivation, of course, was wealth—to
become even richer. Perhaps Æthelred had taken the remains of
his treasury across the sea, and was able to pay Olaf an advance
in Rouen. From the *Anglo-Saxon Chronicle* we know that Thorkell
was paid vast sums in Æthelred's service, and the same must have
been true for Olaf.

Such agreements were always formally concluded in a ceremony of allegiance. Olaf probably swore an oath to Æthelred at a public gathering with many onlookers and witnesses, in a variant of the feudal rituals that displayed a vassal's voluntary submission. The vassal often knelt before his lord and placed his hands in his lord's open palms, before his lord then closed his hands around them.

Great significance was generally attached to ceremonies and rituals in the Middle Ages. For those who lived at this time, an oath sworn before witnesses was like a signed contract is today—an agreement that it would be costly to breach.

This goes hand in hand with the fact that very few people could read and write. Gestures, body language, poses, facial expressions, hand signals and symbolic acts were important, and could express a nuanced set of meanings that would be incomprehensible to a modern onlooker, but which for the people of the age were part of a language that everyone understood—and this went for people from all social classes. Individuals who met on country roads gesticulated to each other from a distance using small hand signals in order to indicate that they harboured no hostile intentions.

Princes showed each other their intentions through more complex means. When Charles the Simple, the King of the Franks, met the German King Henry I in 929, for example, they gathered at the Rhine, each at the head of retinues of equal number. They showed themselves to each other from their opposite sides of the river to make clear their peaceful intentions, set up their camps and waited for an entire day before rowing out into the river in boats of exactly the same size. In the middle of the river they both got into a third boat, where they entered into a peace treaty.

Kings embraced each other and kissed each other's cheeks to show agreement and solidarity. During shared meals, seating positions around the table were extremely important—both at the simplest village gathering and during royal banquets—because this clearly indicated the ranking among those who sat together.

When the most powerful members of society wished to demonstrate to each other and onlookers who was superior or inferior to whom, or that two individuals were of equal status, they did so through theatrical and sometimes slightly absurd demonstrations. When the German King and Holy Roman Emperor Otto the Great and King of the Franks Louis IV met during a church meeting at Ingelheim in 948, they took great care to enter the church, sit down, stand up and walk out again at exactly the same time, almost as if in a choreographed and rehearsed dance. When Christian diplomats from Castile sought an audience with the caliph of Córdoba, the caliph demonstrated his superiority by making the diplomats wait for many days before they were granted entry to the palace. When the gates were eventually opened, the envoys had to walk through a series of antechambers that were designed like a confusing labyrinth, before they were finally allowed to kneel at the caliph's feet. But they always returned to the north with fantastic gifts for their lords, which served to further emphasize the caliph's greatness.

In Christian Europe, where religion was woven into all aspects of community life, the agreement of political alliances and subordination were no exception. When swearing oaths and entering into agreements, one did so in accordance with Christian customs, and practically always through rituals in which priests played a central role. Christian princes were therefore unable to enter into alliances with heathens, so in order to have any dealings with Christian princes at all it was often a necessity for Norse Vikings to become Christians themselves—that is, to be baptized.

In order to be able to trade or enter into minor formal agreements, it was enough to be *primsign*-ed, as were many Norsemen who travelled around Christian Europe, and as Olaf likely had been as a young boy. But when Norse warlords entered into formal alliances or pledged that they would serve Christian princes, they often agreed to be baptized in the proper way.

Baptism and conversion were therefore inextricably linked to political power. Most Norse warlords who had converted to Christianity over the past 200 years had done so in connection with entering into some kind of agreement with a Christian prince. A high-ranking cleric in the prince's service would perform the baptism ritual, while the prince himself stood as the Norseman's godfather. In addition to the baptism ritual, the newly converted also went through a second ritual with their godfather, a kind of vassal ceremony.

It is probably this sort of ritual that William of Jumièges is describing when he writes that Olaf was baptized in Rouen, along with some of his men. Posterity would ascribe Olaf's baptism far greater weight than his alliance with Æthelred—which isn't in the least surprising considering that he was later declared a saint, and all aspects of his story were therefore viewed in the light of this. In reality, it is likely that the baptism formed some part of Olaf and Æthelred's alliance. It was probably similar to that which had happened in Andover nineteen or twenty years earlier, when Æthelred had entered into an alliance with Olaf Tryggvason, who was baptized by Æthelred's bishop, with Æthelred as his godfather. William of Jumièges states briefly that the leader of the ceremony was Richard's brother, Robert, the Archbishop of Rouen, and that he washed Olaf and some of his men in holy water and anointed them with holy chrism.

The baptism ritual may have taken place in Rouen's cathedral, which was in the process of being built, and must have been a grand ceremony witnessed by many of the high-ranking Anglo-Saxon and Norman men and women who were in Rouen at this time. It was a long, complicated and rigid ritual that must have made a significant impression on both those who went through it and those who observed.

First, the priest and those being converted went through a series of religious acts outside the church, most often in the porch just outside the main entrance, before the ritual itself was performed inside. The unbaptized were in the grip of evil, and in order to drive the evil out of them the priest blew on the men's faces, made the sign of the cross and said the words *Recede diabole!*, "Recede, devil!", and *exi ab eo!*, "be gone from him!". The priest then placed salt in their mouths, which since antiquity had been regarded as having a purifying effect, before he continued with a long list of incantations: *Maledicte diabole!*, "Cursed devil!", *Exorcizo te immunde spiritus!*, "I exorcize you, unclean spirits!", *Audi maledicte sathana!*, "Listen, cursed devil!". The priest then recited a number of prayers and extolments to God.

Those who were being baptized renounced the devil three times and answered three questions about their faith. Then, partly or entirely naked, they were immersed in water. The priest then recited the magic formula, which was always the same—*Ego te baptizo in nomine Patris et Filii et Spiritus Sancti*. The baptized were anointed with chrism, the holy salve, and dressed in baptismal robes. The baptismal robes were long and white—the colour of purity and light. It may have been these robes, which the Norse people associated with the new faith, that caused the Christian God to be known in the Old Norse language by the name *hvíti kristr*—the White Christ. At the very end of the ceremony they were handed a lit candle.

All this, simply to enter into a military alliance and obtain more silver! Today, this can seem cynical and calculating. There are also many stories that testify to the fact that Christian missionaries could only shake their heads at how the Danes, whose very souls they were trying to save, primarily regarded baptism as a way to get rich. For example, the German monk Notker of Saint Gall recorded an anecdote at the end of the 800s—which for the monks was funny because it was recognizable—about how the Danes came from the north in large groups in order to be baptized by monks, who with the emperor's support acted as missionaries at the borders of the Danes' lands. Those who confessed their sins and let the monks pour holy water over them each received a white robe, valuable items of clothing and weapons, at the emperor's expense.

The monks soon noticed that the same Danes were returning multiple times, again confessing their sins and being re-baptized in order to take more wealth home with them. In one case, an old Dane was dissatisfied with the baptismal robe he received. Quite forgetting himself, he blurted out that he had never received such an ugly robe in all the twenty times he had gone through the ritual.

However, we have no reason to believe that Olaf was anything but sincere in his new beliefs—if not to the extent that his later hagiographers would have it, perhaps. For the people of the 1000s—whether they confessed to the Christian God or made sacrifices to Thor, Odin and Freyr—the spiritual permeated every-thing and everyone. The spiritual and the secular were inextricably interwoven, impossible to part. The fact that God—or the gods—was at work in the world and could be influenced through rituals and prayer was a given; it was impossible to believe otherwise. This made religion instrumental in a way that can seem strange to us today, but which for people at the time was only natural.

Furthermore, the line between heathenism and Christianity was far from sharp, and the transition from the former to the latter was in no way as abrupt as the Christian monks who described the conversions might have wished it to be. The faith in the old gods appears to have been fundamentally tolerant and open to new ideas. Its chaotic world view, with its competing and shifting deities, had no problem making space for a new God alongside all the old ones.

To the extreme disgruntlement of foreign missionaries, many newly converted people in the north seem to have continued the pre-Christian practice of praying to several gods. Many were an inseparable mix of both Christian and heathen, and simply prayed to the White Christ alongside Odin, Thor and Freyr. Around the year 970, the Anglo-Saxon Bishop Widukind of Corvey, who was deeply involved in missionary work in Denmark, complained that the Danes continued to pray to idols through pagan rituals, despite the fact that they had been Christian for a long time.

Men and women went around wearing items of jewellery both in the shape of the cross and of Thor's hammer, and were even buried with both kinds. Others wore jewellery that featured Thor's hammer shaped like a Christian cross. Coins minted by Viking kings in York in the early 900s feature Odin's raven on one side and the hand of God on the other. A settler in Iceland of Swedish-Irish heritage named Helgi the Lean, who appears in the Icelandic *Laxdœla Saga*, had taken Christianity to the Hebrides and called his farm there Kristnes. But when he set out on sea voyages, he called on Thor. The skalds used a mixture of Christian and heathen symbols, and in Norway scenes from the ancient Norse mythology would continue to be carved into church doorways until well into the High Middle Ages.

In many ways, keeping in with the right gods was comparable to staying on good terms with the right friends and allies in this world. Those who called on a strong God vanquished those who invoked weaker gods.

There was much about the Christianity of the 1000s that was deeply impressive to the Norse people, and which appealed to these travelling kings and warlords who were searching for wealth and power. The people of the White Christ had built the Roman ruins

Olaf and his people saw on their travels, along with the unprec-
edentedly huge cities and castles that they visited and besieged.
They stored knowledge in books and collected dizzying riches in
churches and monasteries. All this bore witness to a mighty deity
that certainly seemed worth calling upon.

For a man like Olaf, there is reason to believe that the White
Christ was primarily a god of war. Christ, as Olaf and his contemporaries encountered him in the wonders of the age's Roman
churches and monasteries, was not the emaciated, tortured and
suffering figure into which he was later transformed, but instead
portrayed as a proud and strong king who wore his wreath of
thorns like a crown. He was surrounded by his disciples during
the Last Supper as a king was surrounded by his court.

Warrior King Olaf's White Christ was the same God whose
cross the Roman Emperor Constantine had commanded his
legionnaires to paint on their shields before the Battle of the
Milvian Bridge in 312; the same God to whom Anglo-Saxon kings
had converted in the 600s because he would ensure them victory
in war if they only prayed and made sacrifices to him; the same
God lauded by Sweyn Forkbeard's skalds because he bestowed
upon their king *gipta hvítakrist*—the White Christ's fortunes
of war—when Sweyn burned villages to the ground along the
English coasts.

Perhaps Olaf already had priests in his company of men before
the baptism ceremony in Rouen; regardless, several priestly scholars entered into his service a short time afterwards. They swore
oaths of allegiance to him and were taken into his *hird*; their
tasks were probably the same as those of the priests in the service of other Christian kings: to teach the king about the faith,
lead him through religious rituals, bless the food he ate and
say intercessory prayers for him and his closest circle. Adam
of Bremen knew the names of four of these men, who later

became renowned leaders in Olaf's Norwegian kingdom—they
were Siegfried, Rudolf, Bernhard and Grimkil. Grimkil, whose
name indicates that he was an Englishman of Norse descent,
later became Olaf's bishop.

*

Æthelred began preparations for the reconquering of his kingdom
as early as the start of February 1013. Together with a group of
his steadfast followers, he sent his youngest son, Edward, in a ship
across the cold English Channel to meet the members of his old
council. Edward was only twelve years old. Permitting his young
heir to represent him was a way for Æthelred to signalize a new
beginning and a better future.

It was still early in February when Edward and his company
went ashore somewhere in Southern England. The king's son met
members of his father's former council and a large assembly of
Æthelred's former subjects at a place that to us remains unknown.
In his unbroken young boy's voice, he spoke in his father's stead
before the gathering. The *Anglo-Saxon Chronicle* summarizes the
speech as follows:

> Then sent the king his son Edward hither with his mes-
> sengers, and ordered them to greet all his people; and said
> that he would be to them a loving lord, and amend all those
> things which they all abhorred, and each of those things
> should be forgiven which had been done or said to him, on
> condition that they all, with one consent, would be obedient
> to him, without deceit.

And the ealdormen did as they were asked. They swore their
oaths of allegiance, and "then established full friendship, by

word and by pledge". The meeting ended with the Anglo-Saxon council declaring "every Danish king an outlaw from England for ever".

While all this was going on in the south, Cnut and the Danish army had barricaded themselves in Sweyn's old headquarters in Gainsborough, evidently completely blindsided by the rapidity with which events were unfolding. Cnut held hectic meetings with his Anglo-Saxon allies, who initiated a grand-scale acquisition of riding horses from the areas under their control. The plan was to supply the entire combined force under young Cnut's command—which consisted of an army of Danish warriors who had followed Sweyn across the sea, as well as loyal men from Northern England—with horses, and then to ride south and mercilessly strike down the uprising. They would "all go out together, and plunder", as states the *Anglo-Saxon Chronicle*.

But Cnut's preparations for the military expedition were not yet finished when the war began just a few weeks later. During Lent of the year 1014, Æthelred sailed across the English Channel at the head of a war fleet. The fleet apparently consisted of Thorkell the Tall and Olaf Haraldsson's combined ships and crews.

Thorkell, who had commanded men during war since before Cnut Sweynsson was born, sailed into the Thames; his ships dropped anchor there to prevent Cnut attacking London. Æthelred was received by his old advisors, probably within London's walls. They held meetings, and Æthelred gave privileges to nobles and members of the clergy. A number of Southern English nobles also joined him, along with their armed bands of men.

Then they marched north. The *Anglo-Saxon Chronicle* states that the king led the army himself, and that he marched towards Cnut "with his full force".

When the scouts reported sightings of the army that was now making its way in their direction at great speed, Cnut and his Danish generals quite simply seem to have panicked. As Æthelred approached, they evacuated chaotically, in great haste. Weapons and equipment were carried aboard sixty warships— seemingly all the ships that were left of Sweyn's magnificent invasion fleet from the previous year. Cnut left the thousands of Anglo-Saxons in the north who had supported him to fend for themselves and face their fate without him, and led all the Danish warriors in his service away. The fleet rowed down the River Trent and out into the Humber Estuary, where it set its course for the open sea.

Back on the mainland, in the area around Gainsborough and York, Cnut's Anglo-Saxon allies were hopelessly outnumbered in the encounter with Æthelred, Thorkell and Olaf Haraldsson's combined military forces. Æthelred's main army trudged into the green fields south of the Humber Estuary. Scores of local peasants began to flee with their families, and the army from the south met little resistance. It was the inhabitants of this area who had supplied Cnut's army with horses, and so to make an example of them Æthelred gave orders to plunder and burn the region, showing no mercy. According to the *Anglo-Saxon Chronicle*, they killed everyone they found alive.

Meanwhile, Olaf Haraldsson led his men in victorious battles. The English chroniclers still do not mention him by name, but traces of him are evident in the Norse narrative tradition. The later sagas describe how Olaf conquered a castle and killed many men at a place whose location remains unknown to us, but which the saga authors called *Jungfurða*. A few years later, Olaf's head skald composed a poem about a battle at a place that in Old Norse was called *Valdi*, possibly the town of Wold at the mouth of the Humber Estuary. Another skald praised his efforts as follows:

King, you brought Æthelred into the land and gave [him]
     his land;

[...]

the battle was hard when you brought Æthelred back to
     the fatherland.

Cnut left the country with his sixty ships in such haste that he
didn't even manage to take his queen along with him—and even
his father's dead body was left behind. Sweyn Forkbeard's corpse
lay somewhere in the north when the Danish army evacuated,
likely in a monastery and in the process of being embalmed, in
preparation to be transported to Denmark in accordance with the
dead king's wishes. It was a humiliating and traumatizing start to
a Danish prince's career.

But Cnut did have something else that was extremely valuable:
on board the fleet were all the hostages that the Anglo-Saxon
nobles had handed over to his father during his victory march
through Middle and Southern England the previous autumn.
Sweyn had continuously sent them north to Cnut, and they
had been Cnut's captives ever since. And there were many of
them.

The hostages were young men—the sons of the Anglo-Saxon
nobility and heirs to estates and titles, representatives of the
next generation of the Anglo-Saxon ruling class. It was hoped
that fear for their lives and health would prevent their families
from breaking the promises they had made. The taking and
giving of hostages was a completely normal part of the age's
diplomacy and warfare, and the most effective method available for ensuring agreements that had been entered into were
respected. When peace and accord prevailed between the parties,
hostages could expect to be treated well and with respect—
indeed, they often led a luxurious existence in the company

of their prison guards, who were their social equals. Hostages were often exchanged both ways, so that a kind of balance of terror was reached.

But Sweyn and Cnut had not given any hostages. And the Anglo-Saxons had broken their promises.

While the armies that were now loyal to King Æthelred slaughtered people Cnut regarded as his subjects, the young Danish king's fleet sailed south along the coast of East Anglia as columns of smoke rose towards the sky across the country behind them. The sixty ships crossed the Thames Estuary and continued southwards. When they came to Sandwich, they dropped anchor. The hostages were brought ashore on the pale beaches below the white cliffs, where soldiers in Cnut's service lopped off all the hostages' hands. Then they cut off their ears and noses. It must have been time-consuming work.

Afterwards, they set them free. As Cnut's fleet disappeared over the horizon and sailed towards Denmark they remained ashore, alive, with bleeding stumps where their hands had been; black wounds instead of ears and noses.

In all likelihood, Cnut—who was only around fifteen years old—was strongly influenced by the older and more experienced warriors from his father's old war council. But what happened to the hostages was done with his blessing and in his name. It was a deeply symbolic act. Cutting off limbs, regardless of whether the victims were permitted to live or whether they were subsequently executed, was a common method of punishment practised by kings in Europe at this time—in response to rebellion, treason and other serious crimes.

Cnut left a wound in the Anglo-Saxon nobility that would take several generations to heal. For the rest of their lives, the released hostages would have to be cared for, nursed and supported by their families—they were now high-born cripples who acted as permanent visual reminders of what happened to anyone who dared to violate an agreement with Cnut. It was a demonstration of resolve and decisiveness—and a warning that Cnut was not out of the running in this bloody game just yet.

His prospects, however, were terrible. The Danish fleet brought him back to a Denmark in which no place had been left for him. His little brother, Harald Sweynsson, was king. And around him was the council Sweyn had established in Denmark. The two young brothers were reunited; Cnut and the men around him attempted to negotiate a partition of the Danish kingdom. Cnut's little brother—and the men around him—refused them.

A short time later, Cnut's Anglo-Saxon wife arrived in Denmark. Ælfgifu of Northampton evaded her enemies and sailed across the sea with her household in a single ship. On board, she had Sweyn Forkbeard's embalmed body, wrapped in a shroud. The two princes buried their father's body in a majestic Christian ceremony, probably in a wooden church in Lund in modern Sweden. During her stay in Denmark, Ælfgifu became pregnant with Cnut's first child.

The two brothers did not become enemies, but set out on a peaceful journey together. They travelled to *Slavia*, Poland, where their mother still lived, having been sent back to her homeland by Sweyn. Cnut and Harald took her back to Denmark with them, where she found a place at court.

The journey's primary objective, however, was not to be reunited with their mother: Cnut and Harald were seeking military support from among their father's old networks. The brothers collaborated on gathering a new army. England would be conquered once more. Sweyn Forkbeard's sons sent messengers to chieftains all across the vast areas their father had controlled and dominated—men who were bound to them through oaths sworn to and old friendships with their father. They made promises, tempting offers of gold, green forests and future positions of power in the rich country across the sea.

In these new war plans, one man above all others was absolutely central—the Jarl of Lade in Trøndelag, the Danish kings' vassal in Norway.

TO NORWAY

GENERATIONS BEFORE Harald Bluetooth conquered his neighbours and created his Danish super-kingdom, another kingdom was created in the far north of modern Norway. Even long before the Viking Age began, the merciless but resource-rich coasts of Hålogaland—the area that stretched north from the Trondheim Fjord along mountainous chains of islands and fjords past Lofoten—were a centre of financial and political power. By the mouths of the great fjord systems that carved their way into the country, Norse chieftains ruled over strategically established power and trading centres, small, densely populated societies that lived by utilizing the nature around them.

From places like Bjarkøy, Bø in Vesterålen and Steigen on Engeløya, the chieftains sent scores of workers and slaves out to collect eggs on the islands in the spring, and on fishing expeditions in the summer. The Hålogaland chieftains sailed north around Gamvik, the mainland's northernmost point, into the Barents Sea, and on into the White Sea surrounded by modern Russia, where they exchanged and traded goods with local tribes who were known as "Bjarmians". They used "Finns"—the Sámi—as hunting specialists during the reindeer- and bird-hunting season in the autumn. The Sámi lived not only in the far north, in *Finnmórk*—"the land of the Finns"– but also much further south than in later times. Their culture and shamanic religion strongly influenced the Norse peoples' own culture and worship. The Hålogaland chieftains on the coast regarded the Sámi as their subjects, and regularly led armed bands of warriors into their territory in order to collect tributes from them.

All this brought in a significant volume of goods that were exotic, luxurious and sought after in Europe, for which the Hålogaland chieftains could earn great sums at the markets further south. Merchants—and often the chieftains themselves—sailed their wide trading ships south, loaded with skins, furs, rope, walrus tusks, whalebone, down and feathers and soapstone. Some of these items were sailed into the Trondheim Fjord and transported east via rivers or overland to Härjedalen and Jemtland, and south into Sweden. But most were taken south along the outstretched and broken North Sea coastline, past south-western Norway and all around the coast into Skagerrak, to Vestfold, from where the goods were transported south into the kingdom of the Danish kings. If one came ashore at night and sailed only with a favouring wind, the journey from Hålogaland to the market town of Skiringssal in Vestfold took a month.

This was the ancient sea route the Anglo-Saxons called *Norðweg* and the Franks *Northvegia*, that is, the "North Way". It was originally a purely geographical name, and did not designate any kingdom or country. But the North Way linked people together. In the still waterways all along the broken coastline lay strategically situated ports, marketplaces and the seats of chieftains; small but important places with wharfs and loading docks and rows of workshops and diminutive buildings. The trade and connections it created bound together local societies from north to south: people from Hålogaland, Trøndelag, Møre, Sogn, Hordaland and Rogaland, descendants of wandering tribes who had settled during the age of migration, all with their own identities to a

lesser or greater extent. The North Way made them all *Norð*
menn—Northmen, or Norwegians.

In the 800s, a north Norwegian chieftain dynasty known as the
Jarls of Hålogaland dominated the northern end of the North
Way. This family gradually expanded towards the south, and
acquired control over the coastal regions that led down towards
the Trondheim Fjord. The family's first certain historical chief
was a jarl named Håkon Grjotgardsson, who around the year 900
waged a victorious war against prominent farmers and chieftains
in Trøndelag. He moved his centre of power south, and established
himself at the old farm and gathering place of Hlaðir—Lade—
which was situated on a peninsula where the mouth of the River
Nidelva led into the Trondheim Fjord, on a ridge with a view of
the fjords in all directions.

Håkon Grjotgardsson became the first Jarl of Lade.

This move to Lade became the start of a rare dynastic success
story. A decade or so into the 900s, Håkon Grjotgardsson was
killed, probably while fighting leading rivals on the coast. But his
son, Sigurd, inherited his title and position of power. We meet
many jarls from this Norse world in skaldic poetry from the Viking
Age; the term originally described no formal title, but was rather
a broad designation of respect for honourable and distinguished
men from good families. The Jarls of Lade used it as an inheritable
princely title, something like a Norse dukedom, which was almost
as exclusive as the title of king. Members of the Lade dynasty
married into the most prominent families from Trøndelag, and
established a solid command over the major farmers in one of
Scandinavia's richest and most densely populated agricultural
areas. This dominance over the coast northwards, and Lade's
central placement between north and south, ensured the Lades
significant income—because in addition to being heavily involved

in trade themselves, they also demanded a share of the goods transported by everyone else in exchange for protection and safe passage. In this way, they built up a unique position of power in the regions that would in time become known as Norway.

At the same time, further south along the old North Way, another large centre of power was growing. In the late 800s and early 900s, Harald Fairhair—who in the later narrative tradition would achieve mythical status—established himself as the king of a kingdom that had its centre of gravity in south-western Norway, and which was strongly influenced by the Anglo-Saxon kingdom across the sea to the south-west. The relationship between Harald Fairhair's many sons and the Jarls of Lade in the north was complex and unpredictable, and for several decades fluctuated between alliances and confrontations; between relative peace and the violent battles for power we can read about in the sagas that describe the earliest times in Norway's history. Harald Fairhair's eldest son, Eric Bloodaxe, made himself worthy of his nickname by killing almost all his brothers; he in turn was supplanted by the youngest of them, Håkon Adalsteinfostre, who returned from England after being raised as a Christian at the Anglo-Saxon King Athelstan's court. Håkon ruled as a Christian king, and is said to have founded the *leiðangr*, a fleet of conscripted warships—a form of coastal defence based on the Anglo-Saxon model. At the assembly in Trøndelag, he was hailed overking of the Jarls of Lade.

In the early 960s, both Håkon Adalsteinfostre and Sigurd Håkonsson—the son of the first Jarl of Lade, Håkon Grjotgardsson—were killed by Eric Bloodaxe's sons. King Håkon died on land of his injuries after a sea battle outside Fitjar in Stord. Sigurd Håkonsson was attacked and burned to death in a fire on a large farm in Stjørdal.

But Sigurd Håkonsson's position of power was inherited intact by his son, Håkon, who became the third Jarl of Lade. He continued his father's battles against Eric Bloodaxe's sons through-out the 960s and 970s.

The young Håkon Sigurdsson was a wily politician and strate-gist, and in this conflict allied himself with the Danish King Harald Bluetooth, whose kingdom was at this time growing into a kind of Norse superpower.

The significant wealth yielded by trade along the North Way was an attractive prospect for the Danish king. Håkon Sigurdsson submitted to Harald Bluetooth's dominion in exchange for his help in defeating and supplanting his rivals, the kings of Western Norway. Harald Greycloak, Eric Bloodaxe's son, was finally killed during an ambush in Limfjorden in Denmark, and his brothers fled to England, never to return.

In reality, this meant the end of Harald Fairhair's dynasty in Norway—although many would invoke this kinship in later times. For the Jarls of Lade, however, the supplanting of the royal family was the start of the dynasty's true golden age. Harald Bluetooth appointed himself King of the Northmen and regarded Håkon Sigurdsson as his Norwegian vassal, but this supremacy was symbolic and theoretical. Håkon Sigurdsson became the first prince with real power over all of Western Norway, from the high north to Agder.

Trøndelag—the core of the kingdom of the Jarls of Lade—was religiously conservative, and a centre of power among the opposition to the new religion that was spreading from the south. Lade was one of Trøndelag's old heathen places of worship. Like his father before him, Håkon Sigurdsson was remembered for his Norse religious beliefs, and as a defender of the ancient ways against the men who sought to break them down in favour of the White Christ. He is said to have personally led grand ceremonies and sacrificial feasts on the farm at Lade.

But the alliance with the Christian Harald Bluetooth made Christianity a political necessity, including for Håkon Sigurdsson.

In the winter of 974, Håkon gathered a large war fleet along the Norwegian coast and led it to Denmark in order to support his king in the war against the German emperor. In Denmark, he consented to being baptized, albeit—as Snorri later described it—extremely reluctantly. According to Snorri, Harald Bluetooth forced Håkon Sigurdsson to take missionaries back to Norway with him after the military expedition ended, but the jarl set them ashore somewhere before they reached his homeland.

Like many others of his time, Håkon Sigurdsson acted like a Christian when abroad and visiting Christian princes, and a heathen when responding to his conservative subjects at home.

Around the year 985, Håkon Sigurdsson broke ties with his Danish overlord. Harald Bluetooth sent a war fleet to attack his obstinate vassal, but the jarl's fleet was victorious, defeating the Danes at the Battle of Hjörungavágr. A few years later, Harald Bluetooth died, and his son Sweyn Forkbeard began his lifelong plundering project in England. Håkon Sigurdsson was now in his fifties. Over the next decade, he ruled as Norway's uncontested prince, the most powerful man who had ever lived in Norway.

Then came Olaf Tryggvason. Håkon Sigurdsson was around sixty years old when in 995 Olaf landed at Moster in Sunnhordland with his army of veterans from the wars in England, having entered into an alliance with Æthelred. Olaf called local free men to an assembly and coaxed and threatened them into hailing him their king. Then he went straight for the throat of the Jarl of Lade.

Rich with English silver, Olaf generously doled out gifts to the prominent men and warriors who entered into his service; the old jarl's authority collapsed almost immediately. Håkon attempted to gather an army, but he simply didn't have enough silver to pay for his men's loyalty in competition with Olaf. His own people revolted. Many of them switched to Olaf's side.

In the later sagas' interpretation of these events the jarl desperately flees before the advancing Olaf, along with his last remaining loyal man, the slave Kark. At night, they hide in a pigpen. In the hope of being rewarded by Olaf, in the darkness Kark cuts off his lord's head, only to be beheaded himself the next day by Olaf, who did not tolerate such dishonourable behaviour. And so Håkon Sigurdsson, Jarl of Lade, falls out of history and into literature. To all appearances, Kark's crime and punishment seem a literary paraphrasing of true events by the saga writers; a dramatization of a time's great paradoxes and moral dilemmas. In this culture, which held fidelity as the highest virtue, it was ultimately always the man with the deepest coin purse who came out on top.

Olaf Tryggvason established himself as King of Western Norway and Trøndelag in a remarkably swift seizure of power. He dismantled the old place of worship at Lade and built a new centre with a church and a royal hall, at an old trading site that had grown into a small town—Nidaros—further south along the River Nidelva. He travelled around the Jarl of Lade's old areas at the head of his army and drove away, killed or subjugated anyone who dared to stand against him.

But Håkon Sigurdsson had sons.

The eldest was named Eric, and he would become the fourth Jarl of Lade. He was in his mid-thirties when Olaf Tryggvason invaded the country and his father was killed. He succeeded in taking himself and his household to Denmark, where he sought protection from Sweyn Forkbeard, Olaf Tryggvason's arch enemy. Sweyn welcomed him with open arms, and to cement the alliance he permitted the Norwegian jarl to marry one of his daughters. Her name was Gyða, and she was Cnut's sister. Eric Håkonsson was now the Danish king's man.

Just a few years later, Eric Håkonsson got his revenge. He was fighting at his father-in-law Sweyn's side in the sea battle at Svolder when Olaf met his end.

Afterwards, with Sweyn's support, Eric returned to Lade and his family lands in Trøndelag, taking Gyða with him. While Sweyn Forkbeard took control of Vik, Eric adopted a position as the Danish king's vassal, ruling over the chieftains along the coast in the north, west and south, with dominion from Hålogaland to Agder, in that which at the Danish king's court was now referred to as "the province called Norway".

For fifteen long years, Eric Håkonsson ruled in Norway with Sweyn's daughter by his side. He reached a ripe old age. Nobody challenged his power, and he was widely respected. As far as we can tell from preserved sources, he participated in not a single one of Sweyn's many military raids on England, nor in the attempt to conquer the country in 1013 that would be the Danish king's last. But in autumn 1014, after his brother-in-law Cnut returned to Denmark with his sixty warships, having lost the kingdom that was meant to be the fruit of his father's three decades of waging war, a messenger came for the Norwegian jarl.

The well-informed and almost contemporaneous account the *Encomium Emmae Reginae*—"The Praise of Emma"—states that of all the prominent men Cnut asked for help to conquer England, Eric Håkonsson, Jarl of Lade, was the most important:

Eirikr, leader and prince of the province which is called Norway—for he also was one of Knutr's officials, had already been long subject to him, and was a man active in war, and worthy of all honour—having received leave, set out with his followers, fell upon a part of the country, seized booty, attacked and destroyed villages, overcame the enemies who met him, captured many of them, and at length returned to his comrades victorious with the spoil.

In the autumn of 1014, Eric Håkonsson made significant preparations for war along the coast of his extensive realm. Warships were readied, and thousands of Norsemen prepared for battle.

Meanwhile, an even larger force was growing under Cnut's direct command on Jutland, consisting of warriors from the Danish island, likely from Sweden too, and probably also from Cnut's mother's Slavic homeland.

The army slowly readied itself to invade England again, but this was a most uncertain and risky business that Cnut, now around sixteen years old, was about to set in motion. Everything was at stake for him. The experienced lords of his war council kept a careful eye on developments in England, and in the summer of 1014 a messenger arrived from the west with news that Æthelred's eldest son had fallen ill and left this world. But Æthelred had many sons. They also learnt of a great flood—that the Thames had burst its banks and submerged several villages, drowning many people.

Cnut's warlords tended their old networks of contacts on the other side of the sea. They were in touch with Thorkell the Tall, and are said to have negotiated with him in an attempt to make him leave Æthelred's side. According to the *Encomium Emmae Reginae*, Thorkell even sailed to Denmark accompanied by nine of his forty warships. After middlemen had assured him that he would not be seized, harmed or killed, he went ashore and discussed the matter with Cnut, face to face. He then sailed back to England. What they agreed upon is unknown.

Cnut and his war council held back. And waited.

*

Early in the autumn of the year 1015, a year after Cnut had fled England, the entire Anglo-Saxon elite gathered for the first time since Æthelred had recaptured his kingdom. The location for this gathering was Oxford, a city that had seen enough of war over the past decade, having been burned by passing Danish armies and rebuilt by its surviving inhabitants time and time again.

Surviving leaders from the north—those who had taken the side of Sweyn and Cnut in the war—were also invited to the great meeting. All serious resistance to Æthelred's royal power was past. The Anglo-Saxon kingdom had moved on to a time for reconciliation and the settling of old conflicts.

Perhaps Olaf Haraldsson was present in the city. He was at least still in the country, along with his army, and presumably by King Æthelred's side. So too was Thorkell the Tall, even though he seems to have negotiated with Cnut independently of Æthelred. He had been paid 21,000 pounds of silver for the assistance he had provided to the English king.

Also present in Oxford was another man Olaf seems to have managed to become personally acquainted with at this time— Eadric Streona. The ealdorman enjoyed a position as a kind of senior minister on Æthelred's council, which managed many of the king's political decisions.

As York had been after Sweyn's death, Oxford was filled with a teeming sea of people as travellers from all across the country sought out the city. Among the many visitors from the north were two thanes by the names of Sigeferth and Morcar. They had sworn allegiance to Sweyn and Cnut, actively gathered support for the Danes in the north and remained loyal to them after Æthelred's return. Like many other prominent Northern men they had stayed away from Æthelred and his court after the war, out of fear for their lives. Now Æthelred promised them free passage and guaranteed their safety.

But there would be no reconciliation. The *Anglo-Saxon Chronicle* states briefly: "In this year was the great council at Oxford; and there Eadric the ealdorman betrayed Sigeferth and Morcar." A more detailed account describes how Eadric lured them to a house he owned in Oxford, as his guests, and guaranteed them safe conduct. Inside the house they were overpowered, and Eadric had them "basely done to death".

Immediately afterwards, King Æthelred himself sent soldiers north, who seized all the farms and houses owned by the two thanes, and forced the servants of their households and the peasants in the areas from which they came to submit. On the king's orders, the widow of Sigeferth was arrested. She was sent south and forced into confinement as a nun at Malmesbury nunnery in Wessex.

Whether it was Æthelred or Eadric Streona who had thought up this plot, and why, we have no way of knowing—but the plan turned out to be a spectacular mistake.

Because at this time, a new, ambitious politician and warlord came to the fore among the conflict-filled upper echelons of the Anglo-Saxon leadership. Æthelred's oldest surviving son, Edmund, was a young man of around twenty and an independent political powerhouse, who had his own household and retinue, his own advisors, his own friends—and his own objectives and motives. His mother was Æthelred's first queen, who had died in Edmund's early childhood. Edmund had grown up in the shadow of his older brother from the same mother, who before dying of an illness just a few months prior had gifted Edmund a 300-year-old sword. Their mother and her kin came from the north, and completely independently of his father and the leading men at court, Edmund had developed a good relationship with the nobility of the region—and not least, with the two men who were murdered. It was Edmund who had negotiated with them on his father's behalf and persuaded his father to promise them safe conduct to Oxford.

Edmund clearly had a strained and not particularly warm relationship with his father; his attitude towards Queen Emma bordered on being openly hostile. He wasn't entirely wrong in regarding Emma and her children as rivals who threatened his own position of power and inheritance now that his older brother was dead. Edmund's relationship with Eadric Streona was no better. When he learnt of how Eadric and his father had ambushed his friends and allies, Edmund reacted violently.

In an act that could almost be regarded as a direct declaration of war against his own father, Edmund gathered his retinue of warriors. He rode to the nunnery at Malmesbury where Sigeferth's widow was confined. After setting her free, he proposed to her. She accompanied him to the north, where Edmund held meetings with prominent local men, who perhaps now more than ever regarded King Æthelred with open animosity. The wedding was soon held somewhere in the north at a location that remains unknown to us, thereby cementing the new alliance that was beginning to assert itself in Anglo-Saxon England's already fragmented political landscape. The men of Northern England flocked to Edmund's growing army.

Æthelred might have dealt with his son's headstrong and antagonistic behaviour and reconciled with him, but at the same time as Edmund broke ties with him he fell seriously ill. He travelled around the southern part of his kingdom with his household, becoming weaker and weaker, until he was finally forced to put up in a small but stately farm complex in Cosham—today's Portsmouth—in south Hampshire. There he lay bedridden as his servants tended to him and his household priests prayed to God for his earthly body and eternal soul.

Meanwhile, the old Northern English rebellion was revived, led by Æthelred's very own son.

*

When news of the rebellion reached Cnut's war council in Denmark, Cnut boarded his waiting warship and, at the head of the fleet that had been gathered off the Jutland coast, he sailed west. Messengers were also sent to Norway, where Eric Håkonsson, Jarl of Lade, was instructed to sail his army to Sandwich, where the forces would unite.

Eric Håkonsson entrusted control of Norway to his younger brother and his young son, who was around seventeen years old—about the same age as Cnut. Then he led a fleet of Norwegian ships manned by thousands of soldiers to the south-west. A poem composed by the Jarl of Lade's skald has been preserved, and describes how the jarl's fleet consisted of many ships of many different sizes, which set out from the Norwegian coast, crossed the sea and sailed south along the coast of England, "so near land that the English plains could be seen".

Once again, Norse warships met just off the pale beaches of Sandwich. The assembled fleet is said to have been the biggest a Danish king had ever commanded in England—larger even than Sweyn Forkbeard's invasion fleet during the conquest of 1013. Cnut held a war meeting with his warlords. He set down prohibitions against all plundering and burning among those of his future subjects who submitted voluntarily.

Then he led the fleet onwards. With bulging sails the ships glided south, past the white cliffs of Dover, before following England's southern coastline to the mouth of the River Frome in Dorset. Without knowing it, they sailed right past the estate where Æthelred lay in his sickbed; the king's household must have seen the fleet as it narrowly missed them. The ships dropped anchor in a snug, sheltered bay, where the army went ashore.

There was now everything to play for in England. On the south coast were Cnut and Eric Håkonsson with their armies—Cnut determined to conquer England or go under in the attempt. In Northern England was Edmund with his army. In the time that followed, the young son of the Anglo-Saxon king would lead his troops with such energy and power that he would posthumously only be remembered as Edmund Ironside—"for his valour", according to the *Anglo-Saxon Chronicle*.

Between them, somewhere in Mercia, was a third army led by Eadric Streona. With Æthelred sick—perhaps even dying for all anyone knew—it was up to Eadric to lead the charge on the king's behalf. He sent messengers to the east and west in a feverish attempt to gather more troops. He found himself in an extremely complicated situation. Should he go north and attack Edmund, or south to attack Cnut?

While the armies sat waiting in their respective parts of the country, Æthelred dragged himself out of the estate where he had lain. Along with his household servants and royal retinue, weak and ravaged by illness, the king rode down the country roads to London where Queen Emma was waiting for him, probably with their sons. The city gates were opened for the royal company, and then closed behind them. The supplies needed to withstand a siege were gathered. The city hunkered down.

It was probably also in or just outside London that the Danish armies in Æthelred's service—Thorkell the Tall and Olaf Haraldsson's forces—were stationed. Neither the Norse nor the Anglo-Saxon accounts mention them.

From the south coast, Cnut and Eric began to advance northwards; Edmund Ironside set his army to march south. Stuck between them, Eadric Streona made a decision and led the royal army north, away from Cnut and Eric and towards Edmund. As the Anglo-Saxon armies approached each other, messengers rode back and forth between the two commanders. The two soon stood before each other, tense and fully equipped for battle. With their armies behind them, Eadric and Edmund negotiated face to face.

They agreed to join forces and fight as one against the Danes. The two armies set up camp side by side and began to prepare for the confrontation with the Danish army that was approaching from the south. But before the Danish army arrived, Edmund changed his mind. He didn't trust Eadric. Fearing that the chronically duplicitous ealdorman would betray him in the heat of battle, Edmund led his army away.

Not long afterwards, the Danish army arrived from the south. Eadric met the Danes at the head of his army, and soon it was he and Cnut who were negotiating face to face. And this time, Eadric ended up changing sides.

The Anglo-Saxon ealdorman swore an oath of allegiance to Cnut as the King of the Anglo-Saxons. For this act of treason, Cnut rewarded Eadric by allowing him to remain Ealdorman of Mercia—but under him. Eadric was permitted to retain his title and all his land under his new lord, with the result that he remained one of the most powerful men in England.

And so the war began. The Anglo-Saxon and later English chronicles and the Norse skaldic poetry that constitute our main sources describe battles and sieges and fires and river-crossings and marches all across the country, around and around, hither and thither.

For a modern observer it is almost impossible to obtain a clear overview of what happened next. We can study the available maps and information about the armies' movements, but the campaign is a messy and confusing jigsaw puzzle of which almost all the pieces are missing. For the people caught up in the middle of it, the situation must have been chaotic. There were now more warriors in England than ever before. Scouts and messengers rode all across the country along the ancient Roman road network.

Fleeing villagers sought refuge behind fortified walls. Men and women buried their valuables in the forest. Panic and rumours spread. Nobody could see where it would all end, and no one could afford to be left on the losing side. Perhaps it was during one of the many skirmishes at this time that the Christian man by the name of Bjor from Southern Norway was killed, whose father later erected a memorial stone at Evje in Aust-Agder with the following inscription: "Arnstein raised this stone in memory of Bjor, his son; he died in the army when Cnut attacked England. One is God."

Cnut's situation was not an easy one. He couldn't obtain supplies for his army by random plundering, because he wanted to become king, and he would hardly be able to win over a country whose population hated him. Meanwhile the Anglo-Saxon armies constantly retreated before him, refusing to meet him in open battle.

During this autumn we are able to glimpse aspects of the young king that would eventually come to define his greatness—a good nose for swift tactical diplomacy, the ability to balance the merciless and terrible punishment of his opponents with magnanimous rewards for his supporters. Areas that opposed Cnut were burned without mercy. "Young ruler, you often saw villages burn before you, saw the villagers scream," an Icelandic skald later stated in order to honour him. But areas that did not resist were spared.

In the wake of Eadric shifting sides—and undoubtedly with the experienced Anglo-Saxon network builder's help—Cnut conducted tense and nerve-wracking diplomacy to lure key persons from the other side over to his, all while his warlords hunted down the enemy armies wherever they went. Cnut promised those who supported him land, money and influential positions.

With Æthelred himself too sick and isolated to be able to gather his own behind him, prominent Anglo-Saxon men broke their bonds of loyalty to him one by one and pledged their support for Cnut.

Among them were several West Saxons from Æthelred's familial lands, who equipped Cnut's army with horses. They also handed over their sons as hostages—solemnly and with heavy hearts, we must imagine, in this kingdom where the sons of many of the most distinguished families walked around as cripples after having had their hands, noses and ears cut off the last time Cnut took hostages.

Thorkell the Tall was also among those who abandoned Æthelred towards the end. He left the king's side, swore an oath of allegiance to Cnut, and entered into his service with his army and his warships. This was, for him, a masterly career move. Cnut rewarded him by making him the Ealdorman of East Anglia.

At some point, Olaf Haraldsson also left the sick Æthelred's side. Perhaps he had fulfilled his obligations under the agreement they had entered into; perhaps he betrayed him. A number of later accounts of various origins concur that Olaf met with Cnut at this time. The two young kings—Olaf probably still only in his early twenties, Cnut a few years younger still—met in a peaceful, orderly fashion. And they negotiated.

This meeting is a disconnected point in Olaf's story. Our earliest available source is the work of the well-informed German churchman and historian Adam of Bremen, who was writing just a generation after Olaf and Cnut's deaths. He obtained his information from Cnut's relatives at the Danish royal court at the time, and wrote that Olaf demanded payment for something he did for Cnut in England; some of the earliest works of Norse history allege the same. But as to what Olaf demanded payment for, we do not know. Perhaps he fought on Cnut's side for a brief time. Perhaps he agreed to leave Æthelred for a certain sum. It is clear that Olaf was not given any English land to govern under Cnut, as were many others. On the contrary, all our oldest sources of information about Olaf's life agree that Cnut and Olaf negotiated their future power dynamics on the other side of the sea, in Scandinavia.

After the meeting, which took place sometime during the autumn of 1015, Olaf was somewhere on the English coast along with his inner core of followers. They boarded two ships and set out to sea, taking their leave of the generation-long war just as it was reaching its bloody crescendo.[1]

It is Olaf's own skald who tells us about this. In one of his poems, he describes how the two ships toiled through the waves on the crossing, atop a rough and stormy sea. And when Olaf and his men again sought land, they were *miðjan Nóreg*, "in the middle of Norway".

The next time we hear about Olaf, also from his skald, he is in Fjaler in Sunnfjord. In a narrow strait in the waterway known as Saudungssund, on the inner side of Atløy and beneath a steep, round mountain, Olaf and his men set up an ambush.

Olaf's victim was the seventeen-year-old Håkon Ericsson, the son of Jarl of Lade Eric Håkonsson. The young jarl was sailing south along the coast—for reasons that are unknown to us now. Neither do we know how much time had passed since Olaf left England, what he had done in the meantime, nor how Olaf knew that the jarl would be passing by.

The obscure skaldic poem tells us only that Olaf attacked the jarl's band of men. After a battle aboard the ships, the jarl's people were overpowered. Olaf took the jarl's ship, and Håkon Ericsson himself captive.

Snorri provides more detail, describing how after overpowering the jarl Olaf gave him his *grið*—a promise of peace and personal safety—in exchange for Håkon renouncing his right to his dominion in Norway, and vowing never to take up arms against Olaf again. Håkon—who of course didn't have much choice in the matter—swore an oath. Olaf gave him back his ship, and Håkon sailed straight to England, to his father and Cnut. It would be more than ten years before he returned to Norway.

After this, Olaf must have sailed north along the forest-clad coasts for days, moving in and out of islands and rocks, past small fishing villages and trading sites at the mouths of fjords, along the jagged coastline of Møre and into the Trondheim Fjord, on down the River Nidelva, past the Lade Peninsula and its ancient places of worship and chieftains' halls, to the little town of Nidaros, where thin columns of smoke rose above wharfs, some small buildings and a little church. Olaf attempted to establish himself right at the heart of the Norwegian realm of the Jarls of Lade, and people in his service began to construct a royal estate in the town.

But the estate would never be finished. Because in Trøndelag remained one final representative of the Lade dynasty in Norway— Eric Håkonsson had a younger brother named Sweyn. Unlike Eric, Sweyn seems not to have been close to the Danish kings, but on the other hand to have had close connections to the east, in Sweden. And in Trøndelag, he put up an overwhelming resistance to Olaf. A preserved poem from a skald in his service describes what happened in few words: Sweyn's people stormed the little town; Olaf and his men retreated. They probably sailed away without making any attempt to fight back. Sweyn's soldiers set fire to Olaf's half-finished construction, and while "fire felled the hall" Olaf and his men sailed south once more, to fight another day.

NOTES

[1] Olaf's skald Ottar the Black calls the two ships *knarrer*—merchant ships. Later in the Middle Ages this was a term used to describe trading ships. In Olaf's time, however, the term was used to refer to all types of ships.

BROAD ANCESTRAL LANDS

HOW ARE WE TO UNDERSTAND all this? What was said between Olaf and Cnut in England is one of the great unsolved mysteries of this story. Did Olaf demand a kingdom in Norway under Cnut's sovereignty? Did he travel to Norway having reached an understanding with Cnut, perhaps even as Cnut's man—or as his enemy? Confusion around these questions was prevalent even among the historians of the Middle Ages; a number of modern historians have also attempted to solve the puzzle. But nobody has ever been able to provide any satisfactory answers.

In the 1950s, the Swedish historian Ove Moberg set out an enticing hypothesis that gained a certain amount of support. He believed that Cnut and Olaf had come to an agreement: Olaf withdrew from England in exchange for being appointed Cnut's new under-king in Norway. Eric Håkonsson, head of the Lade dynasty and Norway's true sovereign, agreed to this exchange because he found himself in a situation through which he could win vast areas in England should they be victorious in the war there. This would explain why Olaf sailed across the sea with only two ships, and why the Jarl of Lade's son left the country having received Olaf's promise of safe conduct.

But this is also a problematic explanation. It is likely that Cnut was willing to make concessions to Olaf; he had, after all, promised his supporters large areas of land and positions of power in England—supporters who included Thorkell the Tall, whom Olaf had fought alongside for years. And for Cnut, Olaf would undoubtedly have been a troublesome and dangerous enemy to have by Æthelred's side in England. But the Jarl of Lade's realm cannot have been something the young Cnut was able to just give away. And it is hard to believe that Eric Håkonsson, Jarl of Lade, would voluntarily renounce all his familial lands—lands for which his forefathers had fought, killed and bled for an entire century; the place where all his power was centred and with which his most important friends and allies were affiliated. The war in England was in no way decided; nobody knew what the final outcome would be. Cnut and Eric might be driven back across the sea.

A perhaps more probable speculation is that Olaf demanded a degree of independence in his control of Vik in south-eastern Norway, where his old familial and inherited lands were situated, and perhaps Cnut granted him this. Knowing full well that the Jarl of Lade's West Norwegian realm was almost empty of warriors—because they were all bound up in an intense battle in England that didn't look like it would be ending any time soon—Olaf might have glimpsed an opportunity to strike a quick bargain and make an easy conquest of this land, too.

Or perhaps Olaf had no clear long-term plan at all. When writing about and seeking to understand history, the fundamental problem is that we always observe past events in the light of their consequences, always in the light of how everything turned out in the end. And when chains of cause and effect line up in the eye of the observer, we project the order we see in retrospect on to people's motives and actions. This is the way in which history is written, and out of it rise great men with grand plans and simple, kingly thoughts: a Caesar who casts the die while crossing the Rubicon, a Harald Fairhair who wishes to unite a kingdom—and an Olaf Haraldsson, who after years of Viking raids returns to his homeland to convert Norway to Christianity.

If we are to understand what happened we cannot think in straight lines, but must rather consider the story as a kind of web of incidents and structures that influence each other in a completely unpredictable way. A web of individuals and great collectives, of both poorly thought-through and brilliant plans, of improvisation—and of chance. Olaf's story is mysterious and there is much we don't know, but one thing is clear enough. He was an opportunist in a world of opportunists, who did the best he could with the cards in his hand. He made plans, like all the other warlord-politicians who dominated his world, but these were short-term and had to be continually revised in line with the shifting circumstances and opportunities around him.

On the other hand, however, there is no doubt that he returned home as a leader with great ambitions. The fact that Olaf crossed the sea with only two ships doesn't necessarily mean that he had disbanded the army that he had spent years leading from war to war. It may have sailed east over the sea in several smaller groups, only to regather around Olaf in Norway.

Eight years had passed since Olaf left his ancestral lands in Vik and ventured out into the world to embark on his career as a warrior. His personality and world view must have been shaped and influenced by the Christian Europe in which he had spent long periods of his life travelling, warring and conducting diplomacy. He had seen and learnt to recognize the ideology of the European kings and emperors. Kings like Æthelred and Robert II strove to assert their authority over obstinate vassals, but the culture that surrounded them gave them a prestige and aura of power—the like of which had never been seen in the Norse world, and which was inextricably linked to Christianity. It was a strong image to encounter for a young warrior king from Scandinavia, who had spent his entire adult life fighting to move up and get ahead in the world.

In the kingdom of heaven, there is but one who reigns and that is he who hurls the thunderbolts. It is only natural that on earth as well there be only one who reigns, under him.

When Olaf arrived in Norway, he obtained a warship for his fleet that was named *Karlhofði*. The name of this ship has traditionally been understood as Snorri interpreted it, as meaning "man's head", with the corresponding notion that a man's head was carved into the prow. Another possibility, and one that is perhaps more likely, is that the ship was in reality named after Charlemagne or Charles the Great, Christian Europe's most famous royal ruler and symbol of power, who in turn had modelled himself on the ancient Roman emperors.

We also know from Olaf's skalds that Olaf compared himself with Olaf Tryggvason, who had defied Danish overkings and been the first person to attempt to unite the old Danish Vik with the traditional Norwegian kingdom to the west and the domain of the jarls to the north. And like Olaf Tryggvason before him, Olaf had the most important means necessary in achieving something like this: more important than any agreement with Cnut, more important than hereditary succession, and more important even than God—he had gold and silver and exotic treasures in great volumes.

Olaf had been one of the recipients of the largest tribute we know of from the Danish wars in England. He had also been paid large sums for entering into Richard of Normandy and Æthelred's service, and on top of this he had all the wealth he must have obtained through trading, plundering, stealing and threatening people on his own for eight years—in the Baltic region, in Frisland, in England and along the coasts and riverbanks of France on his journey along the Iberian coast to al-Andalus. Olaf's victories in war had made him a very wealthy man.

*

Olaf made what appears to have been an unsuccessful attempt to conquer and take control of Nidaros, before sailing to his home region of Vik, arriving there perhaps late in the autumn of 1015. Snorri imagines this homecoming in one of the most artistic and lively sections of his long saga about Olaf, depicting Olaf sailing at the head of his army along the coast of Vestfold, making himself known to his kin and his father's former subjects there, before the army lands and the men pull the ships ashore somewhere in the inner Oslo Fjord. From here, Snorri's Olaf travels into the countryside, past peasants working in the fields, with a company of 100 men, to the great farm at Ringerike that was his family seat. Messengers are sent in advance to provide word of his approach. Upon his arrival, his mother Asta and stepfather Sigurd Syr receive him in the farm courtyard, where the entire household of servants and workers is lined up before a longhouse that has been decorated and prepared for a feast. Asta kisses her returned son; Sigurd greets him and invites him inside. They haven't seen him for eight years, and have managed to have more children in his absence—two girls and three boys, Olaf's half-siblings. The saga names them as Gunnhild, Ingrid, Guttorm, Halvdan and Harald.

In reality, it is likely that Olaf visited his home in Vik several times between his military expeditions and Viking raids of the past few years. As previously mentioned, Normandy and England were less than a week's journey from Vik by ship in favourable winds. And Olaf must have maintained contact with his relatives and network through messengers, regardless. Many of the veterans who had served him for years and followed him to the other side of the world and back were local men from Vik. Olaf had probably deposited most of the wealth obtained from his Viking raids and tribute payments in England for safekeeping with trusted friends in his homeland at regular intervals. It would have been far too risky to take huge volumes of silver and valuables with him on the long journeys he had made in recent years.

It is clear that Olaf laid claim to sovereignty over Vik's core areas immediately after his return. His own skalds proclaimed that he was born to control his "broad ancestral lands" by virtue of being his father's son. Exactly what these "ancestral lands" comprised, we do not know. The area that was known as Vik was large and wide. It included Vingulmork at the innermost end of the Oslo Fjord on the east side; Ranrike, which extended all the way down to the River Göta älv; Vestfold and Agder all the way down to Lindesnes on the west side of the fjord; as well as Romerike and Ringerike in the north.

Olaf also demanded that people submit to him in areas outside Vik, in the north, far from the sea, in the regions around Lake Mjøsa where Danish kings had never obtained any real foothold. These were the areas from which Olaf's mother's family came, and he must have had good connections among the prominent families there.

He encountered significant resistance, however—the villages along the edge of Lake Mjøsa were controlled by prominent farmers and petty kings who were not used to submitting to any overlord. The skaldic odes describe how a number of chieftains or petty kings in this area refused to submit to Olaf. One skald states that there were five of them; another that there were eleven. They banded together, combining their forces to oppose Olaf as a united front.

Olaf and the petty kings in Hedmark came to blows, perhaps late in the autumn of 1015 or during the following winter. Olaf and his experienced warriors were victorious, and the petty kings fled or surrendered. Olaf gave the defeated kings his promise of peace, all except one—the northernmost of them—of whom he made a bloody example by having his tongue cut out.

> Generous king! You have paid with ill punishment the rulers of the land for all their plottings.

> You have driven the rulers away from your land. Each king fled far from you, we know.

> Afterwards you took the tongue of he who lives furthest north.

> Now you rule over that land which five princes held previously; God gave you a great victory. Broad ancestral lands lie under you eastwards towards Eiðar; no warrior has ever before presided over such territory.

Over the years that followed, we have no evidence of open resistance to Olaf in these areas.

Olaf established himself as king with the help of his old friendship networks and familial connections, and by using his military power. But his claims to sovereignty, networks and use of force are only part of the explanation for his rapid seizure of power. Because, as was the case for any king at this time, Olaf's control was also determined by his ability to balance reward and punishment, promises and threats, mercilessness and indulgence. Olaf's use of sheer brute force went hand in hand with his generous distribution of gifts to those who chose to follow him.

The skalds tell of hectic diplomacy and networking as Olaf attempted to gather support in the late autumn and winter of

1015–16. We can imagine extravagant celebrations in the warmth of the great halls in the freezing, snow-covered villages in Vik and the Uplands, where the local elite gorged themselves on food and drink at Olaf's expense, and the storytellers told fantastic tales of voyages sailed across foreign seas, of encounters with strange peoples and battles in far-off lands. And where Olaf made good use of his rich reserves and open-handedly doled out jewellery and beautiful objects of silver and gold, bracelets, money and costly items of clothing to the men who knelt before him, swearing oaths of allegiance. He gifted prominent farms to his allies. His own skalds praise his magnanimity, describing how he handed out treasures; the oldest sagas depict the same. They describe how Olaf gave gold and silver to the men of the Uplands this winter, assuring himself the friendship of many men.

Snorri imagined Olaf's stepfather Sigurd Syr riding around on a horse with a gilded bridle and spurs from Córdoba, which may have been inspired by stories that continued to circulate in Snorri's time about Olaf's exotic gifts from the caliphate. Dirham coins buried sometime in the 1000s have been discovered in the Nordic region and are thought to be from Olaf's journey to al-Andalus.[1]

Olaf was also rich in the honour and prestige that came from being successful in war. This was just as important as material wealth—success bred success. A king's victory meant that he had the fortune and favour of God or the gods on his side. Honour radiated from the king's person all the way down to the simplest warrior in his band of men: this was a man whom it paid to follow.

In order to rule, one had to be formally chosen and hailed as king by the *things*, the most important arena for meetings between kings or jarls and their subjects. These associations, in which free men met and discussed matters of common interest, and settled legal disputes with the help of legally trained men familiar with the ancient customs and laws that had been verbally passed down through the generations, had been the foundational unit of the Norse societal structure since days of old.

Such assemblies were not particular to the Norse world. They are known to have existed in many other places since ancient times, and they played important roles in both low- and high-level government in parts of early medieval Europe. In Anglo-Saxon England the *witan* of the kings had its roots in the so-called *fol-cgemōt*, "folk meeting", of older times—a very similar institution to the Norse *things*.

At Olaf's time, the Norse *things* existed in a variety of shapes and sizes. Men from a single village would gather and hold assemblies locally, but large regional *things* were also organized with thousands of participants who came from afar to attend. It is unlikely that Vik had a single common *thing* in Olaf's time, but the people of Western Norway had met at Gulen at the mouth of the Sognefjord for generations, and this part of the country was regarded as a common legislative area—Gulatingslag. The men of Trøndelag—*Þrœndalog*, "the legislative area of the people of Trøndelag"—had long met on the Frosta Peninsula in the Trondheim Fjord. The free men in the villages around Lake Mjøsa probably held a *thing* on the large old estate at Åker, where the town of Hamar later developed.

Olaf must have travelled around Vik and the Uplands, calling together local *things*. He must have appeared before the peasantry, making speeches to them and presenting his claim to royal power. His future subjects hailed him in the form of an oath submitted by their leaders and representatives. Such ceremonies, where the king's power was legitimized through the free men sym-bolically electing him as their leader, was an ancient Northern European practice. As early as the first century AD, the Roman historian Tacitus wrote that the German custom was to "take a king". The ceremony was probably concluded with the peasants' representatives or men from Olaf's own *hird* lifting Olaf up on to a stone or mound. Frankish annals describe how Norse warriors were in the habit of beating their shields together in order to celebrate newly elected leaders.

It was a busy winter, during which Olaf forged a number of strong alliances in Vik and the surrounding areas. We can glimpse the contours of what looks like a well-thought-through programme of control, in which Olaf depended on powerful local magnates, several of them men who had built their wealth on Viking voyages and trade with faraway lands.

The sagas tell of winter feasts where gifts were exchanged and promises made. To one prominent man Olaf gave a very valuable sword and a farm, to another he gifted a large seagoing ship that was rowed upstream on the rivers to Lake Mjøsa, far from the coast. During such gatherings it is very likely that the priests in Olaf's *hird* baptized those who swore oaths of allegiance to him, and perhaps their family members, too—just as Olaf's mother, his stepfather and Olaf himself had been baptized at Olaf Tryggvason's command when Olaf was a child.

*

At this time, another man also came to Olaf—a man of whom we have a far more detailed and personal description. His name was Sigvat Tordarson, and he was an Icelander. He was young, probably a few years younger than Olaf, with black hair, and a Christian. He was the son of an Icelandic merchant and skald in Olaf's company by the name of Tord, who had followed Olaf in England and probably accompanied him on the long journey to al-Andalus. While his father was away on year-long journeys, Sigvat was brought up by his relatives on a farm beside Lake Apavatn in south-west Iceland.

In the autumn of 1015, or the following winter, Sigvat travelled to Norway where he sought out Olaf and his army and was given a place among the troops, probably by his father Tord's side. He would serve Olaf for years, as an advisor and messenger, with great admiration for his lord, and become a renowned and highly regarded man in the king's service. In his old age and after Olaf's death, he would wistfully look back on the time when everyone knew his name; how he "was once recognized on ships".

We know all this because he tells us about it in his own words. Sigvat Tordarson was a gifted poet, and it is him we have to thank for much of our knowledge about Olaf's life and career. More skaldic poems composed by him have been preserved than by any other Nordic skald before the age of writing, and many of them are about Olaf. His poetry offers a unique and vivid contemporary picture of the king from the viewpoint of one of his own men, depicting Olaf as an inspiring leader held in the highest esteem by those who served him.

> There was no gap in the ranks where I stood proudly in the midst of his men with my sword.

When young Sigvat introduced himself to Olaf for the first time, he did so in the manner that was customary for skalds seeking to enter into a king's service—he offered up a short poem. A brief while later he stood before the king again, probably surrounded by an audience at a feast or at some other location in Vik. This time, he presented a long tributary poem about the king's accomplishments. Sigvat had composed it using the stories of those who travelled with the king, his own father likely among them, and perhaps also included details he had been given by Olaf himself. In fifteen verses, he told the chronological story of fifteen battles that Olaf had fought and won—in eastern Scandinavia, in

England, in Brittany, in Aquitaine and under distant skies in the south. The final verse was about the ambush of Håkon Sigurdsson in Saudungssund, which, at the time Sigvat presented the poem, had happened just a few weeks or months before.

The poem, which was written down and preserved for future generations by Snorri, is our most important source of information about Olaf's bloody career before he came to Norway.

All Norse leaders of a certain rank and status had such court poets in their service, and most of them were Icelanders. Many of them knew each other from their home island, or were related. References are made to female skalds, but most of them were men. Their circle was small—they knew each other and often referred to each other's poems in their verses.

Over the years, a number of skalds served Olaf for shorter or longer periods of time, and we know the names of several of them from their poetry. One skald named Gissur Svarte was nicknamed "Gullbrå" or "Gold Brow", because he had composed a love poem to a beautiful woman with golden eyebrows. Another was named Tormod Bersason, and was Gissur's brother. His nickname was "Kolbrunskald"– or "Coal-black skald"—because he had composed a love poem to a woman with eyebrows that were black as coal. By his own account, when he was around thirty years old Tormod had single-handedly killed six men with his sword. He stayed at Olaf's court one winter, before sailing to Greenland to kill a Norse chieftain there who had taken the life of his foster-brother. His poems included a fantastical tale about Sigurd the Dragon-Slayer, who thrust his sword into the dragon's heart so that it shook in the dragon's chest, and stole the treasure over which the monster had brooded—a story that must therefore have been known among the men of Olaf's *hird*.

One Torfinn "Munnen"—"Mouth"—also followed Olaf for a while. Many years earlier, he had composed poetry for Håkon

Sigurdsson, Jarl of Lade, perhaps before Olaf was born, and so must have been an ageing man by the time he entered Olaf's service. With the exception of Sigvat, the most famous of Olaf's skalds was Ottar Svarte, who was the same age as Sigvat and his nephew. His nickname—Ottar the Black—was probably down to the fact that he, like Sigvat, had black hair. He served the Swedish kings before he eventually joined Sigvat at Olaf's court and composed a great number of tributary poems and odes to Olaf.

The skalds' task was to flatter and praise their employers with beautiful words, whether during the feasts that took place in the princes' dark timber halls, or in the sunlight on board the princes' ships—but always before an audience. Although there may have been exceptions, as far as we know the skalds performed their poetry without musical accompaniment. It was the words themselves—and their rhythm, composition and meaning—that was beautiful, and the poems were probably recited as part of longer stories that were told in prose. The skalds were adaptable men with silver tongues, and their poetry consisted of shameless bragging: about their lord's greatness and proud achievements at sea and on land, about his masculinity and praiseworthy efforts in war, his illustrious conduct and generosity towards his company of men—and especially to the skald himself.

As thanks for all this, the skalds received gifts—swords, bracelets, clothing and fabrics, pouches full of coins, and exotic foods. The first time Sigvat composed a poem for Olaf, Olaf gave him a large gold ring. The second time, the king presented him with a valuable sword. In one ode, Sigvat thanks Olaf for the exotic nuts he received. Serving kings with lavish praise could be an extremely lucrative business, and the skalds could become rich men. One skald who composed poetry for King Cnut received a leather pouch of silver coins that had a total value equivalent to that of 200 cows—all for a single poem.

The skalds also held a unique position in the continually shifting alliances between warlords. They travelled between princes, often serving several lords at once or switching back and forth between them—including between princes who were in open conflict with each other. Such positions were difficult to balance, and could be dangerous. The skalds also fought for their lords in battle. Some of them were taken prisoner, and ended up in delicate situations because they had formerly served their captor's enemies.

Many skalds thematized their complicated relationships to various lords by composing poems about how they were captured and sentenced to death, but managed to escape by coming up with an appropriately beguiling and laudatory poem about their captor. They were never executed, however—the skalds seem to have been protected by a kind of diplomatic immunity, which meant that they could behave in a way that others would never have dared; they could criticize as well as praise. The poems' reliability as historical sources is strengthened by the fact that the skalds performed them in person, before the princes and their men, and so although they often exaggerated hugely, they could hardly lie. Because, as Snorri pointed out two centuries later, to lie would be to offend rather than to flatter. This makes the skalds invaluable sources of information about events that took place before the art of the written word came to the Nordic region. They are our eyewitnesses.

The peculiar and gory skaldic odes are strange historical and linguistic phenomena. Like Anglo-Saxon poets, the Nordic skalds composed their poetry using a strict and mysterious system of linguistic metaphors, kennings, put together in complex rhythmic constructions and rhymes. Some of the metaphors are easy to understand, such as "thought-smith" for skald, or "sea-horse" for ship; but many require detailed knowledge of the Norse mythological imagery and stories to which they refer. This makes the old Norse skaldic poems incredibly cryptic, and borderline incomprehensible for most modern readers—as they most likely would also have been for many contemporary listeners if they were performed out of context—but this also made them resistant to change over centuries of oral retelling. They could only be recited in one single, specific way.

In this bookless culture, in which people's memories were far superior to ours, the poems were memorized and passed on. And so, as if frozen in the patterns of their verses, they broke free of the world that gave rise to them and travelled through time, as the people who passed them on lived their lives, had children and died—for seven, eight, nine, ten generations or more—before the poems were finally written down by the saga writers, who used them as building blocks in the construction of their narratives about the past. Snorri could recite hundreds of skaldic verses by heart—many of which were 200 years old.

Much of what the saga writers composed around the skaldic poems consisted of guesswork, misunderstandings or pure fantasy. But the poems themselves they wrote down more or less unchanged, preserving them, so that they endured like linguistic fossils within the saga texts. They are sealed treasure chests of words that contain encrypted historical information we are able to read today—1,000 years after their creation.

*

While poems were composed, beer was drunk and oaths were sworn in the freezing winter cold of Vik, and Olaf focused on building his network through conversations over shared meals in his feast halls, the battles on the other side of the North Sea raged on, escalating in scope and brutality.

A number of prominent Anglo-Saxon men were now fighting on the side of Cnut, Eadric and Eric Håkonsson—Cnut led one army, Eadric Streona another, and Eric Håkonsson a third. They stormed through areas where the leaders refused to hail Cnut as king, mercilessly burning the fields, towns and villages. In mid-winter of the year 1016, Cnut and Eadric combined their troops and marched into Warwickshire, an area whose leaders refused to submit. In a laconic tone, the *Anglo-Saxon Chronicle* describes how they "ravaged, and burned, and slew all that they could come at".

Edmund Ironside, Æthelred's son, fought on with indomitable energy. He led his army hither and thither throughout the ravaged country, on intense, urgent marches along unpredictable routes, gathering people to him wherever he could. During the winter he returned to London, where Æthelred remained sick and weak. Edmund attempted to raise an army outside the city walls, but the peasants' leaders demanded that the garrison soldiers inside the city come out and join their ranks. When the garrison soldiers refused to leave the safety of London's fortifications, the frightened peasant soldiers fled for home in great flocks. In order to prevent his entire army from disbanding, Edmund now rode into London himself to meet with his enfeebled father.

Father and son were reconciled, and decided to stand together against the enemy. Æthelred left the safety of the city and rode out of London with his son to show his royal personage before the peasantry, and thereby inspire and convince them to fight.

But by this point, the sick old king was likely so paranoid that he was no longer a leader in any real way. In Edmund's war camp, he began to fear for his safety. It was not the Danes he feared, but that someone in his son's circle might be hatching a plot to kill him. He became so afraid that he suddenly left the army and his son's side, and with his escort rode back to the safety of the palace behind London's walls.

Edmund gave up on supporting his father and led his army northwards, into Northumbria, where he met Northern England's most prominent leader—Ealdorman Uhtred of Northumbria— whose headquarters were on the coast at Bamburgh Castle. Uhtred was the same man who three years earlier had received Sweyn and Cnut with open arms in Gainsborough, and led the Northern English aristocracy into the Danish king's embrace. He now realized that his interests lay with Edmund, and joined forces with him.

Edmund Ironside and Uhtred of Northumbria's Anglo-Saxon armies were just as brutal as Cnut's—on Edmund's orders they terrorized, burned and plundered large areas on the east coast in order to make an example of and punish the people there for refusing to march against the Danish army.

Edmund and Uhtred then planned to force Eadric to leave Cnut's side by laying waste to Eadric's home region, so that he would have to march home to defend his people. Uhtred and Edmund led their warriors into Mercia and set to ruthlessly burning the villages there.

This would prove to be a disastrously ill-fated tactical error— and one that changed the course of the war. Cnut and his war council got wind of the fact that Uhtred was on his way south, and while the Anglo-Saxon armies marched into Mercia, Cnut and Eric Håkonsson led their combined armies on an exhausting and urgent march in a long arc around and behind their enemies, via the marshy Fens on the east coast, and from there northwards into Yorkshire—straight into Uhtred's undefended homeland, where they began a violent campaign of terror against Uhtred's people.

The people in the north paid a high price for their leaders' decisions and shifting alliances. Two years had passed since Æthelred's soldiers "slew all the people whom they could reach" in the area around the Humber because the local aristocracy had hailed

Sweyn Forkbeard King of England. Now the Jarl of Lade and Danish king's warriors committed more mass murder in the same region. Through brief snippets of detail, Cnut's skalds permit us to glimpse what happened. Cnut "caused the English to fall" and ensured that "the deep river flowed over the bodies of dead Northumbrians".

When Uhtred learnt that Cnut's army was burning and laying waste to his lands and killing his subjects, he realized that he had been outmanoeuvred. Cnut and Eric Håkonsson's combined armies were far superior to his own. His own lord, Edmund Ironside, had enough on his plate keeping his own forces together, and certainly didn't wish to go north to confront the enemy in open battle. Uhtred had no other choice than to immediately stop his ravaging of Mercia, leave his army and hurry northwards. As he approached, he sent messengers ahead of him to request safe passage—which Cnut granted him. Uhtred rode into the Danes' war camp, where the ageing Northern English ealdorman threw himself at Cnut and Eric's feet and surrendered.

Uhtred's kin had controlled Northumbria from Bamburgh Castle for many generations, but that time was now over. Cnut accepted Uhtred's capitulation and demanded—as usual—that he provide hostages. Uhtred led members of his own family and his supporters in the north in a submission ceremony. The leaders of Northern families gave Cnut their sons as hostages; Uhtred submitted "and all the North-humbrians with him".

Then Cnut had Uhtred summarily executed.

This was a direct breach of Cnut's *grið*, his promise of peace and personal safety, and of the age's conventions regarding how one treated an enemy who had submitted. But this somewhat unchivalrous behaviour was a rational and necessary part of Cnut's greater plan for his future English kingdom. Immediately afterwards, he appointed Eric Håkonsson, Jarl of Lade, as Northumbria's new lord. In doing so, Cnut not only did away with a potentially dangerous rival, but also ensured himself Eric Håkonsson's continued support. It was support upon which he was absolutely dependent in this conquest that was as yet far from secured.

Because at this point, Eric Håkonsson and his advisors must have received news of Olaf Haraldsson's aggressive conduct in Norway. Håkon Eriksson, the jarl's young son, had by now likely arrived in England, having been overpowered by Olaf in Saudungssund and banished from his own lands. By giving control of Northumbria to the Norwegian jarl, Cnut rewarded him for his loyalty and war efforts with a piece of England that was far more valuable than the realm of Lade in Trøndelag, and which gave the jarl the best conceivable reason to continue to support Cnut's cause. With far-reaching power, authority and freedom as Cnut's deputy, from this point onwards Eric Håkonsson was in reality regarded as a kind of viceroy of Northern England.[2]

As Northumbria's lord, Eric Håkonsson continued to use the Norse title of jarl, and this was the first time the title was used in England. It eventually came to replace the Anglo-Saxon title of ealdorman, and continues to be used in England today in its current form—"earl".

*

Developments in England put the Lade dynasty's last remaining representative in Norway—Sweyn, Eric's brother—in a difficult predicament. With the vast majority of the jarls' armed forces now occupied on the other side of the North Sea, where the dynasty's leader now had more to defend and fight for than in his old ancestral lands, Sweyn was in a weak position in relation to the warrior king who had recently arrived in Vik and taken it upon himself to conquer the realm of Lade. Sigvat the Skald describes an arms race, in which Olaf in Vik and Sweyn in Trøndelag each built up their own army. An inevitable showdown was brewing.

Using gold and silver combined with threats and force, Olaf gathered a great army that consisted of many *heiner*—people from the villages of Hedmark in the east of Norway. Sweyn, who cannot possibly have had anything close to Olaf's wealth with which to pay his warriors, didn't manage to gather as many people. Sigvat composed a poem in which Olaf is praised for his open-handedness, while Sweyn is ridiculed for his poverty and stinginess.

> The generous one gained a much greater force for the battle than the mean. The *hird* was merry and ready to fight; the crowds rejoiced.

> But for the friendless leader, he who scrimped on payment, the men were sparse around the banners.

Sweyn Håkonsson's fleet set out from the Trondheim Fjord early in the spring of 1016, and set its course southwards along the coast. The army consisted of the troops Sweyn had managed to gather in Trøndelag, and one of its generals was the local chieftain Einar Thambarskelfir, whose striking nickname meant "wobbly belly"– an indication that he was likely a fairly fat man with an impressive waistline. He had been Olaf Tryggvason's man many years earlier, but had since allied himself with the Jarls of Lade. According to the sagas, he was married to Eric and Sweyn's sister. The army may also have picked up reinforcements in Western Norway on its way south, but it was in no way an impressive force.

Olaf set sail from Vik just before Easter, with a much bigger army. Travelling with the fleet was Sigvat the Skald, who says that he sat in one of the ships as "the warriors cut the sea with their oars". King Olaf himself led the fleet from his royal ship, *Karlhofði*, where he stood at the prow "on the black planks".

The two fleets met each other in the sea east of Agder, "off the broad plain" of the Brunlanes Peninsula, perhaps near the modern village of Nevlunghavn. The date was 26th March 1016, and it was Palm Sunday.

Few incidents were more praised by the skalds and later saga writers than great sea battles. The Norse seafaring and warrior culture provided entertaining and fantastically exaggerated narratives about such clashes, in which the fleets were big as the sea and the sky couldn't be seen for sails, and where the warriors fought like gods. The real sea battles that inspired such fantasies of blood, vengeance and rage were prosaically brutal and fraught with mortal danger.

The verses Sigvat the Skald composed once the sea battle was over can almost be considered an eyewitness account, and are staggeringly detailed for verses so old. He describes how, as the fleet approached the enemy, he sat on a thwart beside a man named Teitr. They prepared for the clash—Sigvat pulled a shirt of mail over his head, and set a helmet forged in Poitou in the kingdom of the Franks over his black hair. From where he sat, he could see Sweyn's forces binding their ships together.

We often hear of fleets being bound together in this way in skaldic poetry and sagas. With lowered sails, the ships were carefully manoeuvred using their oars until they were lined up against each other and it was possible to walk from one to the next, before they were tied together to create a continuous battle platform. When the fleets were within firing range of each other, the battle would begin with the casting of stones and the shooting of arrows. While some of the men shot and cast projectiles, the others protected them with their shields. The skaldic odes describe how, as the distance between the ships shrank, the ringing sound of stones hitting the ships' beams could be heard, mingled with the shouts of the ships' captains calling out orders to their men.

In one of Sweyn's ships was a skald in the jarl's service. He describes how, as the fleets approached each other, Olaf recognized him from the prow of his royal ship and "bade him well". The skald returned the greeting.

Then came the clash. Olaf led the boarding of the enemy ships himself, with his warriors around him and his standard-bearer by his side. Sigvat was also among the men who followed the king—they moved quickly, sticking close together and were "enraged". The hand-to-hand combat on the decks of the enemy's ships is described in detail. The air was filled with the sound of ringing steel as weapons clashed; the blades of swords turned red. Shields were crushed. Injured men fell overboard, down into the ice-cold water. Men fought at both prow and stern. The skalds who described such battles revelled in descriptions of blood. Deck planks are spattered and covered with dark blood, blood runs down between the ships' planks, blood runs down into the sea: "Warm blood fell red on the sea." "Hot wounds gushed blood into the sea." "The green sea, mixed with blood, turned red."

The battle was brief; Sweyn's inferior army crumbled under the pressure of Olaf's assault. Many who gave way before the attack stumbled on the thwarts, fell on to the deck, and were struck down from behind. Soon the gaps between the rowing benches were crammed with the dead and wounded. Sigvat uses the specific word *hrjóða*, "clear". They cleared the enemy's ships.

The skalds also state that many men fell overboard, both living and dead. Some were able to swim to safety, but this was difficult in helmets and chainmail. We hear of dead bodies floating in the water, bodies washed up on beaches, full of sand, bodies sinking to the bottom of the sea—they disappear into the dark depths, but the skalds are still able to imagine them.

> The wave, churned up by a storm, moves their skulls and limbs on the sandy bottom: the sea howls over the warriors.

> Lady, Sunday was not like when a girl brings a man leeks and ale—many a warrior sank under the blades that morning.

And so Olaf defeated his enemies in the Battle of Nesjar, which the later saga writers and modern nation builders would transform into one of the great, decisive moments in Norwegian history. Sweyn Håkonsson's army was destroyed; many of the ships floated empty on the water. Others surrendered. They were Olaf's ships now. "Not a few corpses floated swiftly by the spit of land," Sigvat recalled afterwards.

Many men were taken prisoner, among them the skald in Sweyn's service whom Olaf had recognized and greeted. After a brief period spent as Olaf's captive, he entered into his service. Through his poems, Sigvat merrily praised the men of Hedmark who had fought valiantly alongside him for their king. They had proved that they could do more than drink the king's beer—they could kill for him.

Sweyn Håkonsson survived the battle. He sailed away together with other survivors, Einar Thambarskelfir among them. Their cause was lost. But, strangely enough, they did not go west, to Cnut and Eric Håkonsson in England. The next sources to mention them state that they left anything they were unable to carry and fled east, into Sweden, where Sweyn had friends. The realm of Lade remained behind, wide open and ripe for the conquering.

NOTES

[1] Late-Umayyad coins have been found in England and Sweden, and perhaps also in Norway, which may possibly be from Olaf's expedition. A Spanish Umayyad coin (*dirhem*) from 989–90 has been discovered, together with a Hammudid coin from 1049 (from the Hammudid dynasty in Malaga), perhaps in the area around Bergen. The coin from 989–90 may possibly be from Olaf's expedition. Five Spanish coins have also been found on Gotland, minted between 946 and 1009, together with a larger number of German and English coins, and deposited towards the end of the 1000s.

[2] The jarl witnessed Anglo-Saxon documents in the years 1019–126 (*Diplomatarium Norvegicum IXX*, nos 3, 4, 5).

Brittene igland is ehta hund mila lang.
⁊ twa hund brad. ⁊ her sind on þis
iglande fif geþeoda. englisc. ⁊ brit-
tisc. ⁊ wilsc. ⁊ scyttisc. ⁊ pyhtisc. ⁊
boc leden. Erest weron bugend þises
landes brittes. þa coman of armenia. ⁊ gesætan
suðewearde brytene ærost. Þa gelamp hit þ pyhtas coman   suþan of scithian. mid langum scipu-
na manegum. ⁊ þa coman ærost on norþ ybernian
up. ⁊ þær bædo scottas þ hi ðer moston wunian. ac
hi noldan heom lyfan. forðan hi cwedon þa scottas.
we eow magon þeah hwaðere ræd gelæron. we witan
oþer igland her be eastan. þer ge magon eardian gif
ge willað. ⁊ gif hwa eow wið stent. we eow fultumiað. þ
ge hit magon gegangan. Ða ferdon þa pihtas. ⁊ ge-
ferdon þis land norþan weard. ⁊ suþan weard hit hæf-
don brittas. swa we ær cwedon. And þa pyhtas heom abæ-
don wif æt scottum. on þa gerad þ hi gecuron heora
kyne cin aa on þa wif healfa. þ hi heoldon swa lange
syððan. ⁊ þa gelamp hit ymbe geara rina. þ scotta
sum dæl gewat of ybernian on brittene. ⁊ þes landes sum dæl geeodon. ⁊ wes heora heretoga reoda ge-
haten. from þa heo sind genemnode dæl reodi. Six-
tigum wintrum ær þan þe crist were acenned gaius iuli-
us romana kasere mid hund ehtatigu scipu gesohte
brytene. þer he wes ærost ge swenced mid summum
ge feohte. ⁊ micelne dæl his heres forlædde. ⁊ þa he

TWO KINGDOMS

AS OLAF DEFEATED HIS ENEMIES at Nesjar, Edmund Ironside returned to London with his army yet again in a last-ditch attempt to join forces with his slowly dying father. Followed by a ragtag band of members of the Anglo-Saxon warrior aristocracy and a rabble of peasant soldiers, the king's son rode into a London overflowing with refugees. The war had caused thousands of farming peasants to leave their homes and seek shelter for themselves and their families behind the mighty city walls, where they lived in dreadful and cramped conditions. In the city, Edmund was reunited with his father, but Æthelred's condition was such that it was clear he would never fight again. While the kingdom beyond the walls disintegrated, the paranoid king who was supposed to be its uniting figure sank deeper and deeper into his illness.

Æthelred finally died on 23rd April 1016, St George's Day, one month after the Battle of Nesjar in Norway, having ruled "with great toil and under great difficulties". Thirty-eight long years had passed since he had inherited the kingdom from his murdered brother as a twelve-year-old—his reign was the longest of any English monarch in the Middle Ages. It was also the most violent. Æthelred's time in power had been a more or less continuous war, which he had slowly lost.

The king was buried in the city's cathedral. His queen, Emma, who was in London together with their two sons, now settled all old disputes with her stepson Edmund Ironside. The queen, the bishops and the prominent men of Æthelred's *witan* who were in the city, along with the city's own leaders, came together around the king's son, who was now the only uniting figure with any hope of standing against Cnut. They held a large gathering, and elected Edmund as Æthelred's successor, hailing him the Anglo-Saxon king.

At the same time, Cnut was just a few days' march away in Wessex—Æthelred and Edmund's ancestral lands in Southern England. With the northern parts of the country cowed and in the hands of Eric Håkonsson, Cnut had marched south again. When news of Æthelred's death reached him, he called all his allies to a hailing ceremony in the port city of Southampton, where his fleet was moored and his army was stationed, and where he held court with his band of advisors and warlords—now a merry medley of Danes and Anglo-Saxons; "the bishops, abbots, ealdormen and all the nobles of England, assembled there," writes the chronicler John of Worcester—that is, the entire English elite apart from those in London. They hailed Cnut King of England and swore oaths of allegiance to him; during the ceremony Cnut also swore an oath to be faithful to his duties as their lord. Afterwards, the Danish army boarded their fleet of ships once again and set sail for London.

When word that the Danes were on the way reached Edmund he bade farewell to his half-brothers and Queen Emma, left a strong garrison to ensure London's defence, and led his army and members of his father's old council out of the city so as not to end up trapped in it. In the period that followed, the defence of the city seems to have been led by Æthelred's widow, Emma.

In the mild spring weather of early May, Cnut's fleet came up the Thames and began the most comprehensive siege in London's history. In order to pass London Bridge, which was heavily defended, the Danish warriors hacked and dug a wide trench in a sweeping arc around it as the city's defenders looked on from a distance. They then dragged and hauled their great warships on rolling logs, through the trench and out into the Thames again on the other side.

Eric Håkonsson and his army also came down from the north and joined the siege. With incredible toil and drudgery, Cnut and Eric's soldiers constructed a mound of earth around the entire city, which they then fortified, completely closing London off from its surroundings so that "no one could get in or out". They followed this up by storming the walls and trying to smash open the gates, "and attacked the borough repeatedly, but [the people of the city] withstood them valiantly".

While the Danish army sweated blood before the strongest walls in England, Edmund Ironside led his army into Wessex, straight into the area in which Cnut had just been hailed king. He rode around between the towns and villages, proclaiming that it was he, Æthelred's son and heir to the century-old West Saxon royal dynasty, who was their true lord and king. And with the Danes occupied outside London's walls, Edmund once again managed to transform his mobile war camp into a centre of Anglo-Saxon resistance.

When Cnut's scouts and messengers reported that Edmund was riding around Wessex with a growing army, Cnut divided his army into two. One half he left to continue with the siege of London; the other he led overland, towards his rival. Throughout late spring and early summer, Cnut and Edmund's armies trudged around and around, back and forth, in an exhausting and drawn-out struggle, each attempting to outmanoeuvre the other in the lush fields and forests of Wessex. Thorkell the Tall, Eric Håkonsson and Eadric Streona were by Cnut's side. The war entered its most intense phase—divisions of the armies repeatedly clashed in smaller skirmishes, without conclusive results.

At the end of June, the two main armies finally faced one another outside Sherston, a small village in Wiltshire. The armies advanced, and their front lines locked in one of the bloodiest battles since the Danes had first come to England. According to various accounts, signs of panic arose in Edmund's ranks due to a rumour that the king had fallen, but at the last minute Edmund managed to prevent a mass flight by riding among his troops and showing his face. In a wildly exaggerated version of this story that was written down in the 1200s, in the heat of battle Eadric Streona cuts off the head of a fallen man who looks like Edmund, holds it aloft so Edmund's soldiers can see it, and cries: '*Flet Engle, flet Engle! Ded is Edmund!*'—'Flee Englishmen, flee Englishmen, Edmund is dead!' That such imaginative tales emerged, and that they circulated and lived on for many generations, says much about just how vividly these battles were imprinted on the population's collective memory. The more sober, believable and almost contemporaneous *Anglo-Saxon Chronicle* tells of an exhausting battle without any clear winner: "much slaughter was made on either side, and the armies of themselves separated".

The armies withdrew and continued their clumsy dance around Wessex, plundering the local population in their search for food—and increasingly for fighting men, who were desperately needed. The marches took them north, south, east and west; up, down, back and forth. The Danes took great numbers of livestock from the villages, driving the animals ahead of them in large herds.

Early in the autumn of 1016, Edmund's army marched along the north side of the Thames towards London to free the besieged city. A vanguard he had sent out on a plundering mission ahead of the main troop drowned when their ship capsized in the river.

When Edmund's forces approached, the Danes gave up on their siege and evacuated with their ships down the Thames.

Having liberated London, Edmund marched west again. But the Danes returned to the city and resumed their siege—Edmund turned back and chased them off once more. Several clashes without any conclusive outcome followed. Groups of Danes who strayed any distance from the main army were ambushed and slaughtered by local peasants. Cnut's skalds speak of violent battles in which the Danish warriors struck down their fleeing enemies from behind using spears.

To the Danes' despair, Edmund slowly began to gain the upper hand, and at some point during the autumn Eadric Streona changed sides yet again. Abruptly abandoning Cnut, he went to Edmund and asked for forgiveness. Edmund probably didn't trust the fickle ealdorman, but sorely needed his help and so accepted him.

All at once Cnut was the weaker party, forced to flee before Edmund Ironside's armies. Cnut, Thorkell the Tall and Eric Håkonsson rode through Essex ahead of their marching foot soldiers, their enemies breathing down their necks. In the end, they held a meeting of their war council and decided to turn and fight. They stopped marching and instead prepared for battle at a place known as Assandun, a range of hills likely to be the site of the modern town of Ashdon.

Edmund and Eadric reached Assandun in mid-October 1016. War meetings were held and great speeches were made, through which the leaders on both sides attempted to fire up their men's courage and harden their discipline. On 18th October the armies advanced towards each other.

Thorkell the Tall is said to have personally led the Danes from the front line under his banner, surrounded by selected veterans from his *hird*. His counterpart on Edmund's side was a man

Thorkell had fought against before, who was well known and enjoyed great respect among the Danes—namely the ealdorman Ulfcytel of East Anglia, who had led the Anglo-Saxons during the bloody Battle of Ringmere, all the way back in the year 1010.

The Battle of Assandun was well matched, bloody, long and desperate. According to almost contemporary Anglo-Saxon accounts, the battle surged back and forth for hours as the two sides clashed again and again in terrible hand-to-hand combat, with both sides refusing to yield and neither obtaining any decisive advantage. King Edmund Ironside, who it is worth remembering was only around eighteen years old, fought in the battle himself—several Danes are said to have died by his sword. The day passed into late afternoon as thousands of raging and terrified men fought each other to the death.

Yet again, Eadric Streona was the weight that tipped the scales. As twilight fell, he withdrew his forces from the fray and left the battlefield, abandoning his young king and all his people to their fates. Entire divisions of Edmund's army then collapsed; the men panicked, turned away from the enemy and ran. Many were struck down, stabbed and trampled into the mud from behind; a number of Anglo-Saxon thanes and even several ealdormen were surrounded and killed—among them Ulfcytel himself. An abbot, who was probably there to lead the monks' ritual bearing of relics to bless the troops, was also killed. So many prominent men on Edmund's side fell that the *Anglo-Saxon Chronicle* asserted that "all the nobility of the English race was there destroyed".

One of the fallen was a bishop called Eadnoth, who four years earlier had collected the disfigured body of his colleague Ælfheah of Canterbury, the man who had been put in a cage and later murdered by drunken Danes during the victory feast outside London in 1011. During the Battle of Assandun, he stood out on the battlefield and sang Mass as the fighting raged around him. He was shot, stabbed, beaten or hacked to death. His body was plundered and mutilated by some Danish warriors, who cut off his right hand "for the sake of a ring".[1]

There would be no crushing victory for Cnut, however. King Edmund survived and managed to flee with a core group of some of his best men and parts of his army intact. The Danes had also suffered great losses; dead and dying men from both sides lay strewn across the battlefield. Cnut's skalds and later Scandinavian accounts of what happened at Assandun praise King Edmund for his great courage and fighting spirit.

At the end of October, Cnut's exhausted army pursued the rest of Edmund's forces into Gloucestershire, where in the autumnal cold yet another battle took place in the Forest of Dean. Afterwards, both sides were so weakened by losses that they were willing to negotiate.

After messengers had ridden back and forth between the parties and paved the way for their meeting, and all sides had solemnly sworn to permit each other safe passage, the opponents finally met at a formal gathering in Gloucestershire in early November. Most surviving members of the English nobility, along with high-ranking members of the clergy, travelled to Gloucestershire in order to attend.

Everyone was now so tired of war and exhausted from fighting and marching that they were genuinely willing to find a solution that would end the conflict. Both Edmund and Cnut had realized that no swift victory was within reach for either of them. The sheer scale of death, suffering and destruction was unlike anything even the most experienced war veterans had ever seen, and nobody had anything to gain from letting the conflict continue.

Eadric Streona, who had emerged from the battles with his army intact, took on the role of a kind of mediator between the two kings, who met on an island or *holm* in a river and agreed to make peace, dividing England between them. The territory north of the Thames, excluding London, would belong to Cnut; London and Southern England would belong to Edmund. The two young kings and mortal enemies solemnly swore to this agreement, and kissed and hugged and assumed brotherly poses as dictated by the theatrical diplomatic rules of the age, before they parted ways to establish their separate winter courts in their respective English kingdoms.

And so the story of the Danes' war on England might have ended with the conquest of half a kingdom. But just a few weeks after the parties had gone their separate ways a message arrived from the south. Edmund was dead.

We do not know how the king died. The *Anglo-Saxon Chronicle* states only that Edmund died on 30th November 1016, and that he was buried at Glastonbury a short time later. The king had fought in a number of smaller clashes and great battles in the weeks preceding his death, and it is possible that he fell ill and died of an infected wound.

But rumours also circulated that he had been poisoned. "Edmund, a warlike man, was put out of the way by poisoning to favour the victor," Adam of Bremen wrote later. If this was true, it isn't hard to see who would have had the most to gain from such an act. At the peace meeting just a short time earlier, the two kings had agreed that if one of them should die, the entire kingdom would fall to the other.

Cnut now called prominent men from north to south to a new royal election; there were no other candidates than Cnut himself. He was crowned at a ceremony in London early in 1017, before the gathered English nobility. Archbishop Lyfing of Canterbury, a man who had seen several of his colleagues killed in battle and who himself had been taken prisoner by the Danes some years earlier, set the royal crown upon Cnut's head.

*

At this time, on the other side of the North Sea, Olaf Haraldsson and his army were on a victory procession through Norway—the conquest at Nesjar became the major breakthrough in Olaf's quest for power. Sweyn Håkonsson attempted to gather support in Sweden in order to continue the battle for the kingdom, but he died a short time later—under what circumstances, we do not know. Nor did Einar Thambarskelfir return—instead he settled down somewhere in Sweden, in exile under the Swedish king's protection. Eric Håkonsson and his son Håkon never came back to Norway, instead preferring to remain in their hard-won English earldom. There was nobody left in Trøndelag who was strong enough to oppose Olaf's claim.

A short time after the Battle of Nesjar, Olaf came to Trøndelag with his army. He called free men from the villages around the Trondheim Fjord to a ceremony at which he would be hailed as king. Rather than being held at the people of Trøndelag's traditional *thing* at Frosta, the gathering probably took place at the mouth of the River Nidelva, in the jarl dynasty's centre of power. This was where the people had taken Olaf Tryggvason as their king, and likely the kings of the Fairhair dynasty before him when they obtained sovereignty over Trøndelag. Surrounded by his sworn *hird*, an ever-growing body of followers and a sea of peasants, Olaf Haraldsson followed in their footsteps and was hailed the King of Trøndelag.

Snorri states that Olaf built a royal estate in Nidaros with a permanent seat for Grimkil, one of the priests who had followed him from England and who became Olaf's bishop. According to Snorri, Olaf also built a church in the town, which was dedicated to St Clement, patron saint of sailors—and this may well be true. While sagas like Snorri's tell us a lot about Olaf's kingdom, they are distant and distorted echoes of the events they describe—stories about people who really did exist and events that did indeed take place, although not exactly as related, and perhaps not in the given order. But in 2016, archaeologists found the ruins of a church from the 1000s in Trondheim, with the remains of previous churches beneath it. Tree-ring dating of a wooden pillar from the oldest part of the church showed that the tree was felled at around the time when Olaf established himself in the town, and so this may be the church that Snorri describes.[2]

A short while after the victory at Nesjar, Olaf set out through Harald Fairhair's old kingdom in Western Norway with his army, in order to conquer it. The old kings had controlled the area through a chain of royal estates along the coast, from Jæren in the south to the Sognefjord in the north. Avaldsnes was one of them. The royal dynasty had died out before Olaf was born, but Western Norway was still regarded almost as a separate, independent kingdom. It had come under the Jarls of Lade and Danish kings' symbolic sovereignty, but in practice no one from outside had ever had any significant power over these Western lands.

Western Norway's leading figure was a man of mature years, the very wealthy and widely respected Erling Skjalgsson. In practice, he was regarded as a kind of uncrowned king of Western Norway. Snorri states that he belonged to the might-iest family in the region, and contemporary skaldic poems testify to Erling's almost unparalleled reputation. Olaf's skald Sigvat described him in extremely complimentary terms as "the guardian of the Hordaland", and added that he managed his kingdom well.

Erling maintained connections with influential people to the east and west. As a young man, he had controlled Western Norway under King Olaf Tryggvason's sovereignty, and had probably been baptized at the king's command, much like Olaf and his relatives in Vik. He had married the king's sister, and fathered several sons. After Olaf Tryggvason's fall, he had allied himself with the Jarls of Lade and married off one of his sons to Sweyn Håkonsson's sister.

But despite this, Erling did not intervene when Olaf Haraldsson came to the country and challenged Sweyn's control. When Sweyn and Olaf came to blows at Nesjar, Erling Skjalgsson seems to have simply stood on the sidelines and waited.

Not long after Olaf's victory Erling chose to bow to the new king, swearing an oath of allegiance to Olaf in 1016 or 1017. He became Olaf's *lendmann*, a Norse title that we first hear of in Norway at this time.[3] It was a feudal, aristocratic title given to men who received land from the king in exchange for their fealty. Over time, the title would be superseded by the Latin *baron*.

Olaf also sailed to the high north, and demanded that the people there recognize him as their king. The leading chieftain in Hålogaland was *Þórir Hundr*—Thorir Hund—on the island of Bjarkøy, a rich trader known for his close connections to the Sámi people. It is difficult to form a clear picture of him because he later became an extremely demonized figure in the Church's legends and hagiographies, but he seems to have had a perpetually poor relationship with Olaf. The earliest sources about him, which are poems composed by Olaf's skalds, paint him as a brave, stubborn and belligerent figure. According to Sigvat, he was a "mighty-hearted" man. Thorir Hund was not used to submitting to kings from the south, but chose to do so when Olaf arrived with his powerful fleet. Thorir Hund's brother also swore an oath of allegiance to the new king and became his *lendmann*.

Even chieftains from Hjaltland—the Shetland Islands—are said to have sailed to Norway and sworn their allegiance to Olaf. "No battle-bold king subjugated under himself the islands in the west before you," bragged one of Olaf's own skalds.

It is said to have been during the first years of his reign that Olaf ordered the construction of the first known castle in Norwegian history, a fortified farming town beside the Sarpefossen Falls on the River Glomma, at the point where seafaring ships could move no further into the country. It is fascinating to imagine this young king in his early twenties, self-confident and famous, surveying the area with his company as they are watched with curiosity by the local men, women and children. The small site was already used by traders and ferries, and as a reloading point, where goods were loaded on to smaller rowing boats in order to be transported upriver. A road also crossed the river here, which made it a doubly strategic point.

On Olaf's orders, the workers—probably slaves—dug a 650-metre-long and several-metre-wide trench, and used the excavated stone and earth to build a mound. Trees from the nearby forests were probably felled in their thousands before being de-limbed, split and transported to the building site, where they were set upright side by side atop the mound to form a timbered wall.

Olaf's Sarpsborg was likely similar to the Danish kings' constructions in Denmark and England, and the fortified cities of earth, stone and timber that lay along the coasts both east and west of Denmark. Olaf's ability to command and complete such a work says more about his power than any ode composed by his skalds. Hundreds of people must have been involved, organized into work teams and led by experts who knew how such a castle should be built. Inside the walls, the workers constructed halls, houses, workshops and a church, which the priests of Olaf's *hird* dedicated to the Virgin Mary.

Sarpsborg became a central location in Olaf's new kingdom—a control point and hub in the borderlands facing Denmark to the south and Sweden to the east. He may also have established several similar sites elsewhere in the country, of which we are unaware.

The victory at Nesjar marked the start of a more peaceful period in Olaf's life. The great army with which he had travelled so far must have disbanded when Olaf established himself in Norway, because an army could only be held together in times of continuous war. In a way, this also makes Olaf's story more difficult to write about, because this period of peace meant that the skalds—our most important contemporary witnesses—had less to recount through their poetry. While sporadic preserved tributary poems reveal few concrete details about the course of events, they describe Olaf in turns of phrase that testify to a truly strong position of power: "noble king with your great retinue", "gracious ruler", "mighty ruler", "worthy king", "the brave lord of the people of Trøndelag", "the ruler of the people of Møre", and so on.

More concrete evidence of Olaf's power and ambition is provided by a handful of coins that have been found, imprinted with his name. These show that Olaf, like the Danish kings in the south and Swedish kings in the east, had coin makers in his service. Coins have been discovered from three different mints that belonged to Olaf—they are copies of Anglo-Saxon coins, pennies, with a standardized king's head on one side and a cross or a bird—the dove of the Holy Spirit—on the other, along with a variant of the inscription ONLAF REX NORMANNORUM, *Olaf, King of the Norwegians*. It is possible that they were hammered from English silver that Olaf brought home to Norway. They were not produced in large numbers, but certainly in greater quantities than under Olaf's predecessor Olaf Tryggvason, the first Norwegian king for whom coins have been discovered. They remained in circulation

as a means of payment for a long time, and have been found in
Norway, Sweden, Finland and Poland.

In purely geographical terms Olaf's kingdom was among the
largest in Europe, but in reality his power was in large areas limited to a symbolic sovereignty over established noblemen—and
coins imprinted with the king's name did not change this fact. All
European kings built their power on the natural authority of the
local nobility. In theory, the nobles received the right to rule over
Crown lands from the king; in practice, they often regarded the
land as their own. Like Frankish counts and dukes, and like Anglo-
Saxon ealdormen, men like Thorir Hund and Erling Skjalgsson
were independent leaders, surrounded and protected by household
warriors whose loyalty was not to any king but to their leaders
themselves. Their power was anchored locally, through control
and dominance over the farming population.

At the end of the day, a kingdom in the 1000s was held together
by little more than such men's loyalty, and the idea of a united
Norwegian kingdom under a single king was entirely new. Natives
of the north of Norway were loyal to Thorir Hund and other
local chieftains in the north; those who lived in Western Norway
were loyal to Erling Skjalgsson. According to the sagas, Olaf
visited Western Norway particularly rarely, and on the few times
he did, his trips were brief. By all accounts, it seems that business
generally continued as usual in both Thorir Hund and Erling
Skjalgsson's domains.

On the other hand, Olaf focused great efforts on maintaining
direct control of Trøndelag. The region's location between the
chieftains in the north and the old western kingdom in the south
made control over Trøndelag critical for anyone seeking power
along the old North Way.

Trøndelag became the most important area in Olaf's Norwegian
kingdom alongside his old familial seat in Vik. But even though

the jarls were gone and the region's prominent men were cowed, Trøndelag was an area in which it was tremendously difficult to achieve any real supremacy. The Jarls of Lade had controlled these lands continuously for 100 years, and the old bonds of loyalty among the farming population seem to have been strong. The ancient sacrificial culture was still alive and well in some of the area's villages—something the Jarls of Lade had never sought to prevent, despite being baptized themselves. Olaf was a foreign, Christian king.

Olaf's control was more like an occupation, and Snorri tells of brutal punishments directed at the peasants' leaders and chieftains who refused to submit. At one point, for example, Olaf is said to have led an expedition from Nidaros. Five warships with 300 warriors on board were rowed down the Trondheim Fjord to Mære, a heathen village where the local people still made sacrifices to the old gods. Olaf's forces arrived in the middle of the night, and silently surrounded the houses in the darkness. The most prominent local men were captured and killed, "together with many others". The king took hostages to ensure that their friends and relatives would not revolt, while simultaneously murdering or maiming his enemies. Many villagers fled their homes and even the country. Olaf distributed farms, provisions, items of clothing and household effects among his men as booty, and so "many lost everything they owned". Then he returned to Nidaros.

In an attempt to enforce his authority on Trøndelag, Olaf systematically focused his efforts on cultivating good relationships with immigrants to the area and people of lower rank, in order to undermine the power of the established local chieftains. Especially central to this policy was an old prominent family from Giske on the coast of Møre, the so-called *Ørnungene*—"Eaglets"—who according to their own legend descended from a man who had been found wrapped in silk in an eagle's nest. Four brothers by the names of Kalv, Torberg, Finn and Arne all became Olaf's men. They were connected to chieftains along the coast from north to south, through bonds of blood, marriage and friendship. They were given large estates that had previously belonged to men loyal to the Jarls of Lade. With Olaf's blessing Kalv even took the widow of a chieftain Olaf had killed for his wife, and became stepfather to the fallen enemy's young sons.

Olaf's methods of obtaining control were the same as those used by kings all across Europe. The trick was to divide and conquer by pitting mighty men against each other, supporting one or the other of them in local conflicts, undermining potential enemies by supporting their rivals, and attempting to make people dependent on the king's favour and support. Snorri's saga about Olaf paints a believable picture of him as a man who consciously and methodically tipped people in positions of power off balance, so that they toppled towards each other. He rewarded his new supporters by gifting them treasures from his travels and the farms of his fallen enemies. To some of them, he even married off his female relatives.

In order to block the power of resource-rich and wilful chieftains—including those he had created himself and those who enjoyed great power independently of him—Olaf stationed a number of royal representatives of lower birth at a network of royal estates around his newly conquered lands. They were known as ármaðr, which literally translates as "servant men". These were men who owed their positions of power to the king alone, and were therefore less likely to rebel. Olaf rewarded his apparatus of such sworn representatives with goods stolen from his enemies, and from rivals who left the country. They acted as an extension of his power, and were his eyes and ears where he himself was unable to be present.

In the years he spent as a travelling Viking, the true core of Olaf's machinery of power was his faithful band of warriors, who followed him wherever he went. His *hird* constituted a small but international community, consisting of men from Vik and other areas across the Norwegian kingdom, Icelanders, Anglo-Saxons and probably others besides. Many of these men must have followed Olaf for years—they were veterans from the wars and raids on the great foreign world beyond their homelands. Apart from Olaf himself, the *hird*'s most distinguished figure was a man who held the title of *stallare*, who acted as the leader of the king's *hird* and commander of the army—the king's right hand and close advisor. This title was also in use at Cnut's court in England at around the same time. While Olaf was establishing himself in Norway, his *stallare* was a man by the name of Bjørn. In his poems, Sigvat refers to him as "Bjørn the Stout", and depicts him as a brawny figure who was not only an experienced and hardened warrior, but also wise; a skilled negotiator and a man who gave good advice.

Snorri alleges that Olaf's permanent *hird* consisted of around 120 warriors, which seems probable, but the size of the company varied over time. At one point, Olaf is said to have ridden around with a band of 300 men. Then there was the *hird* clergy, consisting of a small group of mainly Anglo-Saxon scholarly priests who had followed Olaf from England or Normandy.

In the later Middle Ages, a Norwegian king's *hird* would develop into a large and strictly hierarchical organization. Olaf's *hird* was not like this, but it does seem to have been roughly divided into smaller groups with differing tasks, perhaps modelled on Norman or Anglo-Saxon examples. It likely consisted of an inner circle of men who never left Olaf's side, and an outer circle of so-called *gestir*—"guests"—notorious and violent henchmen whom the king had at his disposal and who could be dispatched to "guest" his enemies, which involved everything from threatening and

frightening them to burning down or confiscating their farms—
or, quite simply, beating them to death. Later in the Middle Ages,
these "guests" became notorious because they always travelled
beneath a striking black banner.

The practical exertion of a ruler's power took the form of an
endless journey through the kingdom. The princes of medieval
Europe lived nomadic lives; they were extremely mobile, always
on the move with their retinues. Over the course of the year they
rode from residence to residence, subsisting on local produce and
holding court for a brief period before moving on to visit a holy
site or to lead a military expedition. They lived most of their lives
on country roads; always on horseback, always on their way to
the next destination.

The same was true for Olaf. His kingdom had no capital, no
fixed chancery, no permanent royal residence—everything was
done on the road. Wherever he went, Olaf took along his *hird* and
likely an entire apparatus around it—of servants and associates,
of entertainers and musicians, of people who tended and fed the
horses, who prepared food and kept an eye on the provisions, who
washed clothes, who sharpened swords, who polished harnesses
and maintained equipment.

Olaf and the people who followed him around spent significant
periods of their lives travelling, in ships along the coasts and in
and out of the fjords, and on horseback along the country roads
that linked the inland villages together. The roads were narrow
and rocky, in well-used stretches often hollowed and scooped out,
naturally eroded and shaped by the thousands of human feet that
had trudged and walked the same routes since time immemorial.
They were bridle paths in the summer and sledging trails in the
winter; wheeled carts were not used in Norway until after the end
of the Middle Ages. The roads snaked their way between farms
and villages, taking detours to more remote places, following

ridges where the land was drier since the snow was blown away by the wind and rainwater ran off to lower ground. This meant the roads often climbed and descended steep slopes. The great forests divided people; the crests of the hills bound them together. In both mountains and lowlands, rivers would be waded across at fords. Bridges were rare. At best, a log might serve to keep your feet dry as you crossed.

Olaf's company would have journeyed long distances through wilderness—1,000 years ago settlements in Norway were separated by vast expanses. In Olaf's entire extensive kingdom there were probably fewer than 200,000 people, and most of them were concentrated in strips of farming country, which must have seemed like islands of civilization and culture in a sea of untamed forests and desolate mountains.

The king's company travelled all across the country, their colourful banners and flags visible from great distances away; on horseback along winding mountain passes and through dark pine and spruce forests; in sleighs across snow-covered fields and frozen rivers; through ever-changing weather between royal residences and the farms of chieftains; from small market towns on the coast to inland forest villages; and across the deep snow over the Dovrefjell Mountains in the winter, as Sigvat recounts in one of his many poems. Or as Snorri imagined: "Now Olaf journeyed west, first down the frozen rivers and seas to the sea. But when spring came and the ice melted, they prepared their ships, and when they were sailworthy and had a fair wind, they sailed out and the voyage went well."

Local leading men held banquets for the king's retinue; in turn, the king held feasts for them on the smattering of royal estates where he stayed regularly, and which his representatives kept under surveillance. Here, the representatives were responsible for ensuring the king and his company would receive suitable sustenance, partly from the royal estates' produce and partly in products from local farms.

This provision of hospitality by nobles was the closest this society came to imposing any kind of tax. It was the king's right and privilege to travel around his kingdom with his retinue and eat; the peasants had an obligation to provide the necessary provisions.

The court was not unlike a travelling circus, always on tour throughout the kingdom and visiting the same places, where it both satisfied and exhausted the local hosts before moving on. Travelling with as large a company of followers as possible gave prestige, and nobody was permitted to travel with a larger retinue than the king.

It must have been quite the spectacle to behold hundreds of people travelling together in a single group under flags and banners, with bells jingling on the sleighs and the horses' bridles, making their way into some tiny, out-of-the-way village where the quiet and stillness that characterized all pre-modern agricultural societies otherwise prevailed. The horses would have to be fed. Beds would have to be found for everybody. Prominent locals came to ask for favours; the beseeching poor came to ask for mercy. A royal visit was a huge event. The king showed off his wealth, power and grandeur by holding ceremonial feasts for members of the local upper class; there was drinking and excess. The men in the king's service—and often the king, too—became intimately acquainted with the local women.

Then they left again, and silence fell once more. It might be several years before the procession returned.

Most people never knew where the king was at any given time. During peacetime, the king and his volatile relations with the land's prominent men had a negligible impact on the lives of ordinary people. In the villages, life continued on its quiet course.

*

The sagas depict Olaf travelling around the country in a burning religious fervour. He destroys heathen idols, ridicules heathen men in front of their peers and spreads the true faith through hard means. This is probably an exaggerated portrayal, influenced by the fact that Olaf's story was written down at a time in which he was prayed to as a saint, and when people were looking for an explanation as to why and how the ancient Norse religion and sacrificial culture had been driven out by Christianity.

The earliest sources bear no indication that the Christianization of the country was in any way a priority for Olaf. In the great number of preserved skaldic poems that were composed by Olaf's skalds while he was alive, not a word is ever mentioned about God or Christianization; the same is true of the poems that were later alleged to have been composed by Olaf himself. Their contents are all about battle and war, about daring sea voyages and the warriors' trials and joys, courage and strength. By comparison, Sweyn Forkbeard's skalds claimed that he conquered England with the White Christ's help—not that this should be taken as proof of his piety.

Olaf undoubtedly worked to promote Christianity, but his Christianization project likely differed little, if at all, from those of other Christian kings in his part of the world at this time. The Christianization of Norway was part of a larger trend. It was an unavoidable process, the result of a slow landslide driven by hidden historical structures and forces that no individual was able to truly influence or stop, and which culminated during Olaf's time.

The same thing was happening everywhere on the peripheries of Christian Europe. Kings in new kingdoms simultaneously embraced Christianity all along Christendom's northern and eastern boundaries. The kings in Sweden, King Mieszko in Poland, King Stephen of Hungary and King Bolesław of Bohemia all Christianized their respective kingdoms at around the same time. King Mieszko and King Stephen were also royal saints—they were declared holy by their priests, just as Olaf was in Norway.

This was true of all princes in Christian Europe, who held in their hands more power than their predecessors ever could have imagined. The ancient heathen religion's world view was a complex universe of forces and counter-forces, with many gods who were often in conflict with each other. In the new religion, all legitimate power was concentrated in a single God. It isn't hard to see which world view best suited ambitious kings who sought sovereignty and control over their kingdoms and people.

Olaf's Christianization was therefore an integrated and natural part of the exertion of his power. Like the kings in Europe where he had spent long periods of his life, and like the Christian kings of Western Norway and Olaf Tryggvason before him, he forged alliances with powerful men through rituals of allegiance, in which he demanded that they also be baptized by the priests who accompanied him around the kingdom. When the children of Olaf's allies were *primsign*-ed, Olaf often stood as their godfather, thereby strengthening the bonds between him and both parents and child. A runic inscription on a memorial stone in Oddernes in Vest-Agder names Olaf as the godfather of a prominent man called Øyvind. Sigvat had a daughter named Tófa, and Olaf became her godfather, too. Mass conversions likely happened only rarely, if at all. It was up to the local chieftains to convert their own people.

Churches were erected in many places across Norway in Olaf's time. Most of them were built by prominent men who established private churches on their farms, some of them on Olaf's initiative and others on their own. The building of churches was the custom of the age, and gave status and prestige. These small wooden churches only had space for the prominent men who owned them and their closest family and friends; the priests who led them through the liturgy were part of the men's households. But priests and missionaries were not dependent on having a physical church in order to perform liturgical work. Ceremonies were likely also held outdoors and inside the farmhouses, and ceremonies for larger gatherings may have been performed out in front of the small early churches.

Olaf also built churches in his newly established royal power centres, such as Saint Clement's Church in Nidaros and Saint Mary's Church in Sarpsborg. Olaf Tryggvason, and Harald Fairhair's son Håkon Adalsteinfostre, had in their time consolidated their power over Western Norway by building churches there; Olaf Haraldsson continued the same practice elsewhere in the country. These churches were probably similar to those that were built in royal centres in Denmark at the same time—small and simple, some of them constructed completely out of wood, others partly out of wood and partly out of stone, and based on examples from England. This was a way of maintaining control over the fragile and rickety construction that was Olaf's Norwegian kingdom. Olaf's priests were loyal servants and adept administrators and organizers.

The building of churches and the royal backing of priests further advanced the long process of converting Norse society to Christianity. Missionaries from Christian lands had already been active in heathen Scandinavia for more than 100 years, but the work had been slow and difficult, with many backlashes. The missionaries were brave men, because their work often involved significant risk to their own health—and even their lives. Adam of Bremen, for example, tells of the Anglo-Saxon missionary Wolfred, who travelled to Sweden to convert people during Olaf's reign in

Norway. At a heathen site used for worship and *things* he hacked to pieces a statue of Thor, god of war and thunder, using a battleaxe. The furious locals seized him and stabbed him to death, before dismembering his corpse and throwing it into a swamp. He was just one of a number of missionaries who were killed.

But the situation was quite different when the missionaries were able to operate under the protection of Christian kings. Olaf's priests travelled to Sweden, to Götaland and the islands in the sea to the west of Norway and back, and all around Olaf's kingdom under his protection. Nobody dared touch the priests within the realm for fear of terrible reprisals from the king. The priests performed their missionary work, converting prominent men and training more priests to do the same.

The priests led people through religious rituals in the same manner as did the priests in England, Denmark, France and Italy, observing the same feast days and performing the same cere-monies, and all in the same language—Latin. Instead of many gods—gods for individual districts, gods for individual occupations or actions, gods for war and gods for growth—everyone must now worship one God, who ruled over sun and rain, heaven and earth, war and peace. Instead of gathering a few times a year at the old sites of worship in order to make sacrifices to the district's main gods, people now gathered every Sunday, and on all holy days and during all religious festivals, to attend church services.

The churches helped to undermine the chieftains' traditional power as leaders of religious ceremonies, and linked ever-larger parts of the population through new rituals in a primitive but growing religious organization of which King Olaf was the head. When people bowed before the White Christ, they bowed before Olaf too.

The introduction of Christianity to the Nordic societies was, however, subject to significant continuity in people's everyday lives, and the transition to the new faith and its customs was therefore gradual and slow. Many of the Christian festivals were celebrated at the same time as the old ones, although the priests justified the celebrations in new ways. The old summer sacrifice became Midsummer, the autumn feast Michaelmas and All Saints Day, and the time of the Christmas feast—the midwinter sacrifice—was maintained. The agricultural system upon which the entire society was based continued to function by the same cyclical logic as it always had done.

But the new priests did more than teach the peasants about lofty theological ideas. The Church's liturgy and instruction framed life in a way that anchored theology in concrete everyday activities. A number of saints' days and Masses were introduced, on which it was forbidden to work—instead, everyone would gather to attend Mass in the churches—in addition to the regular Masses held every Sunday. Fridays were fixed fasting days. Church bells began to mark time in a way that must have been completely unfamiliar. They called the people to Mass, to prayer, to funerals and weddings.

The new faith slowly brought about fundamental changes in people's way of thinking. The old-world view was constructed around a horizontal dichotomy between inside and out, near and far. Midgard, the world of humans, and Asgard, the world of the gods, comprised the centre. "The others"—Jotuns, monsters and the Midgard Serpent—remained on the periphery, in the great sea surrounding Midgard or in Utgard. But the new faith was built around a vertical world view which posited the kingdom of heaven at the top, humans in the middle, and hell down below.

In the old culture, the gods and people's forefathers existed in the north, and so people oriented their burial mounds and spaces accordingly. The Christians, on the other hand, oriented themselves towards the east, so that the dead would be able to look upon Christ's countenance on the dawn of the resurrection. Court assemblies in the age of Christianity therefore always began with everyone bowing towards the east.

Under the old customs people burned their dead, or buried them on their home farm. The burial mounds were important symbols of land ownership that denoted descendants' right to the earth. But neither burning nor mounds were compatible with the new concept of resurrection. The Christians buried their dead in collective churchyards.

Even when it came to what and how people ate, the Church had far greater influence than any other authority had ever had before. The early clergy in Norway introduced strict rules regarding what was clean and unclean. It was a sin to eat animals that had died a natural death, or for which the cause of death was unknown; especially strict was the prohibition against eating horsemeat, which the heathens had done as a matter of course. Fasting days were introduced for adults—they made up almost a third of the Church year. On some fasting days it was forbidden to eat meat, while on others eating anything at all was not permitted until the evening.

But the old religion was hard to stamp out. It endured in Trøndelag and Northern Norway for longer than in the rest of the country but continued to exist across the land, becoming more and more hidden and secret, practised in darkened houses and forgotten villages.

Recent research has shown that the pre-Christian religious practices in Norway were strongly influenced by and related to the Sámi religion. Magic rituals whose purpose was to do good or evil might be performed privately or in small groups. Shaman-like women and men brought themselves into a trance, in which they could see into the spirit world and perform *seiðr*, a type of magic. To the disgust of pious Christian monks and priests, this heathen sorcery was often sexually charged, and particularly associated with the female. Heathen men who performed magic sometimes wore women's clothes.

There are credible accounts of women and men performing rituals while wearing painted masks shaped like the heads of pigs, dogs or oxen. In the skaldic poetry, we hear of women and men of the pre-Christian age who sit outside at night, at a crossroads or under a gallows where someone has been hung. We hear of sorcerers and sorceresses who chant and sing, who mumble nonsense and magic words, who meditate and slip in and out of trances and states of ecstasy. Others perform *galdr*, magic incantations that were sung in special high voices, and which are said to have been beautiful to hear. Some were able to mix potions of plants and herbs that brought about hallucinations; some could look into other worlds through magic frames and find hidden objects, in their minds or in the physical world. They could bring about success and disaster, control the weather, catch game and fish, cast curses and cause people to make wild choices and thereby bring about their own downfall. They could send their essence out into the world in the form of a shadow to take the life of an enemy.

The tolerance of the members of the new clergy diminished as their influence increased. In the old rituals they saw devil worship and evil, and terrifying magic. With Olaf's support and backing, the priests victimized the sorcerers and sorceresses through ever more effective means. A couple of generations after Olaf's death, Adam of Bremen wrote that at his time it was known that Olaf "routed out the magicians from the land":

Although all barbarism overflows with their number, the Norwegian land in particular was full of these monsters. For soothsayers and augurs and sorcerers and enchanters and other satellites of Antichrist live whereby their deceptions and wonders they may hold unhappy souls up for mockery by the demons. All these and others of their kind the most blessed king Olaf decreed must be pursued in order that, with their scandals removed, the Christian religion might take firmer root in his kingdom.

Many rulers before Olaf had also been brutal to those who refused to submit to the new God. The sagas assert that Olaf Tryggvason forced a live snake down the throat of a chieftain who refused to convert, and tied sorcerers to stakes in the sea so that they drowned in the rising tide. Whether these claims are true in a literal sense is far from certain, but such stories reflect memories of a violent and terrifying regime. Charlemagne was known as the "missionary with an iron tongue" for the methods he used to force the Saxons to bend to Christ.

However, this violence had little to do with the new religion itself—it was a natural part of a king's manner of ruling. Everyone who sought power in this society had to be prepared to use extreme and spectacular violence—it was a crucial tool for all kings in Europe at this time. It was not a sign of their strength, however, but rather of their weakness. They had no other means of making people act in accordance with their will, or of enforcing their laws. Fear of the king's reprisals and punishment was vital in forcing people into submission.

Æthelred's father, for example, Edgar the Peaceful, who was regarded as a pious and intellectual king, issued an order that people caught thieving in England under his rule would have their eyes put out, their ears, hands and feet cut off, and their nostrils sliced open—before they would be finally scalped and left in a field to be devoured by wild animals.

When Olaf's former employer Richard II of Normandy was young, a great rebellion broke out among the peasants in his dukedom. The rebels held an assembly, and "decided to live according to their own wishes". Richard declared the rebels outlaws, and sent his uncle and a group of knights to force them back into the fold. The knights rode to the assembly, ploughing through the crowds and seizing the rebellion's leaders with terrible force. They then cut off their hands and feet "and sent them, no longer of any use, back to their fellows to restrain them from like conduct and warn them by their own fate against suffering worse. Having seen this the peasants hurriedly dissolved their assemblies and returned to the ploughs."

Olaf's skald Sigvat describes the same kind of severe regime of punishment in Olaf's Norwegian kingdom. Olaf likely had little opportunity to enforce laws and punish criminals and lawbreakers to any great extent, given his modest machinery of power.[4] But when he did mete out punishment, he proceeded in the same manner as other kings. Sigvat praised his lord for punishing thieves by cutting off their hands; assailants and rebels had their arms and legs lopped off. Bandits were beheaded. This was how Olaf created peace and prosperity in the land, and according to his loyal skald, "the high, sloping cliffs seemed to laugh over all Norway while Olaf was alive".

NOTES

[1] Bishop Eadnoth was later buried in the monastery at Ely, a day's journey north of Cambridge. He was laid to rest beside another famous figure who had given his life in the fight against the Danes, namely Byrhtnoth, the ealdorman who was killed at the Battle of Maldon during King Sweyn's very first raid on England in 991.

[2] Tree-ring dating puts the year at 1009 plus or minus five years.

[3] The first time the title of *lendmann* is mentioned is in a poem by Sigvat the Skald, who referred to Erling Skjalgsson as Olaf Tryggvason's "*lendmann*".

[4] In later sagas, Olaf is said to have been concerned with law and order, and to have justly punished criminals on a large scale. This was probably the saga authors' construction, because at their time it was what kings should do. Such *rex iustus* ("just king") depictions are some of the most conventional in medieval works of history, and the portrayal of Olaf as protector of the law was appropriate to the Norwegian royal and ecclesiastical ideology of the 1200s. See e.g. Bagge 2002.

THE GREAT

WHILE OLAF TRAVELLED around his newly conquered Norwegian kingdom and consolidated his power, Cnut did the same in his English one—and the Danish conqueror used brutal tactics. After he was crowned and anointed King of England early in 1017, Cnut ordered that a number of high-ranking nobles whose loyalty he didn't trust be seized and executed. The new king also went after the surviving members of the royal dynasty he had fought.

At least four of Æthelred's sons were still living, and by virtue of their royal blood they were potential future rivals. The greatest threat was posed by the last remaining son from Æthelred's first marriage, Eadwig, who had fought beside his elder brother, Edmund Ironside. Cnut declared him an outlaw and banished him from the kingdom. Eadwig fled. A brief time later, Cnut invited him back, and Eadwig returned—but the king had him killed shortly afterwards.

Edmund Ironside had also fathered two sons, young boys to whom his queen had given birth during the past few years of war, and who can only have been in their infancy. Sources tell us that Cnut sent them away to Sweden, probably with their mother. It was later said in England that Cnut had planned to have the boys murdered after he had got them out of his sight, but they were saved by the people looking after them in Sweden who sent them on to Gardarike, beyond Cnut's grasp. After a period spent in Kiev they are said to have ended up in Hungary, and to have grown up there.

The two sons Æthelred had with Emma of Normandy were also out of Cnut's reach. They grew up protected by their mother's relatives at the duke's court in Rouen.

Having led the defence of the besieged city of London against Cnut's forces, Emma had also left England, sailing in safety to her homeland. To secure his conquest, one of Cnut's first political power plays was to ask for her hand in marriage.

Of course, Cnut already had a queen—Ælfgifu of Northampton. While he had led his army on endless field marches over the past two years, she had borne him two healthy son and heirs—two infants who were cared for in safety far from the war, perhaps in Denmark.[1] Now Cnut set Ælfgifu aside and entered into marriage negotiations with Emma and her relatives. Nobody could give his conquest greater legitimacy than the former king's widow.

The daughter of the Norman duke was at this time around thirty years old—around ten years older than Cnut—and had lived her life at the centre of this drama ever since she had been married off to Æthelred fifteen years earlier. Emma had stood by Æthelred as her brother Richard betrayed him time and again, supporting those who exploited and sought to conquer the English kingdom.

Emma had also borne Æthelred two sons and at least one daughter, and had watched her children grow up surrounded by war. She had seen her new homeland burn and her subjects slaughtered in droves; looked on as her husband's regime tottered and collapsed. She had fled only to return and lead the defence of the besieged London.

But despite her status and central position in this drama, it is more difficult to obtain a clear picture of Emma than of the men around her, for the simple reason that she was a woman. The men who recorded the course of history—mostly monks—almost never mentioned women other than when they were married off or acted on behalf of their husbands or sons. The kings' wives, sisters, mothers and daughters—all of them remain almost invisible to us, even though they were often deeply involved in everything that went on and could be accomplished and independent political players in their own right.

Emma is undoubtedly an example of this. She belonged to the same volatile political culture as the men around her, where personal relationships and political connections were inextricably tangled, and where bitter enemies could transform into allies overnight. For her, Cnut's proposal was an extremely lucrative offer, and one that would ensure her a position as the future queen of a united English kingdom. One of the most important sources from this period is the *Encomium Emmae Reginae*, a tribute to Emma and the people around her written at her request later in life, probably by a Flemish monk. It describes how Cnut initiated the marriage negotiations through messengers, who came to Emma bearing royal gifts. For her part, Emma demanded that Cnut swear a binding public oath that he would never give his kingdom to another woman's son. She would accept his proposal only if Cnut made the sons Emma would give him his sole heirs as future kings of England. Cnut annulled his marriage to Ælfgifu—who was demoted to the rank of mistress—and swore the oath.

Cnut and Emma were married in July 1017. Emma would become an influential figure at the new English court in the country she knew so well, and acted as regent when Cnut was abroad.

At the same time, Cnut negotiated with Emma's family and married off his only sister to Emma's nephew, the son of Duke Richard and heir to the Norman dukedom. The new alliance was thereby anchored by two marriages—a masterful political move by Cnut and his advisors. Cnut's marriage to Emma signalized continuity to the Anglo-Saxon population, while at the same time the alliance with the duke and his kin would make it difficult for Æthelred and Emma's sons to obtain help in Normandy and return to England under the banner of rebellion once they were older.

But Cnut was king of an exhausted English kingdom, and despite his victory his position was not strong. Even though England was infinitely richer than Norway and had a far more extensive and developed royal apparatus, after Cnut's conquest England was in many ways similar to Olaf's Norway. Both kingdoms consisted of four separate parts, of which the king only had direct control over one. Cnut controlled only Wessex and London; the rest of Æthelred's old kingdom he had split up and distributed between his victorious lords.

Eadric Streona was Ealdorman of Mercia, with as good as full independence. Thorkell the Tall was Lord of East Anglia; Eric Håkonsson of Northumbria.

At Christmas in the year 1017 Cnut held court in London, from where he sent a message to Eadric Streona. Eadric was the only high-ranking Anglo-Saxon aristocrat who had emerged from the inferno of recent years unscathed, and who had found himself a position in the new England. Putting it mildly, he had managed this through some impressive diplomatic manoeuvring amid the chaos—through assassinations and murder and a series of abrupt and unexpected changes of side between the warring parties. He always came out on top.

Now Eadric, by this time a middle-aged man, left Mercia and his supporters in the region for the great city beside the Thames. When he and his company arrived, he was seized by Cnut's men. Cnut summarily sentenced him to death, and Eadric was beheaded.

The *Anglo-Saxon Chronicle* states that Eadric was executed "very justly"—he was a widely and deeply hated figure after his many changes of side.

According to the *Encomium Emmae Reginae*, upon delivering the judgement Cnut said: "Pay this man what we owe him […] so that soldiers may learn from this example to be faithful, not faithless, to their kings." The monk and chronicler John of Worcester thought that Cnut feared he would one day fall victim to Eadric's notorious treachery, just as Eadric's former lords, Æthelred and Edmund, had done. With great satisfaction, he paints a literary scene similar to the Norse sagas' story of the slave Kark—Cnut lures Eadric to him by promising to pay him for his services by making him a head higher than everyone else in England, a promise he fulfils by setting Eadric's head on a stake on London Bridge while his headless body is thrown over the city walls, where it lies rotting on the ground because nobody wishes to bury it in consecrated soil.

No one would be judged more harshly in the exacting court of the historians than Eadric—English accounts depict him as an almost fantastically treacherous man. His name became synonymous with opportunism and disloyalty, and he was blamed for much of what went wrong during Æthelred's reign.

In reality, Eadric was probably little worse than many others in his turbulent age of shifting alliances, where anyone who wished to survive had to realize the importance of staying alert and constantly re-evaluate who was friend and who was foe. He was without a doubt extremely skilled, cunning and somewhat unscrupulous, but in the game he had played so masterfully since his youth he finally met his match in the young Cnut.

The fall of the Wessex dynasty—and not least the intense wars and suffering that led up to this defeat—was regarded as a catastrophe among generations of later English historians, and Eadric's posthumous reputation is an expression of their anger.

The writers of English history were little more gracious towards the man who bore the main responsibility for the defeat—King Æthelred himself.

Æthelred remained the king whose reign began with the murder of his own brother and ended with a foreign invasion of the kingdom. Creative chroniclers made fun of him. In Old English, the name Æthelred means something along the lines of "he who is wisely advised". But after his death Æthelred was given the nickname *Unrædas*—"he who is poorly advised". After a few generations, the memory of the king who had reigned for thirty-eight long years had been reduced to a ridiculous carica-ture: "[When enemies threatened the realm] the king, adept and well fitted for sleep, put off such great matters and yawned; and if ever he recovered to the point of rising from his bed, he was immediately overcome by inertia or adverse fortune and relapsed into his miserable state."[2]

The beheading of Eadric Streona marked the start of a larger purge of Cnut's supporters in England. In Mercia, Cnut stationed loyal men—many of them probably of Norse descent. One of them was Håkon Ericsson, the young son of Eric Håkonsson, Jarl of Lade, whom Olaf Haraldsson had driven out of Norway. King Cnut's power and influence grew.

We know far more about Cnut's rule in England than we do about Olaf Haraldsson's in Norway. Cnut was busy, and had much to prove—conquering the country was one thing; controlling it quite another. He was a young king in a large, densely populated land with many regions, and he needed to learn how the Anglo-Saxon system worked.

Cnut inherited a royal Anglo-Saxon machinery of power that was more developed than anything that existed in Scandinavia, but England also consisted of formerly separate kingdoms that had only recently been united, all with their differing customs and traditions, old power structures and leading families. The power of the Crown had to be built upon a fine-meshed network of prominent families and individuals, where the king's role was to function as the spider at the centre of the web. Cnut had to continuously remove potential rivals, but without pushing away the people upon whom he depended. After several decades of war and treason and battle after battle, the country's political circles were simmering with conflicts and bitterness.

Cnut spent a lot of time travelling back and forth between London and Winchester, the largest town in Wessex, and the old power centre of the royal dynasty he had fought and defeated. In Wessex, he surrounded himself with a circle of gifted and loyal advisors consisting of both Anglo-Saxons and Danes. In Winchester, gravestones featuring Norse runic inscriptions have been found, along with objets d'art decorated in a Scandinavian style—including a frieze with motifs from the Norse heroic epic about the dragon slayer Sigurd Fåvnesbane, which must have belonged to people in Cnut's circle. Like his Anglo-Saxon predecessors, Cnut ruled through regular meetings with high-ranking nobles, bishops and other influential men from the English regions.

In order to rule effectively and maintain control, Cnut had to improve his relationships with the bitter Anglo-Saxon noblemen he had defeated, while simultaneously placating those who had betrayed Æthelred because they expected better conditions under a Danish king. He also had to think of the Norse warlords and the men in their service who had fought for him, and who also expected to be rewarded for their efforts.

Cnut handed out property and farms around his kingdom. In the years following the invasion, men who must have followed him from Denmark appear in English documents as landowners and as participants in the meetings of Cnut's council. They have names like Agemund, Bovi, Urk, Hastin, Toga, Healden, Thurstan, Thrumm, Kartoca, Thurgod, Ulf, Theustul and Eusten. Two men named Tokig make an appearance—one of them a priest, the other a soldier. In addition to the introduction of the prominent noble title of "earl", the formal title *huscarl* also makes an appearance in English documents at this time—the Norse term for members of the king's *hird*.

Cnut was surrounded by skilled advisors and he had received a lot of help in ensuring that his conquest succeeded, but there is no doubt that Cnut himself was a political genius. He made not a single false move in the complex task of consolidating his conquest of the great English kingdom, strengthening his position little by little using all the means at his disposal as a European king. The political executions he ordered and the disappearances of potential rivals and people he didn't trust never spun out of control.

For most people who lived in England, Cnut's eventual victory marked the start of a long—and longed-for—period of peace. In order to reassure his war-weary subjects, who had suffered decades of burning and plundering, Cnut announced new laws that protected people's property against seizure and random attacks, and which enabled people to lodge complaints regarding injustices committed against them with his representatives.

Whereas Æthelred had confiscated Church property in order to pay tributes to the Danes and to reward the leaders of his ever more pressured regime, Cnut handed out land and money to the churches and monasteries, thereby winning over the bishops. Queen Emma, a friend of the Church and an eager collector of holy relics, seems to have played an important role in this policy.

Cnut reconciled with Wulfstan, the headstrong Archbishop of York, who in no uncertain terms had cursed the Anglo-Saxon aristocracy for betraying Æthelred, and who had interpreted the Danes' raids on England as God's punishment for Anglo-Saxon sin. Wulfstan was given a central position on Cnut's council, and helped the young king to formulate new laws to govern the Anglo-Saxon kingdom during what would come to be seen as its golden age.

At a large gathering in Oxford, Cnut made a speech to the townspeople and presented himself as the king who would bring back the peace and order that had reigned under Æthelred's father, Edgar the Peaceful. Through oath-swearing ceremonies, people promised to uphold the laws of the kingdom. Cnut gathered together Æthelred and Edmund Ironside's old supporters and made them declare that none of Æthelred's descendants had a right to the throne, in exchange for assurances that they would keep their positions under him.

Later, Cnut placed the cult of Ælfheah of Canterbury—the archbishop who had been killed by Thorkell's Vikings during their victory celebrations in 1011—under his protection and had the skeletal remains moved from London to Canterbury. The move further secured Cnut's position, as such a cult based in London, venerating an archbishop killed by Danes, might otherwise have proved a dangerous breeding ground for resistance against Cnut and his regime.

By 1018 Cnut's control had stabilized, and this year his regime organized a collection of taxes of a scope never before seen in the English kingdom. From all corners of the land a dizzying 82,500 pounds of silver was gathered—a sum greater than all the tributes that had ever been paid to the Danish armies who had plundered the country during the previous decades of war. Nothing says more about Cnut's power and wealth in the kingdom over which he was king.

This collection of taxes had been planned for a long time, and the amassed funds were distributed to Cnut's loyal supporters, Danes and Anglo-Saxons who had helped him to conquer the land. Afterwards, the king disbanded his great war fleet, which had remained moored outside London since his victory, so that it no longer posed any threat to the English people. He retained just forty ships.

At the same time, word arrived from Denmark that Cnut's brother, Harald—Sweyn Forkbeard's other son—was dead.

While Cnut had conquered England, young Harald had ruled over a peaceful Denmark. He probably died of an illness. No rivals remained among Cnut's siblings—only his sister Estrith was still living in Normandy.

In the autumn of 1019, Cnut left Thorkell the Tall as regent in England and set sail for Denmark. He did not cross the sea at the head of an invasion fleet, but instead travelled with just nine ships. Upon arrival, he held meetings with the leading Danish men from his brother and father's earlier regimes. They bowed to him.

In the winter of 1020, Cnut was made king and hailed at the Danish *things*. Just as he had done in England, he gave his loyal supporters key positions in the Danish regions. He appointed learned Anglo-Saxon priests as bishops, and stationed them in Danish towns.

He was only in his early twenties, and was yet to reach the pinnacle of his power.

*

From Norway, Olaf and his inner circle must have watched these developments with a sense of nervousness and unease. The sources reveal nothing concrete about the connections between Olaf and Cnut during these years, or what kind of contact they may have had, but the relationship between them was not good. Much indicates that Cnut had always regarded Norway as his Danish legacy and himself as Olaf's rightful overlord; Olaf's conquest of Norway probably happened without his blessing. Adam of Bremen wrote his work of history two or three generations later, and obtained his information from the Danish court at that time. To him, the situation appeared as follows: "Between Cnut and Olaf, the King of the Norwegians, there was continual war, and it did not cease all the days of their lives, the Danes struggling for dominion, the Norwegians in truth fighting for freedom."

While Cnut's shadow slowly crept closer from the west, Olaf sought out allies in the east, among the lords in the kingdom of Sweden. The history of Sweden at this time is even more obscure than that of Norway. In Olaf's childhood, a Christian king by the name of Olof Skötkonung had ruled in *Sveþuiðu*, "Svitjod", over Swedes and Geats, from a centre close to Sigtuna and Uppsala beside the great Lake Mälaren. Alongside Sweyn Forkbeard and Eric Håkonsson, he had fought against Olaf Tryggvason in the Battle of Svolder. According to Adam of Bremen, he had attempted to build a church in the important heathen cult centre of Uppsala, but encountered significant resistance from heathen chieftains and lost his power in parts of his kingdom. He had two daughters, Ingegerd and Astrid, and a son with the Norse name Anund, who was baptized and given the Christian nickname Jacob.

By the time Olaf Haraldsson returned to Vik and established himself as king, Olof Skötkonung may have been dead; in any case, the strongest man to the east was now a jarl named Ragnvald, who may have been acting as a kind of regent until the king's son Anund Jacob, who was still just a child, came of age. Olaf regarded Ragnvald as the Prince of Sweden, and his equal counterpart. The Swedish jarl was an ally of the Jarls of Lade in Trøndelag, and related to them by blood. It was to Ragnvald that Sweyn Håkonsson and Einar Thambarskelfir had likely fled after the battle at Nesjar.

Some obscure skaldic poems describe how Olaf's warriors took captive twelve men who worked for a Swedish prince, and then hanged them—something that speaks of a warlike state between Olaf and his neighbours in the east at the time Olaf was establishing himself in Norway.

In order to bring Ragnvald over to his side, Olaf sent messengers east shortly after the battle at Nesjar, probably in 1016 or 1017. The leader of this group of messengers was Sigvat the Skald. In a long and fascinating poem, Sigvat describes the journey taken by him and his company, thereby giving us a few rare contemporaneous glimpses into the Swedish kingdom. The journey probably began in newly founded Sarpsborg before passing through Eidskog, and was strenuous and uncomfortable. Sigvat contrasts the comfort he experienced aboard the king's ship, which "flew on the waves", with the difficulties involved in making one's way overland, describing how he whipped his tired and hungry horse eastwards through the deep, dark forests as the sun went down and day and night finally met. Somewhere in the east, he says, he witnessed a heathen fairy sacrifice to Odin—a ceremony that took place in a hall, and which was led by a woman. Along with his company, he finally arrived at "Ragnvald's city", which must have been somewhere in the lush and forest-covered landscapes around Lake Mälaren, with its beaches, side fjords, rivers and islands. He says that women lined the road and watched the band of men from the west as they galloped past on horseback. Upon their arrival Ragnvald received them, and Sigvat negotiated with him on Olaf's behalf.

Sigvat's mission was successful—he describes how he returned home to his king with an agreement that would ensure him friendship and good relations in the east. The Prince of the Swedes and the Prince of the Norwegians promised each other mutual support and reciprocal dignified treatment, along with shelter and safe conduct for each other's sworn men.

When Cnut incorporated Denmark into his growing kingdom a couple of years later, Olaf was determinedly working to strengthen his alliance with his Swedish neighbours. According to Snorri, in 1019 Olaf asked for the hand of Olof Skötkonung's daughter Astrid, Anund Jacob's half-sister. Olaf was in his late twenties; the bride's age remains unknown. Olaf held a wedding ceremony and Astrid became his queen, perhaps in the newly constructed royal timber hall at Sarpsborg, close to the Swedish borderlands. She likely fell pregnant almost immediately, because according to Snorri she gave birth to a girl the following year, on the royal estate at Sarpsborg. Olaf and Astrid had her baptized and named her Ulvhild. She is the first child we know of to be fathered by Olaf.

Like all royal marriages, Olaf and Astrid's was also an expression of a political alliance between two dynasties. Young Anund Jacob, Olaf's brother-in-law, was at this time perhaps in the process of seizing true power within the Swedish kingdom. Cnut posed a threat to him, too—as well as to the Swedish chieftains who surrounded him. Only by combining their forces would the rulers of the Norwegian and Swedish kingdoms have a chance of resisting their far richer and more powerful rival in the south.

At this time, for the first time in history, we can see the contours of a Nordic triumvirate taking shape—the kingdoms that would eventually become the countries of Norway, Sweden and Denmark, led by kings who changed their alliances with each other in line with shifts in the balance of power. A generation earlier, the Swedish King Olof and the Danish King Sweyn had formed a united front against Norwegian Olaf Tryggvason, and crushed him at Svolder. Now the Norwegian Olaf Haraldsson and Swedish King Anund joined forces to obstruct the Danish King Cnut's increasing power.

Some years later, Olaf became a father again—not with Queen Astrid, but with a mistress named Alvhild. According to Snorri, she was the daughter of a prominent man who served at Olaf's travelling court, and very beautiful, but otherwise we know nothing about her. She gave birth to a son—under great distress in the middle of the night, according to Snorri.

Nothing was more important for a king than to father a son. The custom that a king's son must be true-born would not be introduced to Norway until 150 years later, and so from birth this baby boy enjoyed the status that came with being the king's potential successor. The child was named Magnus, apparently at Sigvat the Skald's suggestion, after Karlomagnus—Charlemagne—the famous Christian emperor whose power had extended all across Northern Europe, "because he was the best man in all the world".

*

At some point during these years, according to the sagas, in the year 1024, Olaf and large parts of his machinery of power gathered on the green island of Moster in Sunnhordland, off the coast of Erling Skjalgsson's domain. Before prominent men, the local peasantry and a number of priests and clergymen, Olaf's bishop, Grimkil, lead a large assembly and church meeting.

Grimkil had systematically worked to promote Christianity in Olaf's kingdom for several years. At the meeting at Moster, he now announced a new conversion law, which he must have spent a long time formulating, and which would eventually come to apply to the entire kingdom. It began with the words: "The first in our law is that we shall bow to the east and pray to the White Christ for good years and peace; that we must keep our land well maintained and wealthy and our king in health. Let him be our friend and we his friends, and let the White Christ be a friend to all."

Then followed a long list of prohibitions and rules for the living of Christian lives based on the English example, along with a great number of prohibitions formulated for a Norwegian kingdom in which heathenism was still alive and well. All heathen worship in any form—including sacrifices and praying to idols—was strictly forbidden, as were magic and sorcery. The king's subjects were ordered to observe Masses and Sundays as holy days, and to fast during times of fasting. It was forbidden to marry one's relatives up to distant cousins. It was also forbidden to abandon unwanted babies to die of exposure—a custom apparently practised in the pre-Christian age. Priests would be ensured sustenance, churches would be protected, and bishops would have the right to determine who could become a priest.

It was probably this meeting that the two men who later raised a rune stone on Kuløya in Nordmøre were thinking of when they inscribed the stone with the following words:

> Tore and Hallvard raised this stone for Uljot
> Christianity had been in Norway twelve winters.

A thousand years later, Grimkil's announcement on the island of Moster remains the most momentous and lasting event to occur in Norway during Olaf's time in power, even though the king and his bishop probably led other similar meetings elsewhere in country. The Moster *thing* was the definitive breakthrough in Norway's Christianization.

*

While Christianity and the king's churches certainly helped to bind Olaf's Norwegian kingdom together, Olaf's power was first and foremost built on silver. His kingdom would have been unthinkable without the wealth he had obtained from his Viking raids. The loyalty that supported his power, and which had enabled him to fight his way up to a position of supremacy over Norwegian regions from east to west and north to south, was to a great extent bought.

The necessary generosity and extravagance that had been decisive in Olaf managing to establish himself and increase his power undoubtedly began to drain his reserves. Most of his silver came from England, but with Cnut having taken over the country, that source of income had been cut off. Years spent sitting at the top of his Norwegian hierarchy, in a political system where loyalty only lasted for as long as one's lord's generosity, must have drained Olaf's reserves of wealth.

In the early 1000s, Norway had no system for collecting any significant income from the population in the form of taxes and fines. In Olaf's time, a farmer's duty was limited to providing the king and his men with sustenance when they visited his area—it is also unclear whether this was an obligation that applied to everyone, or only to the tenant farmers on royal property.

From the sagas, we know that Olaf had merchants and hunters in his service, and that he forged partnerships with traders who travelled to the north, south, east and west. According to the sagas, Olaf forbade potential rivals from setting out on Viking raids. This was a way of ensuring peace in the country, and of preventing others from building a power base in the same way that he had—collecting foreign silver and using it to buy loyalty. At the same time, Olaf sent his trusted men out on plundering missions wherever this was still possible, or gave them his blessing to do so—perhaps in a manner similar to how Sweyn Forkbeard had sent plundering expeditions to England while he himself remained in Denmark, but on a much smaller scale. Eyvind Aurochs-Horn, Olaf's man on the west side of the Oslo Fjord, for example, set out on Viking raids in the Irish Sea. The so-called *Legendary Saga of St Olaf* tells of a Viking by the name of Hårek, Olaf's ally and good friend, who brought him booty from his expeditions. But the returns on such enterprises must have been meagre compared to the income Olaf had procured in his heyday as a travelling king of the seas.

Olaf's problems reflect a broader historical change that influenced power relationships in the Nordic countries as the Viking Age drew near to its end. The kingdoms of the Viking Age's seafaring kings were in reality their mobile fleets and the loyal warriors who manned them. They travelled with all their power and were able to journey far and wide, putting ashore almost anywhere—in the Loire Valley, in Ireland, in England, in Normandy. Later in the Middle Ages, as the Norwegian national kingdom developed, these kings moved around less and less, until they eventually hardly ventured beyond their national boundaries. Olaf is a transitional figure between two epochs.

A king in Olaf's position had to use his limited machinery of power in an effective and targeted manner, but just as important was building up a network of followers through friendship and generosity. This was difficult, of course, when one began to run out of funds.

Certain aspects of the Norse narrative tradition clearly bear witness to the fact that Olaf was no virtuoso when it came to political balancing acts. The saga writers composed their stories at a time in which Olaf had been transformed into a holy figure, and was therefore above direct criticism—but they criticized him indirectly by pointing out that the disapproval and criticisms they noted were the opinions of others, and not their own. In their age it must have been well known that Olaf had been highly unpopular in certain circles.

The author of the *Legendary Saga* from the early 1200s lists Olaf's supposed character traits: he was hard, proud and power-hungry, tight-fisted and greedy, says the saga writer, who concludes by asserting that before he became God's martyr, Olaf was "a ruler over this world". Later, using a literary device, the same author also has Olaf himself admit that he was often harder than he needed to be, and that he hadn't governed his kingdom as well as he should.

The greed and hardness for which Olaf was remembered may have been due to his diminishing reserves of silver and the political necessities that arose in the shadow cast by Cnut. In order to rule, Olaf was dependent on the obedience of the people around him, and on obtaining new income. The opposition he faced was strongest in Trøndelag, and so this was where he exercised the most force. This was partly due to the population's heathenism and their old subordination to the Jarls of Lade, but Olaf may also have squeezed the people there extra hard simply in order to pay his supporters elsewhere. Someone always had to pay for the king's generosity.[3]

Olaf's harshest critic among the saga writers is his biographer, Snorri, whose saga can almost be read as an extensive analysis of what Olaf did wrong and what led to his downfall. Snorri was obviously of the opinion that Olaf lacked the ability to fine-tune his actions as the situation dictated—to enter into compromises, as more successful kings were able to do. Although Olaf is the undisputed hero of Snorri's narrative, Snorri also paints a picture of a king who often acted unwisely, who consistently used force to get his own way and who punished the slightest act of insubordination—tactics which often backfired, driving people away from him. Not everything in Snorri's saga is historically accurate—far from it—but it is nonetheless tempting to believe that it captures something central to Olaf's personality and manner of ruling.

Olaf's relationships with prominent Norwegian men, on which his royal power rested, became increasingly poor. Snorri's saga and the older *Legendary Saga* feature a story that had circulated as gossip, and which in the process had probably been adjusted to make the narrative even juicier, but there is reason to believe that it contains a grain of historical truth. The story is the account of a blood feud, a tragedy that shows how the mechanisms of honour and loyalty in this brutal and poor society pressured Olaf into conflicts with the country's mightiest men—conflicts in which neither the king nor the country's leaders really wished to participate.

The saga describes how one autumn in the early 1020s, the crops failed in Northern Norway.[4] The lack of grain forced a young chieftain called Asbjørn who lived on a prominent farm at Trondenes—who on his father's side was the nephew of Thorir Hund, and on his mother's side the nephew of Erling Skjalgsson—to travel south to buy corn. He sailed to his uncle Erling in Jæren.

When he arrived, Asbjørn learnt that King Olaf had prohibited the export of corn from Western Norway in order to ensure adequate provisions there for himself and his company. But Asbjørn purchased some grain regardless.

As he sailed past the old royal estate at Avaldsnes on his way home, Asbjørn encountered Olaf's *ármaðr*, the king's representative and watchman, in his ship with many armed men. The watchman enforced his lord's law and confiscated the grain. Asbjørn sailed home, empty-handed and in disgrace.

Back in the north, Asbjørn was reprimanded by the men of his region for letting himself be pushed around by one of the king's miserable servants of low birth—this brought shame upon not only Asbjørn himself, but also on his friends and relatives. His uncle Thorir Hund told him to pull himself together, defend his honour and take revenge.

The following year, King Olaf was in Western Norway holding court at Avaldsnes, where in the great hall he hosted a magnificent feast for Erling Skjalgsson and the rest of Western Norway's leading men. Also in attendance was Asbjørn. He had spent months burning with humiliation and a thirst for revenge. Among the king's men, he saw the man who had confiscated his corn, and in the middle of the celebrations he decided the time had come. He drew his sword and killed the king's servant right before Olaf's eyes.

He was immediately disarmed and seized by Olaf's men. The king was "very angry", and Asbjørn prepared to die. But then Erling Skjalgsson stepped in. The true Lord of Western Norway was not about to let the king execute a member of his family in his own realm—it would make a huge dent in his prestige. He was surrounded by more loyal and armed men than King Olaf, and so forced the king to spare Asbjørn's life.

This was a dangerous situation. Neither Olaf nor Erling Skjalgsson wished to come to blows—neither of them had anything to gain from it. They therefore entered into a compromise that would allow both of them to maintain their credibility. Asbjørn was permitted to live, but as punishment for the murder he would have to take over his victim's job—the lowly position of representative and watchman—and serve the king.

The conflict might have been resolved there and then, but instead it spun out of control. Some time later, Asbjørn was also attacked and killed on the open sea during a voyage north. The murderers were two of Olaf's servants—they killed Asbjørn not on the king's orders, but to exact revenge. One of them was an old friend of the man Asbjørn had murdered at Erling Skjalgsson's feast.

Thorir Hund was not one to sit idly by while the king's servants killed his relatives. When he—later still—learnt that the man who had murdered his nephew was on his way north, on a trading voyage to Lake Hvitsjøen in King Olaf's service, he followed him across the open sea in his Viking ship and boarded the man's trading vessel. Thorir struck down his nephew's murderer himself.

He then stole all the goods aboard the trading ship—property that belonged to King Olaf.

The conflict did not lead to open enmity between Olaf and Erling Skjalgsson, but after all this any reconciliation with Thorir Hund became impossible. Olaf and the most important and powerful man in Hålogaland were now irreconcilable enemies.[5]

*

On the other side of the North Sea in England, Cnut also shared his power with headstrong men who could prove dangerous rivals. But as Olaf's relations with the leading men of Norway became increasingly difficult, little by little Cnut managed to strengthen his position.

After Eadric Streona's death, Thorkell the Tall was the most prominent man in England after Cnut. Like Cnut and many other victorious warriors, the experienced Danish commander secured the position he had won with fire and murder through marriage to one of his fallen enemies' women. He is said to have married a daughter of Æthelred's named Wulfhild, who unlike the rest of the family had remained in England. She was the widow of Ulfcytel, the ealdorman whom Thorkell had fought in two major battles, first at Ringmere in 1010, and six years later as Edmund Ironside's commander at the Battle of Assandun in 1016, where Ulfcytel was killed.

As the Ealdorman of East Anglia, Thorkell had also taken over the position the slain Ulfcytel had held under the previous regime. In East Anglia, he was surrounded by his followers, loyal veterans whom he had rewarded with land and goods. He travelled with Cnut and many bishops and monks to Assandun, and participated in consecrating a church in memory of the victory they had won there.

His relationship with King Cnut, however, was a turbulent one. Sporadic information in the English sources testifies to a conflict that escalated between the two men before being settled, only to repeatedly flare up again, time after time.

In the autumn of 1021, Thorkell fell into disfavour with Cnut for reasons unknown, and both he and his wife were declared outlaws. Thorkell fled to Denmark with only six ships; in his absence Cnut himself travelled to East Anglia in order to weed out Thorkell's supporters and exert direct control over the area.

But after a time Thorkell returned to England, where he and Cnut were reconciled. In 1023, as collateral in this clearly delicate relationship, they each sent a young son to be brought up in the other's household.

The next information we have about Thorkell is that he was murdered.

The Anglo-Saxon chronicler who tells us this does not reveal why, but he does relate a strange tale in which Thorkell was hunted from town to town and finally beaten to death by an angry mob, who apparently left his body in the wilderness where it was eaten by wild animals and birds. Whether Thorkell really did die in this way and, if so, what led to such a fate, we will never know—but he was dead.

All his possessions fell to Cnut.

The last remaining Norse warlord who shared England with Cnut was Eric Håkonsson, the former Jarl of Lade. He appears in a handful of documents from Cnut's national assemblies, at which he was present. He participated in a large gathering with Cnut in 1023, but then disappears from the sources—he likely died soon afterwards. According to later rumours that found their way into the Nordic and English traditions, Cnut was behind Eric's death.

After this, Cnut remained as the sole ruler over all of England. He was not yet twenty-five, and yet he possessed more power than any previous Danish or English king. For the first time, a real North Sea Empire was in the process of being born. In accordance with the ancient Anglo-Saxon custom, English writers gave Cnut the title *basileus*, which is Greek for "emperor by the grace of Christ". At the same time, his Norse skalds praised him for his lineage descending from the heathen king Gorm the Old. With a united Denmark and a united England behind him, Harald Bluetooth's grandson ruled over resources of a scale that nobody in the Northern world had ever before controlled. These were instruments of power he knew how to use with a combination of ingenuity and aggression, and which meant that he would ever after be remembered as Cnut the Great, or as in the Norwegian tradition, "Cnut the Mighty".

There is a contemporary portrait of the adult Cnut together with Queen Emma in an encomium that they saw with their own eyes, and which we may therefore assume possesses a certain likeness to the people it portrays. Cnut and Emma are the only people in this story of whose appearance we have a vague idea. Emma is depicted as slim and clean-cut, enveloped in a loose, soft, floor-length gown. She is wearing small, dark-coloured, ankle-high shoes, a bracelet around her left wrist and a crown across her forehead, which is partly hidden by a veil that covers her hair and shoulders. The king is presented as a slim man wearing a simple knee-length tunic, tights, bracelets and a cape slung over his shoulder, reaching almost to the ground. He has a broad face, his hair cut short at his forehead, with round eyes and a thick, slightly dishevelled full beard.

In addition to his other lands, Cnut also held dominion over Wales, although the Welsh were not formally his subjects. He

also demanded the submission of Scottish kings in the north—
on one or more occasions during these years they came to his
court and swore oaths of allegiance to him, recognizing his
supremacy.

In the mid-1020s, Cnut turned his gaze towards the north-
east. He began to actively work to re-establish his forefathers'
dominion over Norway, and to incorporate Olaf's kingdom into
his growing empire.

Snorri states that English messengers arrived in Norway in
the spring of 1025, "elegantly equipped for the journey, and with
a sealed letter from Cnut, England's king". Olaf received them.
Before him, the messengers explained that Cnut regarded all of
Norway as his property. Cnut did not want a war—Olaf would
be richly rewarded and Cnut was willing to let him keep his royal
power, provided that he promised to rule as Cnut's Norwegian
under-king. They invited Olaf to come to England to swear an
oath of allegiance and become Cnut's man. The same request
was written down in the sealed letters they carried.

This was a world of hierarchies within hierarchies; the fates
of kings and realms were determined by such choices as the one
that Olaf now faced. "Mighty princes have sold their heads to
Cnut as the price for peace," states one of the poems composed
by Sigvat the Skald, "but Olaf the Stout never surrendered his skull
to anyone in the world; he has often won victory for that reason."

Olaf dismissed the men and sent them back across the sea
with their mission uncompleted. In reality, this was a declaration
of war.

NOTES

[1] The two young boys were the future kings Svein Knutsson and
Harold "Harefoot" Knutsson.

[2] J.R.R. Tolkien would later use the medieval chronicles' caricature of King Æthelred as the literary inspiration for the cursed and paralysed King Théoden in *The Lord of the Rings*. Théoden's evil advisor Wormtongue is said to have been modelled on Eadric Streona.

[3] This builds upon the Norwegian historian Sverre Bagge's discussion of Olaf Haraldsson's reign. See Bagge 2002.

[4] In the early 1000s the climate was significantly warmer than it is today, and corn was grown extensively across Hålogaland.

[5] The story of the escalating feud with Thorir Hund can be found in the oldest sources about Olaf, and perhaps stems from a lost ancestral saga about the chieftain from Hålogaland. In Snorri's saga about Olaf, it is this story that marks the transition to tragedy, when Olaf's successes slip into the defeats he experiences in the second half of the saga.

SILVER COINS FOR THE
KING'S HEAD

WHEN THE SAGAS WERE WRITTEN, nobody who had experienced the events they recounted was still alive—they were simply stories from a distant time. And today, 1,000 years later, it can be hard to grasp that the characters who feature in the old skaldic poems and sagas were once real people of flesh and blood. Their world, just as concrete and rich as ours, is now lost; everything that happened there has been forgotten, or exists only as distant echoes in the stories of others.

Archaeology provides concrete evidence that the reality in which these people lived is the same reality in which we still live today: Viking bone combs, once used to untangle someone's hair; coins that someone held in their hand, fiddling with them perhaps, before passing them on to others; helmets that encased sweaty heads; pots and pans whose contents people once stirred and tasted as steam and delicious smells rose about their faces; an axe that was held in strong hands, and perhaps used to fell, de-limb and whittle timber for a new ship.

In 1996 and 1997, Danish archaeologists discovered ten ancient shipwrecks close to Roskilde's medieval port. The vessels were of various types, sizes and ages. Dating of their timber revealed that the youngest of the ships was built in the early 1400s, the others in the preceding centuries.

The most striking of the ships was also the oldest. In the mud, archaeologists uncovered the remains of the longest ship from the Viking period to be found to date—a vessel almost forty metres in length and three and a half metres wide, with thirty-nine oars and thwarts on each side. It would have been propelled by seventy-eight rowers, and had a total crew of at least 100 men—almost twice the size of the burial ships discovered at Gokstad, Oseberg and Tune, the best-preserved of the vessels that remain from the early Viking Age. This huge ship was constructed from excellent materials; the oak planks of the strakes are up to eight metres long, and almost all the ship's surfaces have been planed. It would have been nimble in the waves—and fast. To all appearances, this was a prestigious vessel—a warship that belonged to someone among the upper echelons of society, a king or a jarl.

Tests performed on the ship's planks show that it was built somewhere around the Oslo Fjord—the trees used to make it were in all likelihood felled in a forest in Vestfold. And tree-ring dating from a particularly well-preserved plank has made it possible to establish accurately when the tree was cut down—the year 1025.

This ship may have belonged to Olaf Haraldsson.

At the time the ship was built, Olaf and his Swedish allies were preparing for the coming war against Cnut. Snorri states that preparations were made all across Olaf's kingdom, and included the construction of new warships. Olaf had a new royal ship built for himself, "a very large ship", which he named *Visunden*—the *Bison*—because it had a carved bison head at the prow. A contemporaneous skaldic poem by Sigvat also describes the ship: "Olaf caused his ship, the *Bison*, to tread the waves; the mighty sea washed the animal's horns."

Olaf's subjects had not experienced conflict on a large scale since Olaf had defeated the Jarls of Lade's army at Nesjar nine years earlier. Now, as war with Cnut drew closer, the same forces that in recent generations had shaped the course of events on both sides of the North Sea came into play once more. Each and every leader below the level of king now had to assess where his future lay—to whom he should be loyal—and try to predict who would win.

Snorri describes how, as Olaf expanded his forces, he received news of a minor catastrophe. Erling Skjalgsson, Norway's most prominent figure with the exception of Olaf himself, had sailed west over the North Sea with four or five ships. With him were his two adult sons. They had left to pledge their allegiance to Cnut.

At around the same time, Thorir Hund also openly broke ties with Olaf. The relationship between the two men had likely been terrible for a long time. Thorir, too, set sail for England with his band of men.

A preserved skaldic poem shows that Hårek of Tjøtta, Olaf's closest ally among the chieftains of Hålogaland, supported Olaf and made ready for battle with his own warships. Many other leading Norwegian men did the same. Olaf mobilized all his military power.

Olaf knew he would never be able to win a full-scale war against Cnut even with Swedish reinforcements on his side, so along with Anund Jacob he planned a surprise attack on Denmark. Uncertain sources imply that Olaf had contact with prominent Danish men who wished to overthrow Cnut. An attack involving enough troops, supported by Danish rebels, would give them the opportunity to occupy cities and castles, and maybe also fortify their positions before Cnut managed to respond. Denmark would be thoroughly plundered. Not only would raiding and looting Cnut's kingdom subject Cnut to great losses, but it would also supply Olaf and his Swedish allies with sorely needed resources in the long-term competition for warriors' loyalty.

*

The plan to stage a surprise attack shows that Olaf and his advisors were keeping a close eye on the political situation in England—as well as that further south in Europe. Indeed, at this time Cnut had his hands full with another political drama—one far larger than that playing out in the north.

One year before Cnut's messengers sailed to Norway and demanded that Olaf submit, Henry II, the German Holy Roman Emperor, died on 13th July 1024. The procedures regulating the succession to Christianity's most prestigious title were complex, and involved princes and high-standing nobles all across Christendom. The system of succession was arranged such that princes, bishops, representatives of various cities—and a long line of other players in the gigantic political patchwork that was the Holy Roman Empire—first gathered to elect a king. The king could then be elected and pronounced emperor, provided he had enough support.

Early in the autumn of 1024, representatives from all corners of the Holy Roman Empire had gathered in Kamba on the eastern bank of the Rhine to elect a king, who in turn would become Henry's successor as the Holy Roman Emperor, at a meeting that soon deteriorated into a tremendous political brawl. Several of the high lords in attendance stormed out of the gathering without taking part in the election and without saying farewell, including the Archbishop of Cologne and Frederick II, Duke of Upper Lorraine.

The title finally fell to a North German prince, Conrad II, who after being crowned king set out on a long procession through the German provinces. This procession lasted almost an entire year until June 1025, a sort of medieval election campaign through which he garnered support for the upcoming imperial election.

The election was of significance for Cnut, because the man who seemed set to become the emperor had long been involved in a border dispute with Cnut's mother's Polish kin. There was a risk that the feud might get out of control, and even spill over into his Danish kingdom.

Cnut therefore allied himself with other princes who opposed the German Conrad's candidature. Along with the Northern Italian Prince of Lombardy, Ulric Manfred II of Turin, and the Northern Spanish kings Alfonso of Castille and Sancho of Navarre, Cnut encouraged William, Duke of Aquitaine in Poitou, to stand as an opposing candidate—the very same Frankish prince whose land our King Olaf had plundered back in 1012 and 1013.

In the run-up to the election, messengers from Lombardy and Spain in the south and from England in the north travelled back and forth to Duke William's court in Poitou. Cnut sent royal gifts of expensive books to William, as well as to selected people in his circle in Aquitaine.

But, finely attuned diplomat that he was, Cnut also made sure to send gifts to Conrad II, the man he was attempting to prevent from becoming the next emperor. If the campaign for William was unsuccessful, a good relationship with the elected emperor would be important. This proved to be a wise approach, because after a time William of Aquitaine gave up on his campaign and withdrew his candidacy.

Conrad, who must have regarded Cnut as a dangerous potential enemy and therefore a correspondingly valuable ally, responded by inviting Cnut to accompany him to Rome and be his witness during the crowning ceremony that would take place there in the spring of 1027. No former Danish or English king had ever before held such an important role in European politics at this top level.

In the summer of 1026, Cnut was still in England, busily preparing for his departure. He would be away for months, perhaps even a year.

This was when Olaf and Anund Jacob launched their attack on Denmark.

*

It was a co-ordinated and large-scale attack on two fronts. Olaf's army began their campaign in the Trondheim Fjord, with Olaf sailing in his enormous and newly built ship the *Bison* along the outstretched and jagged Norwegian coast at the head of a fleet that probably carried several thousand men, including many peasant soldiers from the coastal regions. Also on board were a number of leading men from all across the Norwegian kingdom. From the coast of Vestfold, the fleet swept across the Skagerrak to Denmark.

At the same time, Anund Jacob sailed south from Sweden's Baltic coast at the head of his Swedish war fleet, towards Scania, which at this time was part of the Danish kingdom. But the young Swedish king seems not to have led his troops himself. The skalds relate that his war fleet was under the command of a general named Ulf, possibly a son of the aforementioned Jarl Ragnvald.

The Danish islands and peninsulas were considerably more populous than the more sparsely inhabited Norwegian and Swedish regions. Farming villages were strewn across the flat, fertile landscape, not unlike in Anglo-Saxon England. In all the years the Danish warriors had ravaged the English kingdom, Denmark itself had been spared any great conflict. But varied and fragmented sources now describe a violent attack on the Danish kingdom. The Swedes burned their way south along the Baltic coast of Scania; Olaf's Norwegian fleet attacked the "flat plains" of Zealand. Olaf sailed around the island's coasts before landing and leading his army into the interior on plundering raids among the defenceless farming population. According to Snorri, "the inhabitants were robbed, some killed, others taken prisoner and carried off to the ship in chains; anyone who was able to fled and nobody put up any resistance. King Olaf ravaged the area violently."

In a poem about these events, Sigvat says that Olaf, "feller of the Danes", also ravaged and burned great areas of Scania. Battles raged as far south as Hedeby in Schleswig-Holstein, modern Germany. On 2nd August 1026, Cnut's bishop, Eikkhard, was murdered there, in all likelihood while defending his diocese.

It must have taken at least several days for word of the attack to reach Cnut in England. In great haste, the king gathered all the soldiers and ships available on England's south and east coasts. Accompanied by his *hird* of warriors, he boarded a great warship, a *drakeskip*—dragon ship—and led the fleet east "as the oars glittered", because "there would be no plundering in his land", as one skald expressed it.

Having crossed the sea, Cnut sailed into the Limfjord in northern Jutland. By this time, the attack had probably been under way for several weeks. In Limfjord, presumably while the Norwegian and Swedish forces burned and raided villages further east with the help of Danish rebels, Cnut obtained reinforcements of loyal Danish troops.

Olaf and his Swedish allies seem to have severely underestimated Cnut's military capabilities. Their forces hadn't obtained any real foothold on the Danish islands when Cnut crossed the sea; they seem to have been caught off guard by how quickly Cnut mobilized and by the size of the army he managed to pull together at such short notice. According to Snorri, Cnut's fleet was twice the size of the united fleets Olaf and Anund Jacob had managed to gather over the long period during which they had prepared and planned the war.

It seems like an exaggeration, but Cnut's fleet was apparently so large that just the sight of it made the Norwegians and Swedes retreat before him. Olaf and Anund Jacob's fleets sailed east together, while Cnut chased after them through the narrow Øresund, around the southern tip of Scania and into the Baltic. The fleets clashed in a sea battle off the shallow sandy beaches of the Bight of Hanö, where the great River Helge runs out into the Baltic Sea. The battle had no clear outcome.

A smattering of historical notes also mention battles on land in Scania early in the autumn. The *Anglo-Saxon Chronicle* states that Cnut lost many men in a battle there, and that the Swedes "had possession of the place of carnage". This could mean that the Swedes were victorious, or be a poetic way of stating that it was the Swedes whose dead lay strewn across the battlefield. The skalds who later composed poetry about the battle praise both sides for fighting valiantly, but again mention no victor. Nor did these skirmishes provide any clear conclusion. Neither Cnut nor Olaf and his Swedish allies managed to obtain any obvious upper hand in the war.

As autumn settled in and the weather turned colder, time was running out for Cnut. He could no longer delay his departure for Rome, and was forced to leave the situation in Denmark unresolved. He left his war fleet under the command of his loyal Danish or English warlords, with orders to keep the fleet together and block the Øresund Strait, which separates modern Denmark from Sweden. Then he hastened back to England.

Back home, he gathered a large company of Danes and Anglo-Saxons worthy of a European king, who would accompany him to Rome. After a brief and hectic stay he boarded a ship once again, and along with bishops, priests, servants and the men of his *hird*—all with their own horses—he crossed the English Channel and put ashore near Calais, from where the long journey through the European continent would begin.

Meanwhile, time worked in Cnut's favour. Chasing the enemy into the Baltic Sea and blocking the Øresund was quite the stroke of military genius—easy to implement but absolutely annihilating for his rival. Forces loyal to Cnut also blocked the Great Belt and the Little Belt, two other straits between the Danish islands and mainland, thereby ensuring that Olaf and Anund Jacob's fleets were effectively bottled up in the Baltic Sea. The Swedes could sail home—which they promptly did. During the autumn, Anund Jacob withdrew from the war. He—or his leaders—gave the soldiers leave, and the Swedish army disbanded. Olaf's fleet was now alone, with nowhere to go. He had sailed into a trap.

War fleets at this time only carried enough supplies to last them a few weeks. They were completely dependent on plundering food during their voyage, or on travelling home to collect more food during the course of the expedition. While the crews of the Danish fleets blocking the straits leading out of the Baltic lived on supplies provided by the Danish king's subjects around them, it was difficult for the crews of the Norwegian fleet to obtain more food. According to Snorri, there were significant splits and great frustration in Olaf's circle of leaders as they discussed what they should do. It was in these waters that Olaf Tryggvason had met his end when his fleet was crushed by Sweyn Forkbeard. Should they now simply wait for Cnut's fleet to withdraw, or attempt an attack against Cnut's greater forces?

Olaf waited. The supplies dwindled and the weather turned colder as Olaf's fleet lay moored somewhere off the east coast of Scania. Cnut's scouts kept an eye on them from land. According to what was said in Snorri's time, parts of Olaf's army slowly crumbled away as his men went ashore and were lured over to the other side by Cnut's people. Morale was low.

One of those who abandoned the army was Hårek of Tjøtta, one of the most important men in Olaf's war council and an experienced sailor and warrior. He is said to have left Olaf's side and sailed away in a single ship with his men. He made it through the Øresund—perhaps sneaking through the blockade unseen in the night, perhaps by cutting a deal with Cnut's forces. Then he sailed past the Danish islands and continued north along the Norwegian coast, towards his seat in Hålogaland.

Like Olaf and many other Norse leaders, Hårek too was a master of the skaldic arts. He composed a poem that Snorri later wrote down and therefore saved, in which he proclaimed that he had preferred not to give the women of Scania reason to laugh as he walked home, and had therefore fearlessly defied Cnut's mighty fleet in his ship.

Olaf, however, did not have that option. Sometime later in the autumn he made the difficult decision to abandon the ships and led his army on the long journey home overland. The ships were likely sailed into harbours controlled by Anund Jacob's people and left there. According to Snorri, some of the ships were burned to prevent them from falling into the enemy's hands. Then the soldiers began to walk.

In this we can glimpse the contours of a human and military catastrophe—a death march. The leaders had horses, or perhaps obtained them from their allies in Sweden, but the vast majority of the men in Olaf's army had to make it all the way from the south-east coast of Sweden to Norway on foot.

The journey must have taken many weeks. Most of the supplies the army had brought from Norway and plundered in Denmark would have been long since consumed, and it must have been extremely difficult to supply the men along the way. They likely robbed the local population in the areas through which they marched—as all armies on the march had always supported themselves—but their trek passed through the sparsely populated Swedish kingdom. For long stretches, the ranks of Olaf's soldiers trudged through deep, deserted and silent forests where almost nobody lived. Autumn turned into winter, and the forests through which they passed froze. The army was not equipped for this— the soldiers had no winter clothes, nor warm shoes suitable for walking such long distances.

Many must have perished—it is hard to imagine otherwise. But what is certain is that when Olaf emerged from the eastern forests into Norway, perhaps some way into the winter of 1027, it was at the head of an army so small and so weakened that it no longer posed any threat to Cnut.

*

That same autumn and winter, Cnut travelled through Europe; his journey to Rome took the form of a pious pilgrimage made in God's honour. An eyewitness account from Saint-Omer near France's northern coast states that Cnut's company made a stop there, and describes how the king entered a monastery in order to bestow costly offerings upon the abbey's church. In a theatrical demonstration of humility and religious ecstasy, he bowed repeatedly and kissed the stone floor as tears ran down his cheeks and he beat his breast with his fist.

Moving from city to city, the company proceeded slowly to the south-east. A German chronicle describes how a cripple was healed in a monastery in Cologne, and how Cnut, the King of the Englishmen, was part of the proceedings. Early in the winter the group reached the Alps, which they crossed through a pass, before they continued south through Lombardy. They arrived in Rome in March 1027.

The holy city that in the Roman Empire's prime had housed a million inhabitants was a pale shadow of its former glorious self, but nevertheless an impressive sight to behold for any traveller in the Europe of the 1000s. Rome probably had as many permanent residents as London—around 20,000. Palaces and residences had been built into the Roman ruins. The crowning of the emperor was the most important event in Europe, and mighty figures from far and wide had come to the city with their retinues. Cnut met and exchanged gifts with princes from some of the oldest royal houses in Europe. He visited the graves of Peter and Paul, as well as other churches both within and outside Rome.

Conrad II was crowned Holy Roman Emperor on 26th March 1027 by Pope John XIX. The Pope blessed the new emperor—who was given the names Caesar and Augustus—and crowned his wife Gisela as Holy Roman Empress. The crowned emperor was slowly and solemnly led to a seat between two ceremonial royal witnesses. One of them was Cnut.

The new emperor is said to have showered Cnut with gifts. In a separate ceremony, the Pope gave one of Cnut's English bishops the pallium—the vestment that is draped around the shoulders and hangs in a long strip at both front and back—and which was the formal symbol of the bishop's appointment by the Pope. Cnut himself also conducted long conversations with Pope John; they discussed who would take over the episcopal position in Hedeby after Bishop Eikkhard, who had recently been murdered in the war against the Norwegians and the Swedes.

At this time, Cnut cannot have known that he had defeated Olaf and his Swedish allies. On his way back from Rome, he sent a messenger to England on a fast horse ahead of the main party, with a letter addressed to all his English subjects, which was probably intended to be read aloud by heralds. In the letter, he stated that at Easter he had met the Pope and the emperor and many other princes, and held many discussions with them on behalf of his subjects. But before he could return to England, he must travel to Denmark in order to make peace with the antagonistic Norwegians and Swedes who had attacked his land.

Some time later, Cnut arrived in Denmark, where he is said to have commanded executions, including at Roskilde. These were probably part of a targeted purge of the Danish nobility, to remove people who had supported or collaborated with Olaf and the Swedes. Then Cnut sailed back to England.

At this time, several of the skalds who served Olaf were travelling through Cnut's kingdom, and one of them was Ottar the Black. One of his preserved tributary poems was likely performed before Cnut in England during this period. Ottar greeted "the king of the Danes, of the Irish and of the English and of the Island-dwellers",[1] and using dramatic turns of phrase praised Cnut's accomplishments—both his conquest of England and his successful defence of Denmark against Olaf and Anund Jacob's attack. He boasted about how Cnut had held his territory against two princes, and in battle "sated the raven's hunger" with the corpses of his enemies.

It's not clear where Sigvat was while the battles raged during Olaf's attack on Denmark, but afterwards he visited Cnut too. He says that he arrived in England with an Icelandic friend by the name of Bergr. They had set sail from Norway in a ship and first made their way to Rouen in Normandy, perhaps on a trading voyage, or possibly on a diplomatic mission for Olaf. Sigvat later remembers how he docked at Rouen's wharfs and moored his ship at the city wall. From Rouen they sailed on to England, where they visited King Cnut—perhaps at one of Æthelred's old palaces, in Winchester or in London. At first, they met with hostility among

Cnut's people. According to Sigvat's own account, Cnut's guards refused to permit them access to the great hall when Cnut held court, probably because Sigvat was Olaf's man. Sigvat was forced to use his powers of persuasion in order to get in.

As previously mentioned, the skalds moved freely between lords, but now Sigvat was truly in the enemy's camp. At his English court, Cnut was surrounded by Olaf's opponents. By his side was Håkon Ericsson, the last remaining member of the Lade dynasty. He had served Cnut since Olaf had driven him out of Norway, and controlled areas of land that included Mercia, Eadric Streona's former region. He was now a mature man in his thirties, surrounded by his deceased father's old supporters. Erling Skjalgsson and his sons were likely also at Cnut's court at this time, as were Thorir Hund and the people he had brought across the sea from Hålogaland. One of them was Hårek of Tjøtta, who according to Snorri had been Olaf's most kindly disposed supporter in the north of Norway. He had cut his ties to Olaf completely after making his way through the blockade in the Øresund, however, and he too had now pledged his allegiance to Cnut.

Perhaps all these men were at Cnut's court at the same time as Sigvat, who witnessed an open discussion of how best to do away with Olaf. In a later poem, he states that he understood that Olaf was in grave danger—so grave that his best option would have been to flee up into the mountains and stay there, beyond Cnut's reach.

Nevertheless, Sigvat performed his skaldic verses in honour of the English king before Cnut in his hall. He lauded Cnut's honourable conquest of England and the exile of Æthelred's dynasty—as well as how Cnut sailed across the sea "under dark sails" in order to defend Denmark against Sigvat's own lord, Olaf. Cnut appreciated this tribute enough to reward Sigvat with half a mark of silver and his friend Bergr with a sharp sword, and both received "glittering bracelets".

Afterwards, Sigvat returned to Norway and once again allied himself with Olaf. According to Snorri, Sigvat went to Sarpsborg in Vik, where the Norwegian king sat with the remnants of his army—now significantly reduced after the march through the Swedish forests several months earlier. He was in a miserable state. People were deserting him left, right and centre—and his reserves of money and treasure were almost completely exhausted.

Because he had visited Cnut's court and been paid by him for his skaldic services, Sigvat had to defend himself against accusations of treason in Olaf's presence. Over the subsequent period, he composed several poems in which he comes across as somewhat fawning, and in which he avowed his fealty.

> Say, mighty king, where you have decided on a seat for us at your table; all the inside of your hall is agreeable to me.

> […]

> Cnut, generous with treasures, asked me if I wanted to be of service to him as to Olaf. I declared that one lord at a time was fitting for me, and I thought I answered truthfully; as should every man.

Through the poems, we glimpse a tense atmosphere surrounding a quick-tempered and paranoid king on the verge of losing control.

Snorri paints the same picture—as Olaf's power crumbled, he reacted with the use of force and violence against his own people, with the result that he drove even more of his former supporters into his rival's arms. Snorri describes how Olaf led his shrinking band of followers northwards, through the forests of Hedemarken, where provisions could be found. The company passed through the villages beside Lake Mjøsa, from large farm to large farm, where local leaders fed the king's men.

One of the men who followed the king northwards was Kalv Arnesson—Olaf's key man in Trøndelag and a member of his inner circle. On the journey through North Hedmark, the company stopped at the farm of a young man with close ties to Kalv. His name was Tore, and he was descended from a prominent family in Trøndelag, the son of Olve of Egge—one of the heathen men Olaf had had killed. Kalv Arnesson was his stepfather—because Kalv, as previously mentioned, had taken over the murdered man's farm, widow and household.

While Olaf's company was stationed in the area, with Olaf himself quartered in Tore's farm in Hedmark, the king learnt that Tore had received a gold ring as a gift from Cnut. Olaf reacted with irreconcilable anger, and had Tore put in chains. Kalv Arnesson begged for mercy for his stepson, as did several others, but Olaf would not be moved. He had Tore killed.

We can almost imagine Snorri shaking his head at his hero in dismay as he continues: "This murder caused great vexation, both in the Uplands and even more in Trøndelag, where lived most of Tore's kin. It weighed very heavily upon Kalv that the young man should meet such an end."

Tore's elder brother, Grjotgard, was also in Hedmark. When he learnt of his brother's death he fled into the forest with a group of men, from where they made raids on the king's men. Snorri states that Olaf's soldiers chased the small group of rebels through the forest from village to village, and that in the end Grjotgard barricaded himself in a small cottage on a farm while the king's men surrounded it. When Olaf arrived on the scene, Grjotgard came out. Instead of surrendering, he stabbed and slashed at those around him with his sword, and succeeded in killing one of the king's men. He, in turn, was immediately slaughtered. On Olaf's orders, most of the other men from the group of rebels were also killed. Then Olaf's company turned south again.

Instead of launching an open attack against Olaf, Cnut undermined his power. He maintained extensive contact with prominent men in Norway, attempting to lure them over to his side. He used the same tactics he had employed when he took control of England, and which Olaf had used when he had come to power in Norway eleven years earlier: he bought men's loyalty with gold and silver, and promises of future influence.

The same men who had taken Olaf's silver and given him his kingdom were now given the opportunity to tear themselves free of him by a king who offered them better conditions. "In truth, it can be said of Cnut that every man who came to him and wished to be his friend, and whom he found worthy, had his hands filled with coins. He was therefore especially well liked," says Snorri.

Cnut showered the people who left Olaf's side with gifts, and this is also confirmed by English sources. The chronicler John of Worcester later wrote that "Cnut, King of England and Denmark, received intelligence that the Norwegians held their king Olaf in contempt on account of his meekness and simplicity, his justice and piety. In consequence, he sent large sums of gold and silver to certain of them, earnestly entreating them to reject and depose Olaf, and submitting to him, accept him for their king. They greedily accepted his bribes, and caused a message to be returned to Cnut that they were prepared to receive him whenever he chose to come."

Many treasure troves have been discovered in Norway which were buried in the 1020s and 1030s, containing huge numbers of English silver coins imprinted with Cnut's likeness and mark. These are probably the remains of the silver Cnut sent to Norway in order to pave the way for his invasion.

Sigvat the Skald faithfully composed poetry for his king, and took up a similar position to that assumed by the Anglo-Saxon Archbishop Wulfstan of York a decade earlier, when he had reprimanded leading Anglo-Saxon men for leaving Æthelred's side to pledge their allegiance to Sweyn Forkbeard.

> Enemies of the prince go there with open purses; people are repeatedly offered solid metal for the not-for-sale king's head.

> Every man should know that his lot will be in Hell if he sells his gracious lord for silver coins!

Cnut worked through loyal Norwegian allies and deputies—and the most important of these was Erling Skjalgsson. During 1027, the most prominent man in Western Norway left his sons with Cnut in England, and returned to his homeland to challenge Olaf. According to Snorri, Erling's company contained messengers from Cnut, who also carried plenty of gold and silver. While Olaf was on the other side of the country, Erling made use of his loyal network in Harald Fairhair's old kingdom, and—with significant help from Cnut's money—began to gather an army.

At the same time, messengers who served Håkon Ericsson, descendant of the Jarls of Lade, were active in Trøndelag. They spread the news of the jarl's imminent return, and rebels began to gather and organize. Olaf seems to have lost contact with his people there, perhaps because they turned away from him. According to Snorri's account, Olaf wasn't prepared to risk travelling to Trøndelag because his own *hird* was small and becoming ever smaller, and "what he heard from the north hinted that it would be anything but peaceful there". The peasants in the Uplands were also hostile and restless, and Olaf regarded the situation as so unsafe that he retreated to Vik.

At the core and most loyal area of his crumbling kingdom, Olaf worked intensely to re-establish his army, but he had few or no remaining funds with which to do this. Rumours swirled that Cnut was in the process of assembling an enormous army, and people were afraid. In the autumn of 1027, Olaf gathered all the warships and crew that were available in the Oslo Fjord. After Olaf's loss of almost his entire war fleet in the Øresund, the military force with which he managed to set out to sea was not a large one—according to Snorri, it mostly consisted of small boats belonging to peasants. In the south, Cnut's great fleet was still assembled in Danish waters. Olaf led his small fleet, manned by his most loyal crew members, westwards along the coast.

In December, a time of year when few ships could be seen out on the seas, Olaf attacked Erling Skjalgsson. Erling had assembled a large fleet and had many longships, but somehow—in a manner the sources neglect to explain—Olaf successfully lured him into a trap in the Boknafjord in Ryfylke. Erling and a small band of men were sailing either into or out of the fjord when Olaf attacked them.

The sea battle is described in detail in a poem that Sigvat composed not long afterwards; he tells of a violent and overwhelming attack. Olaf and Erling's ships lay side by side in the ice-cold water, and Olaf's warriors boarded Erling's vessel—the two leaders' men fought each other with swords between the thwarts. While "warm blood fell into the wide ocean", Olaf fought in the battle himself. One by one, Erling's men were struck down. In the end, Erling remained alone, the sole survivor, "far from friends, at the stern of his empty ship". The battle was over.

Erling was a mature man, likely an ageing chieftain, admired and renowned. He did not ask for mercy. Instead, he cried out to Olaf: 'Eagles should fight face to face!'—that is, great men should fight face to face. Then he was struck down and killed right there on the spot by one of Olaf's men, Aslak "the Bald" from Fitjar— Erling's own second cousin.

Sigvat was Olaf's loyal man, but he later condemned in harsh words what he regarded as the murder of a defenceless man of honour who had surrendered. "I did not drink my drink very happily at Christmas on the day when they told me of the betrayal of Erling [...] Aslak has committed a crime against his kin; kin-killing cannot be condoned; one should look to the old ways."

One of the few preserved skaldic poems said to have been composed by Olaf himself is also about Erling's death. In Snorri's time, it was said that Olaf composed this poem shortly after the battle. Olaf adopts a less sentimental and significantly more aggressive and uncompromising tone than his skald. Through the dense undergrowth of later writings that sprang up around Olaf's posthumous reputation, Olaf perhaps tells us in his own words about the forces that controlled his world.

Little joy will the army have tonight in Jæren; the raven tore its meal from the corpse; robbing my power boded ill for him; enraged, I crossed the warships; hunger for land and power leads to the deaths of men.

Later, Erling's *hird* priest, Alfgeir, raised a memorial cross for his lord. It has been moved many times, but is said to have been visible from the road leading into the small market town that would later develop into the city of Stavanger, right at the heart of Erling's realm. On the cross are carved the following words:

"Priest Alfgeir raised this stone for Erling, his lord, who alone was betrayed when he fought against Olaf."

Olaf might have killed Erling, but Erling's entire network was still intact. His adult sons, who would inherit Erling's power and connections, lived on, ready to avenge their father. In the period that followed their father's death they took control of his troops. The skaldic poems and accounts in the sagas depict a chaotic situation in which Olaf sailed up and down the northern coast of Western Norway, sending people into the country in a vain attempt to keep his supporters united. He lost contact with many of them. In the south, Erling's sons were too strong to be confronted openly. Nor did Olaf dare sail into the Trondheim Fjord to the north.

Everyone understood that a great and decisive confrontation with Cnut was approaching– and nobody wanted to be on the losing side. Snorri rattles off the names of prominent men who abandoned Olaf, or with whom he lost contact: Erling of Gjerde, Aslak from Finnøy, Rut from Vigg and Torgeir from Kvistad all opposed Olaf, whether openly or in secret. Tord from Steig in Gudbrandsdalen and Brynjulv Ulvalde in Vestfold now kept their distance. And Aslak from Fitjar—the man who had killed Erling Skjalgsson—also left the king. He was attacked and killed by Erling's sons, somewhere along the coast.

Kalv Arnesson, the key figure in Olaf's regime in Trøndelag, whose stepson Olaf had executed, according to Snorri, saw that the only chance he had to retain the status and power he had won in Trøndelag under Olaf was to become Cnut's man. He too sought out Olaf's rival—and Olaf's ranks began to look very thin.

In the spring of 1028, Cnut sailed from England to Denmark. According to the *Anglo-Saxon Chronicle*, he sailed at the head of fifty warships. It was a small fleet compared to the fleets from the wars in England, which had consisted of 200 or more ships, but a larger fleet was not necessary. By his side were a number of prominent Norwegian men, the most distinguished among them being Jarl Håkon Ericsson. Thirteen years had passed since he had been attacked by Olaf in the Saudungssund and thereafter travelled to England. Cnut intended to give him his father's old position in Trøndelag, and to let him control all of Norway as his vassal.

Once again, Cnut's fleet gathered in the Limfjord in northern Jutland, where the ships that had blocked the Øresund joined forces with the king. Then Cnut sailed north.

They came to Norway in peace. They sailed north along the coast, and nowhere did Cnut's soldiers go ashore to burn towns or villages. Just as the young Cnut and his father had been welcomed as liberators by Æthelred's subjects in Gainsborough in Northern England fifteen years earlier, the adult Cnut was now welcomed by Olaf's subjects in Norway. Huge crowds were waiting for them. Cnut was hailed as king by the people of Trøndelag at the local *thing*, and presented his vassal, Håkon of Lade. The free men's representatives swore oaths of allegiance to their king and to their jarl.

Sometime during the summer, probably as Cnut's fleet approached from the south, Olaf steered his few remaining ships between the islands of the Møre coast and into Tafjorden. He left them on a beach below the steep, dark mountainside, and led his people on foot up into the mountains. The little group walked down stony paths towards the east. Olaf had been reduced to a fleeing refugee within his own kingdom.

Olaf attempted to gather more people to him in the Uplands, but was apparently opposed by the men he himself had stationed in positions of control there. They had little interest in fighting a war that could not be won, regardless of any feelings of loyalty and patriotism they may have had towards their king.

After the hailing ceremony in Nidaros, Cnut and Håkon sailed back south along the Norwegian coast with the fleet. In the autumn of 1028, they moved slowly from *thing* to *thing*, receiving oaths of allegiance from the local free men; Cnut is said to have handed out great volumes of silver and gold. Just as high-ranking Anglo-Saxon men had done during the conquest of England, a number of Norwegian leaders and prominent farmers offered their sons or brothers to Cnut as hostages. "In this way, the king secured people's allegiance," Snorri explains.

When Cnut and Håkon arrived in Vik in the autumn, Olaf fled the country. He travelled east, into Sweden, with his household of men, women and servants. Unless they had already been sent to safety in the east, Olaf must have taken Queen Astrid and their daughter Ulvhild with him, along with Magnus, his son by his mistress. Ulvhild was around six or seven years old, Magnus four or five.

Behind them, the free men's representatives swore allegiance to Cnut at Vik's *things*. Even part of the Swedish kingdom fell to Cnut at this time. We are unaware of the specific circumstances that led to this—but Cnut titled himself "Cnut, King of all England, and of Denmark, Norway, and part of Sweden". After playing the role of Olaf's ally during the failed sea attack on Denmark, Anund Jacob had probably been forced to give up his lands.

Astrid seems to have stayed with her relatives in Sweden, perhaps with their daughter, while Olaf moved on after a short stay, probably because it was unsafe for Anund Jacob to protect them. At the head of a small core of his most fanatical followers—a few prominent Norwegian men and a handful of *hird* warriors who had followed him through thick and thin and killed and bled for him for years—he sailed onwards, towards the east. His son Magnus he took with him. They sailed further and further from Cnut, into areas Olaf had plundered on Viking raids in the eastern regions twenty years earlier, when he was a young man.

Olaf's royal power over Norway was lost, and he would never win it back. Thirteen years had passed since he returned home from England. He was probably in his late thirties. His kingdom was now limited to the decks of a handful of Viking ships; his subjects to the men aboard them. They crossed the Baltic Sea, sailed into the Neva Bay, and disappeared down the rivers into Gardarike.

*

Cnut didn't remain on the eastern side of the North Sea for long. England was the heart of his empire now, and having banished his rival and securing his dominion over Norway, in 1029 he sailed back across the sea. Håkon Ericsson did the same. The dynasty Håkon had re-established in Norway was old—almost a century of jarl rule makes Olaf Haraldsson's thirteen years as king seem like nothing but a minor intermezzo. But Håkon Ericsson also owned significant areas of land and held strong interests in Cnut's England, where he had spent around half his life.

Håkon probably followed Cnut back to England because he and Cnut planned further to strengthen the bonds between them and their families. Cnut offered the jarl the hand of his niece—a girl or young woman named Gunnhild—and this was part of the consolidation of his conquest of Norway. Late in the autumn, Håkon was at sea in his ship with his crew in the Pentland Firth, the waters between the Orkney Islands and the Scottish mainland, on his way back to Norway.

He was never seen again. The ship was wrecked, and went down with everyone and everything on board. Nobody knew exactly what had happened, but one thing was certain—no male heirs remained of the once so prolific Lade dynasty.

In the winter of 1030, Cnut began looking at other men he could employ to control Norway. Olaf's former man Kalv Arnesson was one of the candidates he considered, but in the end Cnut found another solution. As previously mentioned, Cnut had sworn an oath to his queen, Emma, that only the sons she gave him would be able to inherit the throne in England. But Cnut also had two small sons with his first queen, Ælfgifu of Northampton, the woman who many years earlier had sailed across the sea to bring the dead body of Cnut's father to him, but who had been shoved aside and demoted to the rank of mistress when Cnut married Emma. Cnut appointed his eldest son with Ælfgifu the King of Norway. The boy was named Sweyn—after Sweyn Forkbeard— and was still in his late childhood.

His mother would accompany him and stay with him in Norway, as would one of Cnut's bishops by the name of Sigurd, and Kalv Arnesson, who became the little king's protector in his new homeland. In the spring of 1030, they set sail for Norway.

At the same time, Olaf returned.

His stay in Gardarike is somewhat obscure—little is known about what he and his company did in the great land in the east. They had sailed along the Russian rivers into the domain of Prince Yaroslav the Wise, the Christian ruler of Novgorod and Kiev, who had Norse roots and maintained close contacts with the Nordic world. According to the sagas—and this is probably true—Olaf lived in exile under Yaroslav's protection, most likely in or around Novgorod, where Yaroslav's court was located at the time.

News of the Jarl of Lade's death also spread along the Russian rivers and soon reached Olaf, who saw a chance to regain control of his lost kingdom. In the spring of 1030, leaving his son Magnus in safety under Yaroslav's protection, Olaf sailed out into the Baltic Sea once more. His Norse *hird* was now reinforced by a group of Slavic warriors, who accompanied him with Yaroslav's blessing.

First the company journeyed to Gotland, where Olaf seems to have stayed for a time, probably while his messengers sought out old allies in Norway and in Sweden. Olaf then left the island, and sailed across to the Swedish mainland. He was reunited with Queen Astrid and his brother-in-law Anund Jacob, according to Snorri in Uppsala, and secured himself the Swedish king's support. A group of Swedish warriors entered his service, and this became the core of Olaf's new army.

Meanwhile, Olaf's spies reported on what was happening back in Norway, and how Cnut's little son Sweyn had arrived in Vik. The young king was travelling through the country in order to be taken as king at the *things*, and was surrounded by a large army loyal to Cnut. Olaf's route back to his home region—where he had begun his long journey to fame and power, and where he still enjoyed a certain loyalty among the population—was consequently blocked.

Olaf therefore led his small army northwards into the border regions, and entered his old kingdom close to Lake Mjøsa in the Uplands, where no enemy soldiers were present. He attempted to gather more men, but he had nothing to offer them. The area's inhabitants turned out to be hostile towards him, and Olaf withdrew eastwards again.

Early in the summer of 1030, Olaf's little army was on the march north once more, moving through the dense forests of the borderlands. Olaf's objective must have been to bypass his enemies and enter Trøndelag from the east in order to take Nidaros, the most important power centre of his lost kingdom. Perhaps he thought that if he could take the city quickly, and persuade and pressure the local noblemen to support him, he would be able to gain a foothold and negotiate with Cnut. He was in desperate need of more men, and on the way north recruited locals from the villages in the Swedish forests. Snorri states that Olaf promised to reward those who served him faithfully and fought well with his enemies' land and property, with the result that "a vast number of people joined his cause, people from the forests, some of them outlawed bandits".

Small groups of warriors also came from the west of Norway and joined Olaf's company, led by old supporters with whom Olaf had re-established contact. The army was a mixture of heathens and Christians, Slavs and Norsemen, outlawed and free. Some Icelandic skalds were also present—men who had followed Olaf for a long time, among them Torfinn Munnen, who by this point must have been an old man. Sigvat, however, was not there. He was on a pilgrimage to Rome—perhaps he had followed Olaf into Gardarike and then travelled on from there. One of the skaldic odes tells us that the man who bore Olaf's field banner was named *Þórðr*, Tord; he is one of the few members of Olaf's *hird* of warriors for whom we are given a name. Bjørn the Stout, Olaf's trusted *hird* leader, was also present.

This ragtag army trudged and traipsed along the trails that ran through the deep and wild summer-green forests, through valleys and vales, along streams and rivers, over hills and mountains. The journey took several weeks. At the height of the hottest period of the summer, they entered Verdal from the east.

They were expected—their enemies had likely been watching them for a long time. Up ahead of them, on the other side of the valley, awaited an army led by Norwegian chieftains. One of these was Kalv Arnesson; by his side were Hårek of Tjøtta and Thorir Hund. They had all once been Olaf's men, but they would extend him no warm welcome—they now served King Cnut and his son. The Norwegian army grew quickly as local peasants took up their arms, afraid and angry at the foreign army's entry into their valley from the east—everybody knew what foreign soldiers did to the local people's farms and families. Cnut himself was in England, but according to Snorri his bishop was present, and made inspiring speeches about victory and honour and Christ.

One of the very last testimonies about Olaf from his own lifetime is a poem by one of the skalds who accompanied him on this final march. The poem describes how Olaf held a war council with his men. His scouts had observed the army blocking the road up ahead, and the council now discussed what they should do. One of the proposed suggestions involved spreading out and burning down the local villages "like scrubland", to force the peasant soldiers to return home to save their houses and families.

But this never came to pass. Instead, just as he had done so many times before, Olaf chose to fight. On 29th July 1030 the two armies clashed near a farm known as Stiklestad, part of a densely populated rural community at the innermost end of the valley. The subsequent battle would become one of the most fabled incidents in Nordic medieval history, swelling and expanding into an event of mythical proportions in the later sagas. At the time, however, it was just another battle in the long succession of violent showdowns that made up Olaf's bloody career. Olaf's army was outnumbered, but held the higher ground; his *hird* of warriors also consisted of more experienced men than those who stood against him. Olaf gave the signal to attack. The skalds who later described the battle told of arrows flying through the air in both directions, of spears that were thrown as the lines of men approached each other—scenes similar to many others in Olaf's long career as a warrior. And, as usual, Olaf himself fought on the front lines, with his best men close about him.

But this time, things went disastrously wrong for Olaf. Early on in the battle his *hird* was surrounded and overpowered, and in the storming chaos of thrusting and hacking metal weapons, Olaf was struck. Around him, man after man fell. His banner-bearer was killed, and Olaf's banner—the army's uniting insignia, and

Olaf's symbol and mark—dropped to the ground for all to see. Panic spread through Olaf's ranks. His men broke and ran from the battlefield and into the surrounding forests.

Again, dead and wounded lay scattered in the summer grass, but this time, Olaf himself was among them. He would never rise again. He died, as he had lived, by the sword. In the end, the simple and true epitaph he had composed for a fallen enemy some years earlier also became his own: "Hunger for land and power leads to the deaths of men."

*

On the other side of the North Sea, Cnut remained victorious as the age's great conqueror—after Olaf fell, there was nobody left who could challenge his power with any credibility. England, parts of Ireland and Scotland, the Orkney Islands, Denmark, Norway and parts of Sweden were all under Cnut's control: he had concluded a political life's work that can only be regarded as one of the most successful and formidable enterprises in European medieval history. Loyal deputies ruled in his name in every corner of a vast kingdom that spanned both mountains and seas—the like of which had never before existed.

It didn't last, however. How could it? This kingdom was not one built to last. Cnut died on 12th November 1035—five years after Olaf—as the mightiest ruler in Western Europe after the Holy Roman Emperor. But his life's work went the way of countless other kingdoms throughout history that had been built on blood and silver around strong leaders—it crumbled to nothing.

In the latter half of the 1030s, the North Sea Empire dissolved amid conflict and divisions between Cnut's sons and descendants on both sides of the sea. For a time, England was divided in two between the half-brothers Harold, who ruled in the south, and

Harthacnut, who held the north. Only after they were both dead did Æthelred's remaining son, Edward the Confessor, return to England to be crowned king of a reluctant and obstinate aristocracy consisting of a mixture of Danes and Anglo-Saxons.

At this time, the Scandinavian countries were no longer part of the same kingdom. In Norway, Cnut's regime, centred around Ælfgifu and Cnut's young son Sweyn, introduced new taxation laws after the Anglo-Saxon model in order to ensure income for the Crown. This was the start of a lengthy process that would continue for centuries, through which the Norwegian kingdom of the Middle Ages would be slowly built—modelled on the English one. But at the time, the new laws were extremely unpopular. They placed a heavy burden on both prominent noblemen and the farming population—a demand no former Norwegian king or jarl had ever made of his people. And when Cnut died, the Norwegian noblemen rebelled, just as they had done against Olaf. They brought home Olaf's son Magnus from Gardarike, and with him as their uniting figure drove Sweyn and Ælfgifu from the country. In the 1040s, with Olaf's young son as their leader, they waged violent attacks on a leaderless Denmark, where the population was subjected to treatment similar to that inflicted upon England by Cnut and his father some decades earlier, with annual raids that left large-scale death, suffering and destruction in their wake.

A uniting symbol for the new regime that now arose in Norway was found in the memory of Olaf Haraldsson. Olaf's old Anglo-Saxon bishop, Grimkil, who was still living in Norway, declared that his fallen lord was holy, just as many Anglo-Saxon kings in England had been declared holy after their deaths. People experienced miracles beside Olaf's grave. And so, in one of the strangest transformations of medieval Europe, the memory of the warrior king Olaf was converted into a cult revering him as a Christian saint. Over the following centuries, the cult of St Olaf would grow to become one of Northern Europe's most popular, and Olaf a figure of enormous symbolic significance in Norway's religious and national mythology.

The North Sea Empire did not survive the man who created it, but the kingdoms on either side of the North Sea continued to exist as a common political arena—one in which Scandinavian and Anglo-Saxon players persisted in competing for power and influence—and dreams of reuniting the region shaped the politics of ambitious Norse kings for several decades to come.

The last of them was Olaf's younger half-brother, Harald Hardrada, who came to power in Norway at the end of the 1040s. With a base in Norway and a great army at his command, which he paid using plundered silver, he attempted to become the next Cnut. Having waged war for years to take control of Denmark, he finally crossed the North Sea to conquer England in the fateful year of 1066. He died in his attempt, along with thousands of his men, three days before the Normans landed on the south coast.

It is said that history is written by the victors, but half a century after Cnut conquered England, neither his descendants nor those of his opponents remained victorious. The Norman invasion became what the Danes' conquest never did—a lasting turning point that changed the course of history. It was the start of a new age.

Although ordinary people in England likely experienced a significant degree of continuity, the Anglo-Saxons' glory days were over. After the Norman conquest, the Anglo-Saxon social elite were destroyed. Many were killed. Many left England, never to return. Some fled to Ireland or Scotland; others to Scandinavia, and settled there. In Scandinavia, they found a new world that was also in flux—the Viking Age itself was coming to an end. The Scandinavian kings were becoming more and more like other

European kings, and their opportunities to exploit their neighbours in the north so ruthlessly would soon disappear completely.

Towards the end of the eleventh century, an increasing number of Anglo-Saxon and Scandinavian warriors for whom there was no longer a place in the regions around the North Sea chose to band together, and journeyed to foreign beaches to seek their fortunes. Many ended up as bandits or mercenaries in the service of the Christian princes and Byzantine emperors in the Mediterranean. To the people who encountered them, they must have seemed exotic and foreign—like people from another world. And nobody could discern any difference between them.

NOTES

[1] This term probably refers to the people of the Orkneys, although it could also refer to those of Shetland and the Hebrides.

CHRONOLOGY

pre-950   Gorm the Old is buried in Jelling. Harald Bluetooth becomes king of the Danes.

c.960   Harald Bluetooth is baptized.

970s   Border wars between Harald Bluetooth and Otto I, King of Germany and Holy Roman Emperor.

974   Håkon Sigurdsson, Jarl of Lade, participates in Harald Bluetooth's war against the emperor.

975   Edgar the Peaceful, King of the Anglo-Saxons, dies. A comet is seen in the sky. The king's eldest son, Edward, is crowned king.

978   King Edward is murdered by Æthelred's thanes in Corfe. Æthelred is crowned the Anglo-Saxon king, probably at around twelve years old.

979   Seven Viking ships plunder the coast of Wessex, the first recorded Viking attack on England in several decades.

979–89   Escalating wave of Viking attacks along the English coasts.

c.981   Harald Bluetooth builds the Danish ring castles.

c.986   The Battle of Hjörungavágr. Håkon Sigurdsson, Jarl of Lade, frees himself from Harald Bluetooth's supremacy.

c.987   Harald Bluetooth is killed during a rebellion. A period of unrest follows in the Danish kingdom.

c.990   Sweyn Forkbeard establishes himself as the Danish king. Olaf Haraldsson is likely born around the same time, perhaps a little later.

991   The Battle of Maldon. Æthelred pays the Danes 10,000 pounds of silver in tribute.

992, 993   The Danish armies ravage England.

994   Great siege of London. Æthelred pays 16,000 pounds in tribute. Olaf Tryggvason makes peace or enters into an alliance with Æthelred, and is baptized.

995   Olaf Tryggvason comes to Norway. At around the same time, Håkon Sigurdsson of Lade is killed by one of his own. Olaf conquers the lands of the Jarls of Lade and establishes himself as King of Norway.

997–99   The Danish fleet sets up a winter camp on the Isle of Wight and ravages England for three summers in a row.

c.997–99   Olaf Tryggvason conquers Vik, and perhaps has Sigurd, Asta and Olaf Haraldsson baptized.

999 or 1000   Sweyn Forkbeard fights Olaf Tryggvason in a sea battle at Svolder. Olaf Tryggvason is killed. Eric Håkonsson of Lade takes over his old ancestral lands and Sweyn re-establishes his father's supremacy over Norway.

1001, 1002   The Danish army ravages England.

1002   13th November, St Brice's Day. Æthelred orders the mass murder of Danes in England. Massacres occur at several locations in the country.

1003–04   Danish armies ravage England.

1005   Famine in Northern Europe. The Danish army sails back to Denmark due to problems obtaining supplies.

1006   Eadric Streona murders Ealdorman Ælfhelm of York.
       Ælfhelm's sons are blinded. Palace coup. Eadric becomes
       Ealdorman of Mercia.

       The Danish army returns and ravages England on a
       scale never before experienced.

1007   Æthelred pays 36,000 pounds in tribute and in doing so
       purchases two years of peace.

1007, 1008   Young Olaf Haraldsson leads an army on Viking raids
       in the east.

1009   Spring. Olaf Haraldsson joins Sweyn Forkbeard's plun-
       dering army, which is led by Thorkell the Tall.

       Summer. Olaf Haraldsson probably participates in the
       plundering of Tiel.

       The Danish army receives 3,000 pounds outside
       Canterbury to spare the city and its environs.

       Autumn. Plundering of Southern England. London is
       besieged. Olaf Haraldsson fights by London's "wharfs".

1010   Spring. The Danish army moves to Ipswich.

       5th May. The Battle of Ringmere.

       Summer and autumn. Æthelred's army collapses; large
       parts of the kingdom are overrun and plundered on a
       scale never before seen.

1011   Winter, spring and summer. Negotiations lead to a break
       in warfare.

       September. Olaf participates in the storming and plun-
       dering of Canterbury.

       Late autumn? Olaf Haraldsson fights at an unknown
       place called *Nýjamóða*.

1012   Easter. Archbishop Ælfheah is murdered.

1012 Summer. Æthelred pays 48,000 pounds in tribute to Thorkell's army. The Danish army is disbanded. Thorkell enters into Æthelred's service with forty-five warships.

Late summer? Olaf enters into Duke of Normandy Richard II's service, fights against Count Odo of Blois and burns Dol Castle in Brittany.

Autumn? Olaf sails south, participates in the plundering of the Loire Valley against William Duke of Aquitaine, continues south along the coast of Spain, where he leads several raids on land before he finally reaches *Karlså*, probably Cádiz.

1013 May. Córdoba is plundered and burned by a Berber army. Caliph Hisham II is killed.

Spring, summer? Olaf sails north. Plunders the Loire Valley in the kingdom of the Franks once more.

Summer and autumn. Sweyn Forkbeard and Cnut invade England. Sweyn is hailed as king in the English villages. Cnut marries Ælfgifu of Northampton. Æthelred flees to the Isle of Wight. London surrenders.

Autumn? Olaf arrives in Rouen.

1014 Early winter. Æthelred and Thorkell flee to Rouen just after Christmas.

February. Sweyn Forkbeard dies on his way to York. Cnut is hailed the new king. Anglo-Saxon rebellion.

That same winter? Olaf enters into Æthelred's service. Is baptized in Rouen.

Spring. Summer. Æthelred reconquers England with Olaf and Thorkell's help. Olaf fights at *Jungfurða* and *Valdi*. Cnut flees back to Denmark.

Autumn. Cnut prepares for a new invasion together with Eric Håkonsson, his Norwegian ally.

1015   Early autumn. Æthelred holds a national assembly in Oxford. Eadric Streona has Siferth and Morcar murdered. Edmund Ironside leads a rebellion. Æthelred falls seriously ill.

Autumn. Cnut and Eric Håkonsson invade England. Chaotic battles. Eadric Streona and Thorkell the Tall switch to Cnut's side. This autumn or sometime later, Eadric becomes Cnut's ealdorman in Mercia and Thorkell Cnut's jarl in East Anglia.

Same autumn. Olaf and Cnut negotiate regarding future power dynamics in Scandinavia. Olaf leaves England and sails to Norway, overpowers Håkon Ericsson of Lade in the Saudungssund, attempts to establish himself in Nidaros, flees after a confrontation with Sweyn Håkonsson, takes Sigvat the Skald into his company and is hailed as king in Vik.

1016   Winter? Olaf conquers areas previously belonging to a range of petty kings in the Uplands and is also taken as king here.

Same winter. Cnut and Eric Håkonsson outmanoeuvre their enemies, execute Uhtred of Bamburgh and take Northumbria. Eric becomes, either immediately or sometime later, Northumbria's new jarl.

25th March, Palm Sunday. Battle of Nesjar. Olaf fights Sweyn Håkonsson and Einar Thambarskelfir.

23rd April. Æthelred dies in London.

Spring. Edmund is hailed the English king in London; Cnut is hailed the English king in Southampton.

Early summer. London is besieged.

June. The Battle of Sherston.

18th October. The Battle of Assandun.

1016   November. Cnut and Edmund Ironside make peace in Gloucestershire.

         30 November. Edmund Ironside dies.

1016–c.1019 Olaf is hailed as the Norwegian king at *things* around the country. Erling Skjalgsson, Thorir Hund and prominent Norwegian men from north to south submit to his supremacy. Olaf establishes the fortress city of Borg at Sarpefossen in the River Glomma, and probably a royal household and church at Nidaros. Olaf enters into agreements of peace and friendship with the princes in the Swedish kingdom.

1017   Early in the year. Cnut is crowned King of the Anglo-Saxons in London. Banishes Æthelred's relatives and supporters.

         July. Cnut marries Emma of Normandy.

         Around Christmas. Cnut executes Eadric Streona.

1018   Cnut collects 82,500 pounds in England.

         Cnut's brother Harald, King of Denmark, dies.

1019   Autumn. Cnut inherits his brother's royal power in Denmark.

         Around the same time, Olaf marries Astrid, Anund Jacob's sister, according to the saga in Borg.

c.1020   Olaf's first child, his daughter Ulvhild, is born.

1021   Cnut declares Thorkell the Tall outlawed. They reconcile.

c.1022   A conflict between Thorir Hund's nephew and one of Olaf's men escalates into a dangerous feud between Olaf and Thorir Hund.

1023   Cnut and Thorkell the Tall exchange sons. A short time later Thorkell dies and his possessions in England fall to Cnut.

Eric Håkonsson appears in English documents for the last time. He likely died shortly afterwards. His possessions in England fall to Cnut.

*c.*1024   Olaf's other known child, Magnus, is born.

The Moster *thing*. Olaf's *hird* bishop, Grimkil, establishes a permanent church organization in the kingdom.

13th July 1024. Henry II, German Holy Roman Emperor, dies.

4th September 1024. Large German national assembly in Kamba. Conrad II is elected as King of Germany and candidate for emperor.

1025   The saga's uncertain dating. Cnut's messengers demand that Olaf submit to Cnut's supremacy. Olaf refuses.

Olaf and Anund Jacob prepare for war. Olaf's shipbuilders probably start construction of the *Visunden*.

1026   The saga's uncertain dating. Erling Skjalgsson and his sons enter into Cnut's service. Thorir Hund breaks ties with Olaf and seeks out Cnut.

Summer. Olaf and Anund Jacob attack and ravage Denmark.

2nd August. Cnut's bishop in Schleswig is killed in battle.

Late summer/early autumn. Knut fights Olaf and Anund Jacob's forces in the sea battle at Helgeå. Various battles on land and at sea in the Øresund and Scania. Cnut's fleet blocks the Øresund.

Autumn. Cnut sets out for Rome.

Late autumn, perhaps winter. Olaf's fleet is disbanded. Anund Jacob's army is sent home. Olaf leads his army back to Vik on foot.

1027   Easter. Cnut witnesses the crowning of Conrad II as Holy Roman Emperor in Rome.

Summer. Cnut is back in Denmark, where he punishes those who have been disloyal before returning to England.

December. Battle between Olaf and Erling Skjalgsson in the Boknafjord. Erling Skjalgsson is killed.

1028   Spring. Cnut sails to Denmark along with Håkon Ericsson and gathers his fleet in the Limfjord.

Summer. Cnut's fleet sails to Nidaros. Cnut is hailed king in Trøndelag. Olaf flees to Vik.

Autumn. Cnut and Håkon set out on a victory procession along the Norwegian coast. Olaf flees first to Sweden, then on to Gardarike.

1029   Summer. Håkon Ericsson sails to England, and his ship is wrecked on the way back to Norway.

1030   Spring. Cnut's mistress, Ælfgifu, his son Sweyn and Kalv Arnesson arrive in Norway. Olaf arrives in Gotland.

Summer. Olaf walks towards Stiklestad.

AFTERWORD

THIS IS NOT THE STORY of a particular king, country or people. It is a story about the mechanisms of power and money and politics in this lost world—strange and distant, but also eerily similar to our own. To me it has felt like an anti-nationalistic project, an attempt to escape the restraints and boundaries of our times, and the mentality of modern national identities, when trying to understand a past when those borders and mentalities did not yet exist. The Northern region of 1,000 years ago was a fluctuating and intertwined world with no real borders, where people, money and ideas moved around, freer and more unbound that we are used to imagining. One cannot really understand the history of England in this period without understanding Scandinavian history, and one cannot really understand Scandinavian history without understanding English history. This book is my effort to describe one small part of a past that we very much share.

The events described in this book played out in an age when the line between reliable historical information on the one hand, and the myths, legends and narratives of later ages on the other, is often blurred, and sometimes impossible to draw clearly for historians. My aim has been to write a coherent, documentable account based on primary sources and on insight from 150 years of historical, archaeological and philological research, without tiring my readers with long clarifications, discussions and reservations. This is a difficult balance to achieve, since all our knowledge of this distant age is fundamentally uncertain. In other words, much interpretation and many academic deliberations lie hidden behind the text.

I would like to extend huge thanks to my editor, Ingrid Eia Ryvarden. Without her this book would never have existed, because it was she who came up with the idea of a new work about the kings of the Viking Age and the Middle Ages. She has provided invaluable support and help throughout the entire process of writing this book. I have also received exceptional help from Professor Hans Jacob Orning and Professor Jón Viðar Sigurðsson, both of whom have acted as my historical consultants at the University of Oslo. My partner, Ane Bjølgerud Hansen, has not only read, listened to and commented on the text, but also shown me great patience—for which I am extremely grateful. I would also like to thank the following people, who have all helped me in various ways, and who are listed here in no particular order: my former supervisor at the University of Oslo, Arnved Nedkvitne, Roy Jacobsen, Harald Endre Tafjord, Óskar Guðmundsson, Geir Waage, Geir Gullbekk, Atle Næss, Mette Karlsvik, Kai Petter Østberg, Margit Walsø, Thorvald Steen, Sigrun Slapgard, Frode Iversen, Are Skeie Hermansen and Timothy Bolton.

I, of course, am solely responsible for the final product.

ILLUSTRATIONS

Frontispiece, images of coins: Æthelred: Nationalmuseet, Copenhagen; Olaf: Oldsaksamlingen, University of Oslo; Cnut: Nationalmuseet, Copenhagen.

p. 34. An Anglo-Saxon king with his *witan*. From the *Anglo-Saxon Hexateuch*, "the six books", from the early 1000s and including scenes and figures from the Old Testament depicted in the contemporary Anglo-Saxon style (London, British Library, Cotton MS Claudius B IV, f. 59r).

p. 68. The Vikings arrive. Illumination from a French manuscript, *c.*1050–1150 ("Illustrations de la vie de saint Aubin d'Angers", Bibliothèque nationale de France, Département des manuscrits, NAL 1390).

p. 100. Tools of war. A selection of axes and spears from *c.*1000, discovered in the area around London Bridge (Museum of London).

p. 128. Anglo-Saxon world map from the first half of the 1000s, probably created in Canterbury. East is at the top, west at the bottom. In the bottom-left corner are the British Isles, with the Scandinavian Peninsula above, labelled "Thule". At the bottom, at the centre of the map, are the Pillars of Hercules— the mythological gateway to the Mediterranean Sea and the final stop on Olaf Haraldsson's journey (British Library, Cotton MS Tiberius BV).

p. 166. The White Christ. Crucifix, the triumphant Christ, depicted as a king wearing a crown, Åby, Jylland (Nationalmuseet, Copenhagen).

p. 196. Warrior's helmet from the late 900s, found in a heathen burial mound on the old farm at Geirmundbu in Ringerike, in Olaf's home region (Kulturhistorisk Museum, University of Oslo).

p. 216. Silver treasure from Cuerdale in Lancashire in Northern England (Trustees of the British Museum).

p. 242. Page from the *Anglo-Saxon Chronicle*, the Peterborough manuscript. The first lines read: "The island of Britain is 800 miles long and 200 miles broad; and here in this island are five tongues: English, British, Scottish, Pictish, and Latin" (Wikimedia).

p. 274. Cnut and Emma, portrayed in 1031, probably with a certain likeness. An angel sets the crown on Cnut's head and simultaneously points to God, in order to demonstrate that Cnut ruled in accordance with God's will, with God's blessing. New Minster Liber Vitae (The British Library Board, Stowe 944, f.6).

p. 300. "The vizier", chess piece from Italy, 1100s (Cabinet des médailles, Paris).

REFERENCES

This is not an academic work, but below follows an overview of the most important sources and literature I have consulted. Due to space limitations and in order to avoid unnecessary repetition, I rarely refer to reference works and the most fundamental historical works I have used, which are Matthew et al. 2004; Danstrup 1982; Krag 1995; Gunnes 1976; Andersen 1977; *Norsk biografisk leksikon* (NBL 1) 1921; *Svenskt biografiskt lexikon* (SBL) 1917; *Dansk biografisk leksikon* 1979; *Norsk biografisk leksikon* (NBL 2) 1999; Holmsen 1961.

1241

Snorri's last days
Kålund 1904; McGrew 1970; Sigurdur 1973; Guðmundsson 2009; Hødnebø and Magerøy 1979; Nordal 2002

Reykholt
Harðardottir 2002; Sveinbjarnardottir 2002; conversations with Óskar Guðmundsson and Geir Waage on site

Snorri the historian and Olaf's saga

Krag 2011; Kraggerud 2018; Driscoll 2008; Eikill 2008; Salvesen 1990; Beckman 1915; Johnsen 1922; Storm 1893; Bagge 1991, 2015b, 2010b, 2002; Bagge and Nordeide 2007; Whaley 1991; Brown 2012; Krag et al. 2003; Krag 2009, 2002, 1995; Flokenes 2000; Friis-Jensen et al. 2010

A REGIME FACING RUIN

God's messengers

Whitelock 1961; Williams 1871; Duby 1983; Holtsmark 1981; Schove 1986; Godden 1994; Landes et al. 2003

The West Saxon kings

Higham and Ryan 2013; Lavelle 2002; Stenton 1971; Whitelock 1961; Tudor 1995

England's first Viking Age and the Anglo-Saxon national assembly

Williams 2010; Morris 2014; Keynes 1980; Loyn 1984; Higham and Ryan 2013; Whitelock 1961; Campbell 2000; Williams 1999; Tudor 1995; Konshuh 2016; Williams 2003; Keynes 2004; Hill 1978; Andersson 1987; Lavelle 2002

England's silver

Howard 2003; Pye 2015; Loyn 1984; Lacey 1999; Higham and Ryan 2013; Clark 1980

The Battle of Maldon in the year 991

Higham and Ryan 2013; Whitelock 1961; Clark 1968; Neidorf 2012

Harald Bluetooth's kingdom

Pentz 2013; Williams et al. 2013; Jensen 2008; Haywood 1995

Sweyn Forkbeard

Jensen 2008; Keynes and Campbell 1998; Campbell 1949; Warner 2001; Greenway 2002

Olaf Tryggvason in England

Higham and Ryan 2013; Whitelock 1961; Neidorf 2012; Andersson 1987; Sawyer 1987; Lavelle 2002; Howard 2003; Darlington et al. 1995; Sawyer 1971, 1987; Williams et al. 2013; Sigurðsson 2007, 2012

"Satan's bonds are now indeed slipped"

Godden 1994; Landes et al. 2003; Wormald 2001

The St Brice's Day massacre

Greenway 2002; Van Houts 1992; Higham and Ryan 2013; Lavelle 2002; Whitelock 1961; Keynes 1980; Williams 2003; Darlington et al. 1995

"Like a fire which someone had tried to extinguish with fat"

Greenway 2002; Darlington et al. 1995; Whitelock 1961; Higham and Ryan 2013

The great famine of 1005

Whitelock 1961; Higham and Ryan 2013; Keynes 1980

Eadric Streona's palace revolution

Greenway 2002; Whitelock 1961; Higham and Ryan 2013; Darlington et al. 1995; Lavelle 2002; Bolton 2017; Williams 1999, 2003

The Danish army's plundering expedition of 1006

Greenway 2002; Higham and Ryan 2013; Whitelock 1961; Darlington et al. 1995; Lavelle 2002; Williams 2015

Ethelred's fleet

Whitelock 1961; Higham and Ryan 2013; Howard 2003; Sandwich, Kent Archaeological Assessment Document 2004; Darlington et al. 1995

THE WARRIOR'S GOOD LIFE

The size of the Danish army
Keynes 1980; Higham 2000; Whitelock 1961

The men of the Danish army
Keynes 1980; Bolton 2017; Jansson 1966

Óláfr digri
Kraggerud 2012; Harsson 2000; Schjødt and Magerøy 1979e, 1979f; Gade 2009b

Vik and the wider world
Lunde 1986; Tschan 2002; Skre 2013; Skre and Stylegar 2004; Nedkvitne and Norseng 2000; Jesch 2001; Tschan 2002; Storli and Alm 1995

The old and the new religion
Sigurðsson 2003, 2011; Gunnes 1976; Fletcher 1997

Olaf Tryggvason and Olaf's baptism
Lie 1970; Robinson 1921; Schjødt and Magerøy 1979f; Salvesen 1990

Svolder
Tschan 2002; Eikill 2008

"East on the salt sea"
Townend 2012a; Jónsson 1967; Ashby 2015; Whaley 2012

On Viking raids and warrior culture
Howard 2003; Fletcher 1997; Jesch 2001, 2005; Whaley 2012; Townend 2012a; Price 2002; Holtsmark 1970; Ellis 1943; Gade 2009a

Olaf's skald
Poole 2012a

The plundering of Tiel

Jesch 2001; Besteman H. A. 1990; Bachrach 2012; de Vries 1923

The first attack on Canterbury

Jesch 2001; Whitelock 1961; Higham and Ryan 2013; Roesdahl 1998; Williams et al. 2013

FIRE AND SMOKE

Europe

Bartlett 1994; Duby 1983; Lacey 1999

Plundering in the south

Keegan 1978, 1993, 1998; Lavelle 2002; Greenway 2002; Whitelock 1961; Keynes 1980; McGlynn 1994

"God help us all. Amen."

Keynes 1980

The campaign of 1009–12

Whitelock 1961; Darlington et al. 1995; Howard 2003

The siege of London

Vince 1990; Clark 1980; Jesch 2001; Blackburn 2011; Moberg 1941; Keynes and Campbell 1998; Campbell 1949; Whitelock 1961; Schjødt and Magerøy 1979e

London's "bryggjar"

Jesch and Whaley 2012; Jesch 2001; Campbell 1949; Clark 1980

Ulfcytel Snillingr

Joleik 1931; James Campbell 1949

Ringmere

Joleik 1931; Norman Blake 1962; Roesdahl 1998; Jesch 2001; Whitelock 1961; Jesch and Whaley 2012; Townend 2012a; Darlington et al. 1995

"spoiling some wretched people of their property and slaying others"

Townend 2012a; Whitelock 1961; Darlington et al. 1995

The storming of Canterbury

Jesch and Whaley 2012; Townend 2012a; Whitelock 1961; Darlington et al. 1995; Greenway 2002

Nýjamóða

Jesch and Whaley 2012; Jesch 2001

Ælfheah's martyrdom

Whitelock 1961; Warner 2001; Darlington et al. 1995

Peace 1012

Higham and Ryan 2013; Whitelock 1961; Keynes 1980; Keynes and Campbell 1998

MIDGARD

In the service of the Norman duke

Breese 1977; Van Houts 1992; Crouch 2002; Stafford 1997; Musset 1954; Searle 1988; Jesch and Whaley 2012

Plundering the Loire Valley

Downham 2004; Chavanon 1897; Jónsson 1967; Jesch and Whaley 2012; Jesch 2001; Munch 1853

On the slave trade

Higham and Ryan 2013; Downham 2004; Jesch 2001; Lunde and Stone 2012

On ships, the sea and rune stones

Steen 1934; Pentz 2013; Jensen 2008; Snædal 2004

Previous Viking voyages to the south

Rando, Pieper and Alcover 2014; Birkeland 1954; Roesdahl 1998; Allen 1960

The Bishop of Tui

Chronicon Lusitanum 1796; Johnsen 1916; Munch 1853; Whaley 2012b; Fletcher 1992; Schjødt and Magerøy 1979e

Karlså

Birkeland 1954; Johnsen 1916

HVÍTI KRISTR

Sweyn Forkbeard's plan

Bolton 2017; Campbell 1949; Van Houts 1992; Howard 2003

The invasion

Tyler 1999; Pentz 2013; Whitelock 1961; Lavelle 2002; Van Houts 1992; Winroth 2012; Williams 2003; Townend 2012b; Howard 2003

Sweyn's death

Bolton 2017; Whaley 2012b; Whitelock 1961; Higham and Ryan 2013; Carroll 2012

Rituals

Althoff 2004; Fletcher 1992

The baptism in Rouen

Holtsmark 1981; Van Houts 1992

Notker's account
Fletcher 1999; Grant and Moring 1905

Christianity and heathenism
Fletcher 1999, 1997; Schreiner 1967

New battles in England
Flokenes 2000; Warner 2001; Campbell 1949

Preparations for a new invasion
Cinthio 1997

Olaf at war
Flokenes 2000; Johnsen 1922; Eikill 2008

TO NORWAY

The old North Way
Stylegard 2015; Price 2002

The history of the Jarls of Lade and the Kings of Western Norway
Schjødt and Magerøy 1979c, 1979a, 1979f, 1979d, 1979b; Krag 2011, 1995, 2002; Bagge 2010a, 2015a; Driscoll 2008; Salvesen 1990; Eikill 2008

Preparations for war
Campbell 1949; Townend 2012a

The meeting at Oxford
Thomson and Winterbottom 2007; Whitelock 1961; Greenway 2002; Darlington et al. 1995

Edmund Ironside's rebellion
Hill 1978; Whitelock 1961; Higham and Ryan 2013

The invasion in 1015

Campbell 1949; Whitelock 1961; Birkeli and Hauge 1995

"so near land that the English plains could be seen"

Carroll 2012

"Young ruler, you often saw villages burn before you, saw the villagers scream"

Townend 2012b

Olaf and Cnut

Jónsson 1965; Driscoll 2008; Schjødt and Magerøy 1979e; Van Houts 1992; Tschan 2002; Salvesen 1990; Krag 1995; Moberg 1941; Bagge 2015b, 2002;

Olaf travels to Norway

Townend 2012a; Whaley 2012; Schjødt and Magerøy 1979e; Driscoll 2008; Eikill 2008; Andersen 1977

Sweyn burns Olaf's half-finished halls

Gade 2012a

BROAD ANCESTRAL LANDS

About the thinking of the kings

Englund 2000; Moberg 1941; Krag 1995; Bagge 2015b, 2002

"In the kingdom of heaven..."

Monk Rodulfus Glaber cited in Duby 1983

Olaf establishes himself in Vik

Scott 2016; Schjødt and Magerøy 1979e; Krag 1995; Andersen 1977; Church and Brodribb 1877

Subjugation of the petty kings
Krag 1995; Townend 2012a; Jesch 2012a

Skaldic poetry
Jónsson 1967; Jesch 2001; *Fostbrødrenes Saga* 1876; Whaley 2012c, 2012a

Sigurd Fåvnesbane
Fulk 2012c

Nesjar
Whaley 2012a; Poole 2012b; Jesch 2001

TWO KINGDOMS

The war in England 1015–16
Whitelock 1961; Campbell 1949; Keynes and Campbell 1998; Townend 2012a; Keynes 1980

"with great toil and under great difficulties"
Tschan 2002; Darlington et al. 1995

Cnut and Eric's siege of London
Whitelock 1961; Keynes and Campbell 1998; Carroll 2012; Hermann and Edwards 1986

'Flet Engle, flet Engle!'
Greenway 2002; Whitelock 1961; Townend 2012b

The Battle of Assandun
E.O. Blake 1962; Whitelock 1961; Greenway 2002; Darlington et al. 1995; Keynes and Campbell 1998; Hermann and Edwards 1986

ONLAF REX NORMANNORUM
Andersen 1977; Bagge and Nordeide 2007; Bagge 2002, 2015b; Krag 1995; Schjødt and Magerøy 1979e; Driscoll 2008; Salvesen 1990

Erling Skjalgsson
Jesch 2012c, 2012b

Sarpsborg
Johannessen et al. 2015; Schjødt and Magerøy 1979e; Eriksson 1995

Coins
Gullbekk 2016; Skaare 1976

The hird
Imsen 2000; Jónsson 1965; Hødnebø and Magerøy 1979; Fulk 2012b

The travelling king
Selnes 1995

Christianization
Tschan 2002; Fletcher 1999, 1997; Reuter 1991

Brutality
Schjødt and Magerøy 1979f, 1979e; Gade 2009b; Jesch 2012a; Fulk 2012b

THE GREAT

Cnut consolidates his power in England
Lawson 1993, 2004, Bolton 2017, 2009; Tschan 2002

The fall of Eadric Streona
Darlington et al. 1995; Thomson and Winterbottom 2007; Andersson 1987

Olaf and the Swedish kingdom
Moberg 1941; Tschan 2002; Fletcher 1997; Jesch 2012a; Ljungkvist and Frölund 2015

Sigvat's journey east
Fulk 2012a

The feud with Thorir Hund
Schjødt and Magerøy 1979e; Jónsson 1965; Bagge 1998, 2002

Cnut and Thorkell
Joleik 1931; James Campbell 1949; Keynes and Campbell 1998; Darlington et al. 1995; E.O. Blake 1962; Whitelock 1961; Bolton 2017; Rumble 1994

The messengers
Schjødt and Magerøy 1979e; Eikill 2008

"Olaf the Stout never surrendered his skull to anyone in the world"
Fulk 2012b

SILVER COINS FOR THE KING'S HEAD

Visunden
Stylegar 1996; Bill 2013

European complications
Chavanon 1897; Bolton 2017

Erling Skjalgsson and Cnut
Schjødt and Magerøy 1979e

The attack on Denmark

Bagge 2002; Schjødt and Magerøy 1979e; Bolton 2017, 2009; Saxo et al. 2000; Weibull 1911; Munch 1853; Moberg 1941; Townend 2012c, 2012b; Gade 2012b

Cnut's journey to Rome

Tschan 2002; Keynes and Campbell 1998; Bolton 2017, 2009; Townend 2012c

Cnut's letter

Lange 1849, volume 19, number 11; Gunnes 1989, volume 1, number 26; Thomson and Winterbottom 2007

Cnut ensures his control in Denmark

Bolton 2017, 2009; Townend 2012c, 2012b; Gelting 2002

The skald caught between two kings

Townend 2012c; Jesch 2012d; Townend 2012b

Olaf's men receive gold from Cnut; Olaf's power crumbles

Fulk 2012b; Schjødt and Magerøy 1979e; Darlington et al. 1995

The attack on Erling Skjalgsson

Jesch 2012b; Schjødt and Magerøy 1979e; Krag 1995; Poole 2012a

The shipwreck in the Pentland Firth

Darlington et al. 1995; Driscoll 2008; Schjødt and Magerøy 1979e; Whitelock 1961

Sigvat on his way to Rome

Fulk 2012b; Whaley 2012a; Jesch 2001

On the road to Stiklestad

Jesch 2012a; Schjødt and Magerøy 1979e

SOURCES

Alexander, Michael (trans.). 2003. *Beowulf. A Verse Translation* (London)

Andersson, Theodore M. and Kari Ellen Gade. 2000. *Morkinskinna: The Earliest Icelandic Chronicle of the Norwegian Kings 1030–1157* (Ithaca, NY)

Barlow, Frank. 1992. *Vita Edwardi Regis: The Life of King Edward Who Rests at Westminster* (Oxford)

Blake, E.O. (ed.). 1962. *Liber Eliensis.* Camden Third Series (London)

Blake, Norman (ed.). 1962. *Jómsvikinga Saga: The Saga of the Jomsvikings* (Stockholm)

Campbell, James. 1949. "Supplement til Jómsvíkinga Saga", in *Encomium Emma*, ed. James Campbell (London)

Carroll, Jayne. 2012. "Þórðr Kolbeinsson, Eiríksdrápa", in *Poetry from the Kings' Sagas 1: From Mythical Times to c.1035. Skaldic Poetry of the Scandinavian Middle Ages 1*, ed. Diana Whaley (Turnhout)

Chavanon, Jules (ed.). 1897. *Adémar de Chabannes, Chronique* (Paris)

Chronicon Lusitanum. 1796. (Madrid)

Church, A.J. and W.J. Brodribb (eds). 1877. *The Agricola and Germania of Tacitus* (London)

Clark, George. 1968. "The Battle of Maldon: A Heroic Poem", *Speculum*, 43

Darlington, R., P. McGurk and J. Bray. 1995. *The Chronicle of John of Worcester: The Annals from 450–1066*, trans. Thomas Forester (Oxford)

Driscoll, M.J. (ed. and trans.). 2008. *Ágrip Af Nóregskonungasogum. A Twelfth-Century Synoptic History of the Kings of Norway* (London)

Eikill, Edvard (trans.). 2008. *Fagerskinna. Sagaen om Norges konger* (Stavanger)

Eithun, Bjørn, Magnus Rindal and Tor Ulset. 1994. *Den eldre Gulatingslova* (Oslo)

Ekrem, Inger and Lars Boje Mortensen. 2003. *Historia Norwegie* (Copenhagen)

Flokenes, Kåre (trans.). 2000. *Den legendariske Olavssaga* (Stavanger)

Fulk, R.D. 2012. "Þormóðr Kolbrúnarskáld, Lausavísur", in *Poetry from the Kings' Sagas 1: From Mythical Times to c. 1035. Skaldic Poetry of the Scandinavian Middle Ages 1*, ed. Diana Whaley (Turnhout)

Fulk, R.D. 2012. "Sigvatr Þórðarson, Lausavísur", in *Poetry from the Kings' Sagas 1: From Mythical Times to c.1035. Skaldic Poetry of the Scandinavian Middle Ages 1*, ed. Diana Whaley (Turnhout)

Fulk, R.D. 2012. "Sigvatr Þórðarson, Austrfararvísur", in *Poetry from the Kings' Sagas 1: From Mythical Times to c.1035. Skaldic Poetry of the Scandinavian Middle Ages 1*, ed. Diana Whaley (Turnhout)

Gade, Kari Ellen. 2012. "Þórðr Særeksson (Sjáreksson), Róðudrápa", in *Poetry from the Kings' Sagas 1: From Mythical Times to c.1035. Skaldic Poetry of the Scandinavian Middle Ages 1*, ed. Diana Whaley (Turnhout)

Gade, Kari Ellen. 2012. "Þórðr Særeksson (Sjáreksson), Flokkr about Klœingr Brúsason", in *Poetry from the Kings' Sagas 1: From Mythical Times to c.1035. Skaldic Poetry of the Scandinavian Middle Ages 1*, ed. Diana Whaley (Turnhout)

Gade, Kari Ellen. 2017. "Háttatal", in *Poetry from Treatises on Poetics. Skaldic Poetry of the Scandinavian Middle Ages 3*, ed. Kari Ellen Gade and Edith Marold (Turnhout)

Gelting, Michael H. 2002. *Roskildekrøniken* (Højbjerg)

Giles, J.A. 1914. *The Anglo-Saxon Chronicle* (London)

Grant, A.J. and A. Moring (eds). 1905. *Early Lives of Charlemagne by Eginhard and the Monk of St Gall* (London)

Greenway, Diana (ed.). 2002. *Henry of Huntingdon: The History of the English People, 1000–1154* (Oxford)

Gunnes, Erik (ed.). 1989. *Regesta Norvegica, 1 822–1263* (Oslo)

Halvorsen, Eyvind Fjeld and Magnus Rindal. 2008. *De eldste østlandske kristenrettene* (Oslo)

Hermann, Pálsson and Paul Edwards (eds). 1986. *Knytlinga Saga: The History of the Kings of Denmark* (Odense)

Holtsmark, Anne (trans.). 1970. *Orknøyingenes Saga* (Oslo)

Horn, Fr. Winkel (trans.). 1876. *Fostbrødrenes Saga* (Copenhagen)

Hødnebø, Finn and Hallvard Magerøy (eds). 1979. *Soga om Eirikssønene*, transl. Steinar Schjøtt and Halvard Magerøy, *Noregs kongesoger* (Oslo)

Hødnebø, Finn and Hallvard Magerøy (eds). 1979. *Soga om Olav Tryggvason*, transl. Steinar Schjøtt and Halvard Magerøy, *Noregs kongesoger* (Oslo)

Hødnebø, Finn and Hallvard Magerøy (eds). 1979. *Soga om Harald Hårfagre*, transl. Steinar Schjøtt and Halvard Magerøy, *Noregs kongesoger* (Oslo)

Hødnebø, Finn and Hallvard Magerøy (eds). 1979. *Soga om Olav den heilage*, transl. Steinar Schjøtt and Halvard Magerøy, *Noregs kongesoger* (Oslo)

Hødnebø, Finn and Hallvard Magerøy (eds). 1979. *Soga om Håkon den gode*, transl. Steinar Schjøtt and Halvard Magerøy, *Noregs kongesoger* (Oslo)

Hødnebø, Finn and Hallvard Magerøy (eds). 1979. *Soga om Håkon jarl*, transl. Steinar Schjøtt and Halvard Magerøy, *Noregs kongesoger* (Oslo)

Imsen, Steinar (ed.). 2000. *Hirdloven til Norges konge og hans håndgangne menn* (Oslo)

Jesch, Judith. 2012. "Sigvatr Þórðarson, Erfidrápa Óláfs Helga", in *Poetry from the Kings' Sagas 1: From Mythical Times to c.1035. Skaldic Poetry of the Scandinavian Middle Ages 1*, ed. Diana Whaley (Turnhout)

Jesch, Judith. 2012. "Sigvatr Þórðarson, Poem about Erlingr Skjálgsson", in *Poetry from the Kings' Sagas 1: From Mythical Times to c.1035. Skaldic Poetry of the Scandinavian Middle Ages 1*, ed. Diana Whaley (Turnhout)

Jesch, Judith. 2012. "Sigvatr Þórðarson, Flokkr about Erlingr Skjálgsson", in *Poetry from the Kings' Sagas 1: From Mythical Times to c.1035. Skaldic Poetry of the Scandinavian Middle Ages 1*, ed. Diana Whaley (Turnhout)

Jesch, Judith. 2012. "Sigvatr Þórðarson, Vestrfararvísur", in *Poetry from the Kings' Sagas 1: From Mythical Times to c.1035. Skaldic Poetry of the Scandinavian Middle Ages 1*, ed. Diana Whaley (Turnhout)

Jesch, Judith. 2012. "Sigvatr Þórðarson, Vikingarvísur", in *Poetry from the Kings' Sagas 1: From Mythical Times to c.1035. Skaldic Poetry of the Scandinavian Middle Ages 1*, ed. Diana Whale (Turnhout)

Johnsen, Oscar Albert (ed.). 1930. *Saga Ólafs konungs hins helga* (Oslo)

Joleik, Albert (ed.). 1931. *Soga um jomsvikingane: norrøn grunntekst og nynorsk umsetjing* (Oslo)

Jónsson, Finnur. 1927. Flateyjarbók (Copenhagen)

Jónsson, Finnur. 1965. *Heimskringla. Saga Óláfs hins helga* (Oslo)

Jónsson, Finnur. 1965. *Heimskringla. Ynglingasaga* (Oslo)

Jónsson, Finnur. 1967. *Den norsk-islandske skjaldedigtning* (Copenhagen)

Kraggerud, Egil. 2018. *Theodoricus. De antiquitate regum Norwagiensium. On the Old Norwegian Kings* (Oslo)

Kålund, K. 1904. *Sturlunga saga* (Copenhagen)

Keynes, Simon. 1980. *The Diplomas of King Æthelred "The Unready" 978–1016. A Study in Their Use as Historical Evidence* (Cambridge

Keynes, Simon and Alistair Campbell. 1998. *Encomium Emmae Reginae, Camden Classic reprints*, ed. Alistair Campbell (Cambridge)

Killings, Douglas B. 1991, 1996. *The Battle of Maldon: A Verse Translation*, http://english.nsms.ox.ac.uk/oecoursepack/maldon/translations/killingsfull.htm

Lange, C.C.A. (ed.). 1849. *Diplomatarium Norvegicum I–XXII* (Kristiania)

Lie, Hallvard. 1970. *Egils saga* (Oslo)

Lunde, Paul and Caroline Stone (trans.). 2012. *Ibn Fadlan and the Land of Darkness: Arab Travellers in the Far North* (London)

McGrew, Julia. 1970. *Sturlunga saga* (New York)

Musset, L. 1954. "Le satiriste Garnier de Rouen et son milieu", *Revue du Moyen Age Latin*, vol. 10.

Pauli, R. and Benjamin Thorpe (eds). 1900. *The Life of Alfred the Great. To Which Is Appended Alfred's Anglo-Saxon Version of Orosius* (London)

Poole, Russell. 2012. "Óláfr inn helgi Haraldsson, Lausavísur", in *Poetry from the Kings' Sagas 1: From Mythical Times to c.1035. Skaldic Poetry of the Scandinavian Middle Ages 1*, ed. Diana Whaley (Turnhout)

Poole, Russell. 2012. "Sigvatr Þórðarson, Nesjavísur", in *Poetry from the Kings' Sagas 1: From Mythical Times to c.1035. Skaldic Poetry of the Scandinavian Middle Ages 1*, ed. Diana Whaley (Turnhout)

Riley, Henry (ed.). 1853. *Annals of Roger de Hoveden: Comprising the History of England and of other Countries of Europe from AD 732 to AD 1201* (London)

Robinson, Charles H. (ed.). 1921. *Anskar, The Apostle of the North, 801–865. Translated from the Vita Anskarii by Bishop Rimbert his Fellow Missionary and Successor* (London)

Rollason, David (ed.). 2000. *Symeon of Durham: Libellus de exordio atque procursu istius, hoc est Dunhelmensis, ecclesie. Tract on the Origins and Progress of this the Church of Durham* (Oxford)

Salvesen, Astrid (trans.). 1990. *Historien om de gamle norske kongene* (Oslo)

Saxo Grammaticus, Peter Zeeberg and Maja Lisa Engelhardt. 2000. *Saxos Danmarkshistorie* (Copenhagen)

Skard, Eiliv. 1930. *Passio Olavi. Lidingssoga og undergjerningane åt den heilage Olav* (Oslo)

Storm, Gustav. 1893. *Otte bruddstykker af den ældste saga om Olav den Hellige* (Kristiania)

Titlestad, Torgrim, Elizabeth Ashman Rowe, Birgisson Bergsveinn, Edvard Eikill, et al. 2014. *Flatøybok* (Hafrsfjord)

Thomson, Rodney Malcolm and Michael Winterbottom. 2007. *William of Malmesbury: Gesta Pontificum Anglorum, The History of the English Bishops* (Oxford)

Townend, Matthew. 2012. "Óttarrsvarti, Hǫfuðlausn", in *Poetry from the Kings' Sagas 1: From Mythical Times to c.1035. Skaldic Poetry of the Scandinavian Middle Ages 1*, ed. Diana Whaley (Turnhout)

Townend, Matthew. 2012. "Óttarrsvarti, Knútsdrápa", in *Poetry from the Kings' Sagas 1: From Mythical Times to c.1035. Skaldic Poetry of the Scandinavian Middle Ages 1*, ed. Diana Whaley (Turnhout)

Townend, Matthew. 2012. "Sigvatr Þórðarson, Knútsdrápa", in *Poetry from the Kings' Sagas 1: From Mythical Times to c.1035. Skaldic Poetry of the Scandinavian Middle Ages 1*, ed. Diana Whaley (Turnhout)

Tschan, Francis J. 2002. *History of the Archbishops of Hamburg-Bremen* (New York)

Tudor, Victoria. 1995. "Reginald's Life of St Oswald", in *Oswald: Northumbrian King to European Saint*, ed. C. Stancliffe and E. Cambridge (Stamford)

Van Houts, Elisabeth M.C. (ed. and trans.). 1992. *The gesta Normannorum ducum of William of Jumièges, Orderic Vitalis, and Robert of Torigni* (Oxford)

Warner, David A. 2001. *Ottonian Germany: The Chronicon of Thietmar of Merseburg* (Manchester)

Whaley, Diana. 2012. "Bersi Skáld-Torfuson, Flokkr about Óláfr helgi", in *Poetry from the Kings' Sagas 1: From Mythical Times to c.1035. Skaldic Poetry of the Scandinavian Middle Ages 1*, ed. Diana Whaley (Turnhout)

Whaley, Diana. 2012. "Þorfinnr munnr, Lausavísur", in *Poetry from the Kings' Sagas 1: From Mythical Times to c.1035. Skaldic Poetry of the Scandinavian Middle Ages 1*, ed. Diana Whaley (Turnhout)

Whitelock, Dorothy. 1961. *The Anglo-Saxon Chronicle: A Revised Translation* (London)

Whitelock, Dorothy. 1979. *English Historical Documents: 1: c.500–1042* (London)

LITERATURE

Abram, Christopher. 2015. "Modeling religious experience in Old Norse conversion narratives: The case of Óláfr Tryggvason and Hallfreor Vandræðaskáld", *Speculum*, 90.1

Allen, William Edward David. 1960. *The Poet and the Spae-Wife: An Attempt to Reconstruct Al-Ghazal's Embassy to the Vikings* (Dublin)

Althoff, Gerd. 2004. *Family, Friends and Followers: Political and Social Bonds in Medieval Europe* (Cambridge)

Andersen, Per Sveaas. 1977. *Samlingen av Norge og kristningen av landet: 800–1130* (Bergen)

Andersson, Theodore M. 1987. "The Viking policy of Ethelred the Unready", *Scandinavian Studies*, 59.3

Andersson, Theodore M. 1994. "The politics of Snorri Sturluson", *The Journal of English and Germanic Philology*, 93

Ashby, S. 2015. "What really caused the Viking Age? The social content of raiding and exploration.", *Archaeological Dialogues*, 22.1

Bagge, Sverre. 1991. *Society and Politics in Snorri Sturlusons's Heimskringla* (Berkeley)

Bagge, Sverre. 1998. *Mennesket i middelalderens Norge. Tanke, tro og holdninger 1000–1300* (Oslo)

Bagge, Sverre. 2002. "Mellom kildekritikk og historisk antropologi. Olav den Hellige, aristokratiet og rikssamlingen.", *Historisk Tidsskrift*, 81:1

Bagge, Sverre. 2010. *From Viking Stronghold to Christian Kingdom* (Copenhagen)

Bagge, Sverre. 2010. "Warrior, king, and saint: The medieval histories about St Óláfr Haraldsson", *Journal of English and Germanic Philology*, 109.3

Bagge, Sverre. 2015. "Olav den Hellige som norsk konge (1015–28)", *Historisk Tidsskrift*, 94:1

Bagge, Sverre. 2015. "Borgerkrig og statsutvikling", *Historisk Tidsskrift*, 94:1

Bagge, Sverre and Sæbjørg Walaker Nordeide. 2007. "The Kingdom of Norway", in *Christianization and the Rise of Christian Monarchy: Scandinavia, Central Europe and Rus' c.900–1200*, ed. Nora Berend (Cambridge)

Barrow, Julia. 2007. "Demonstrative behaviour and political communication in later Anglo-Saxon England", *Anglo-Saxon England*, 36

Bartlett, Robert. 1994. *The Making of Europe: Conquest, Colonization, and Cultural Change, 950–1350* (London)

Batey, Colleen E. and James Graham-Campbell. 1996. *Vikingenes verden* (Oslo)

Beckman, Natanael. 1915. *Vetenskapligt liv på Island under 1100- och 1200-talen, Maal og Minne*

Bennett, Judith M. and C. Warren Hollister. 2006. *Medieval Europe: A Short History* (Boston)

Besteman, H.A. 1990. *Medieval Archeology in the Netherlands* (Utrecht)

Bill, Jan. 2013. "Langskibet Roskilde 6", in *Viking*, ed. Gareth Williams, Peter Pentz and Matthias Wemhoff (Copenhagen)

Birkeland, Harris. 1954. *Nordens historie etter arabiske kilder* (Oslo)

Birkeli, Fritjov and Kjell O. Hauge. 1995. *Tolv vintrer hadde kristendommen vært i Norge* (Gjøvik)

Blackburn, M.A.S. 2011. *Viking Coinage and Currency in the British Isles* (London)

Bolton, Timothy. 2007. "Ælfgifu of Northampton: Cnut the Great's 'other woman'", *Nottingham Medieval Studies*, 51

Bolton, Timothy. 2009. *The Empire of Cnut the Great: Conquest and the Consolidation of Power in Northern Europe in the Early Eleventh Century* (Leiden)

Bolton, Timothy. 2017. *Cnut the Great* (New Haven and London)

Breese, Lauren Wood. 1977. "The persistence of Scandinavian connections in Normandy in the tenth and early eleventh centuries", *Viator*, 8

Briggs, Keith. 2011. "The battle-site and place-name Ringmere", *Notes & Queries*, 58.4

Brink, Stefan. 2012. *Vikingarnas slavar: den nordiska träldomen under yngre järnålder och äldsta medeltid* (Stockholm)

Broch, Just. 1937. *Veier og veivesen i Norge: fra de eldste tider til veiloven av 1851* (Oslo)

Brøgger, A.W. 1946. *Stiklestadslaget* (Oslo)

Brown, Nancy Marie. 2012. *Song of the Vikings: Snorri and the Making of Norse Myths* (New York)

Bugge, Alexander. 1905. "Vesterlandenes indflydelse paa nordboernes og særlig nordmændenes ydre kultur, levesæt og samfundsforhold i vikingtiden", *Videnselskapets Skrifter*, 1

Byock, Jesse Lewis. 1994. "Modern Nationalism and the Medieval Sagas", in *Northern Antiquity: The Post-Medieval Reception of Edda and Saga*, ed. Andrew Wawn (London)

Campbell, James. 2000. *The Anglo-Saxon State* (London)

Cantor, Norman F. 1994. *Inventing the Middle Ages* (New York)

Cinthio, Maria. 1997. "Trinitatiskyrkan i Lund – med engelsk prägel", *Hikuin*, 24

Christys, Ann. 2012. "The Vikings in the South through Arab Eyes", in *Visions of Community in the Post-Roman World: The West, Byzantium and the Islamic World, 300–1100*, ed. Walter Pole, Clemens Gantner and Richard Payne (Abingdon)

Christys, Ann. 2015. *Vikings in the South: Voyages to Iberia and the Mediterranean* (London)

Clark, John. 1980. *Saxon and Norman London* (London)

Clover, Carol J. and John Lindow. 2005. *Old Norse-Icelandic Literature: A Critical Guide* (Toronto)

Collins, Paul. 2013. *The Birth of the West: Rome, Germany, France, and the Creation of Europe in the Tenth Century* (New York)

Coolen, Joris. 2015. "The elusive Norse harbours of the North

Atlantic: Why they were abandoned, and why they are so hard to find", in *Häfen im 1. Millennium AD: Bauliche Konzepte, herrschaftliche und religiöse Einflüsse*, ed. Thomas Schmidts and Martin Vucetic (Mainz)

Cox, Rory. 2015. "The Ethics of War up to Thomas Aquinas", in *The Oxford Handbook of Ethics of War*, ed. Seth Lazar and Helen Frowe (Oxford)

Cross, Katherine Clare. 2014. *Enemy and Ancestor: Viking Identities and Ethnic Boundaries in England and Normandy, c.950–c.1015* (London)

Crouch, David. 2002. *The Normans: The History of a Dynasty* (London)

Danstrup, John (ed.). 1982. *Kulturhistorisk leksikon for nordisk middelalder fra vikingtid til reformationstid* (Copenhagen)

de Vries, Jan. 1923. *De wikingen in de lage landen bij de zee* (Haarlem)

Dobat, Andres Siegfried. 2015. "Viking stranger-kings: The foreign as a source of power in Viking Age Scandinavia, or, why was there a peacock in the Gokstad ship burial?", *Early Medieval Europe*, 23.2

Downham, Clare. 2004. "England and the Irish-Sea Zone in the Eleventh Century", in *Norman Studies XXVI: Proceedings of the Battle Conference 2003*, 26, ed. John Gillingham (Woodbridge)

Downham, Clare. 2012. "Viking ethnicities: A historiographic overview", *History Compass*, 10.1

Dronke, Ursula (ed. and trans.) 1997. *The Poetic Edda: Vol. II: Mythological Poems* (Oxford)

Duby, Georges. 1983. *The Age of the Cathedrals* (Princeton)

Ellis, Hilda Roderick. 1943. *The Road to Hell: A Study of the Conception of the Dead in Old Norse Literature* (London)

Englund, Peter. 2000. *Den oövervinnerlige* (Stockholm)

Eriksson, Anna-Lena. 1995. *Maktens boningar: norska riksborgar under medeltiden*, Lund studies in medieval archaeology (Stockholm)

Fleming, Robin. 1991. *Kings and Lords in Conquest England* (Cambridge)

Fletcher, Richard. 1992. *Moorish Spain* (Los Angeles)

Fletcher, Richard. 1997. *The Conversion of Europe: From Paganism to Christianity 371–1386 AD* (London)

Fletcher, Richard. 1999. *The Barbarian Conversion: From Paganism to Christianity* (Berkeley)

Friis-Jensen, Karsten, Jon Gunnar Jørgensen and Else Mundal. 2010. *Saxo og Snorre* (København)

Fæhn, Helge. 1980. "Dåp", *Kulturhistorisk leksikon for nordisk middelalder fra vikingtid til reformationstid* (Copenhagen)

Fæhn, Helge. 1980. "Fadder", *Kulturhistorisk leksikon for nordisk middelalder fra vikingtid til reformationstid* (Copenhagen)

Gade, Kari Ellen (ed.). 2009. *Poetry from the Kings' Saga: Vol. 2* (Turnhout)

Gelting, Michael H. 2004. "Elusive Bishops: Remembering, Forgetting, and Remaking the History of the Early Danish Church", in *The Bishop: Power and Piety at the First Millennium*, ed. Sean Gilsdorf (Münster/Hamburg/Berlin)

Gillingham, John. 2011. "Christian Warriors and the Enslavement of Fellow Christians", in *Chevalerie et christianisme aux XIIe et XIIIe siècles*, ed. M. Aurell and C. Girbea (Rennes)

Godden, Malcolm. 1994. "Apocalypse and Invasion in Late Anglo-Saxon England", in *From Anglo-Saxon to Early Middle English*, ed. Malcolm Godden, Douglas Gray and Terry Hoad (Oxford)

Green, John Richard. 1904. *A Short History of the English People* (London)

Gräslund, Bo. 1986. "Knut den store och sveariket: Slaget vid Helgeå i ny belysning", *Scandia*, 52

Guðmundsson, Óskar. 2009. *Snorri: Ævisaga 1179–1241* (Reykjavik)

Gullbekk, Svein Harald. 2016. "Olavsikonografi på mynt. De eldste fremstillingene av Olav Haraldsson, Hellig-Olav og helgenkongen", in *Helgenkongen St Olav i kunsten*, ed. Øystein Ekroll (Trondheim)

Gunnes, Erik. 1976. *Rikssamling og kristning ca. 800–1177* (Oslo)

Hadley, Dawn M. 2006. *The Vikings in England: Settlement, Society and Culture* (Manchester)

Hadley, Dawn M. and Julian D. Richards. 2000. *Cultures in Contact: Settlement in England in the Ninth and Tenth Centuries. Studies in the Early Middle Ages, 2* (Turnhout)

Halvorsen, Svein. 1995. *Vikingene og den iberiske halvøy* (Oslo)

Harðardottir, Guðrun. 2006. "The Physical Setting of Reykholt According to Sturlunga Saga", in *Reykholt som makt- og lærdomssenter*, ed. Else Mundal (Reykjavik)

Harsson, Margit. 2000. *Stein: en storgård på Ringerike* (Hole)

Haywood, John. 1995. *The Penguin Historical Atlas of the Vikings* (Harmondsworth)

Haywood, John. 2015. *Northmen. The Viking Saga 793–1241 AD* (London)

Heide, Eldar. 2012. "The Early Viking ship types", *Sjøfartshistorisk årbok*

Henriksen, Vera and Gro Eriksson Stoll. 1985. *Hellig Olav: historien om vår nasjonalhelgen* (Oslo)

Higham, Nicholas J. 2000. *The Death of Anglo-Saxon England* (London)

Higham, Nicholas J and Martin J Ryan. 2013. *The Anglo-Saxon World* (New Haven and London)

Hill, David (ed). 1978. *Ethelred the Unready: Papers from the Millenary Conference* (Oxford)

Hjardar, Kim and Vegard Vike. 2011. *Vikinger i krig* (Oslo)

Hødnebø, Finn and Hallvard Magerøy. 1979. *Noregs kongesoger* (Oslo)

Holmquist, Lena. 2011. *Birkas Garrison and its Warriors* (Wolin)

Holmsen, Andreas. 1961. *Norges historie fra de eldste tider til 1660* (Oslo)

Holtsmark, Anne. 1981. "Kometer", *Kulturhistorisk leksikon for nordisk middelalder fra vikingtid til reformationstid* (Copenhagen)

Howard, Ian. 2003. *Swein Forkbeard's Invasions and the Danish Conquest of England, 991–1017* (Woodbridge)

Innes, Mathew. 2000. "Danelaw Identities: Ethnicity, Regionalism, and Political Allegiance", in *Cultures in Contact: Scandinavian Settlement in England in the Ninth and Tenth Centuries*, ed. Dawn Hadley and Julian D. Richards (Turnhout)

Jacobsson, Sverrir. 2015. "Erindringen om en mægtig personlighed: den norsk-islandske historiske tradisjon om Harald Hårfagre i et kildekritisk perspektiv", *Historisk Tidsskrift*, 94:1

Jacobsson, Sverrir, Viðar Pálsson and Helgi Þorláksson. 2018. "Reykholt as a Centre of Power", in *Snorri Sturluson and Reykholt. The Author and Magnate, his Life, Works and Environment at Reykholt in Iceland*, ed. Helgi Þorláksson and Guðrún Sveinbjarnardóttir (Copenhagen)

Jansson, S.B.F. 1966. *Swedish Vikings in England: The Evidence of the Rune Stones* (London)

Jensen, Kurt Villads. 2008. *Danmarks krigshistorie 700–1814* (Copenhagen)

Jesch, Judith. 2001. *Ships and Men in the Late Viking Age: The Vocabulary of Runic Inscriptions and Skaldic Verse* (Woodbridge)

Jesch, Judith. 2005. "Literature in Medieval Orkney", in *The World of Orkneyinga Saga*, ed. O. Owen (Kirkwall)

Jochens, J. 1987. "The politics of reproduction: Medieval Norwegian kingship", *American Historical Review*, 92

Johannessen, Live and Jan-Erik G. Eriksson. 2015. *Faglig program for middelalderarkeologi: byer, sakrale steder, befestninger og borger* (Oslo)

Johnsen, Oscar Albert. 1922. *Olafs saga hins helga: efter pergamenthaandskrift i Uppsala Universitetsbibliotek* (Kristiania)

Johnsen, Oscar Albert. 1916. *Olav Haraldssons ungdom indtil slaget ved Nesjar 25. mars 1016*, Videnselskapets Skrifter (Kristiania)

Johnsen, Oscar Albert. 1930. *Olav den helliges personlighet og livsverk* (Hamar)

Jones, Michael. 1988. *The Creation of Brittany: A Late Medieval State* (London)

Jónsson, Finnur. 1924. "Snorri Sturlasson i Norge", *Historisk Tidsskrift*, 5:5.

Jónsson, Finnur. 1967. *Tidsregningen i det 9. og 10. årh. særlig hvad Norge angår* (Oslo)

Jørgensen, Anne Norgard, John Find, Lars Jørgensen and Birthe Clausen (eds). 2009. *Maritime Warfare in Northern Europe: Technology, Organization, Logistics and Administration 500–100* (Copenhagen)

Keegan, John. 1978. *The Face of Battle* (Harmondsworth)

Keegan, John. 1993. *A History of Warfare* (London)

Keegan, John. 1998. *War and Our World: The Reith Lectures* (London)

Keynes, Simon. 1980. *The Diplomas of King Æthelred "the Unready", 978–1016: A Study in Their Use as Historical Evidence* (Cambridge)

Keynes, Simon. 2004. "Æthelred II (c.966x8–1016)", *Oxford Dictionary of National Biography*

Kjesrud, Karoline and Nanna Løkka (eds). 2017. *Dronningen i vikingtid og middelalder* (Oslo)

Koht, Halvdan. 1914, "Sagaenes oppfatning av vor gamle historie", *Historisk Tidsskrift*, 5:2

Koht, Halvdan. 1920. "Kampen om Norge i sagatiden", *Historisk Tidsskrift*, 5:4

Koht, Halvdan. 1920. "Medførte kristendommens innførelse et makttap for det gamle aristokrati?", *Historisk Tidsskrift*, 5:4.

Konshuh, Courtnay. 2016. "Anraed in their Unraed: The Æthelredian Annals (983–1016) and their Presentation of King and Advisors", *English Studies*, 97.2

Krag, Claus. 1995. *Vikingtid og rikssamling 800–1130* (Oslo)

Krag, Claus. 1999. "Rane Kongsfostre og Olav Geirstadalv. Om utviklingen av to sagaskikkelser", *Historisk Tidsskrift*, 78:1

Krag, Claus. 2000. *Norges historie fram til 1319* (Oslo)

Krag, Claus. 2002. "Myten om hårfagreættens odel", *Historisk Tidsskrift*, 81:2–3

Krag, Claus. 2009. "Olav 2. Haraldsson Den Hellige", *Norsk biografisk leksikon*

Krag, Claus. 2009. "Harald 3 Hardråde", *Norsk biografisk leksikon*

Krag, Claus. 2009. "Sigurd Halvdansson Syr", *Norsk biografisk leksikon*

Krag, Claus. 2012, "Rikssamlingshistorien og ynglingerekken", *Historisk Tidsskrift*, 91:2

Krag, Claus, Bjørn Myhre, Sverre Bagge, Lars Hamre and Ole Jørgen Benedictow. 2003. *Prehistory to 1520: The Cambridge History of Scandinavia* (Cambridge)

Kraggerud, Egil. 2012. "Hellig-Olavs dåp hos Theodoricus Monachus og i hans kilder", *Collegium Medievale*, 25

Krambs, Karsten Laust. 2018. "Saint Olave, King of Norway, Olav den Hellige: Are his raids to England based on a 1200s poem?" (Academia.net.)

Lacey, Robert. 1999. *The Year 1000* (New York)

Landes, R., A. Gow and D.C. Van Meter (eds). 2003. *The Apocalyptic Year 1000* (Oxford)

Langslet, Roar and Knut Ødegård. 2011. *Olav den hellige. Spor etter helgenkongen* (Oslo)

Lavelle, Ryan. 2002. *Aethelred II: King of the English, 978–1016* (Stroud)

Lawson, M.K. 1993. *Cnut: The Danes in England in the Early Eleventh Century* (London)

Lawson, M.K. 2004. *Cnut: England's Viking King*, The Medieval World (London)

Liestøl, Aslak. 1953. "Runekrossen i Muséparken i Stavanger", *Stavanger Museums årbok* (Stavanger)

Liestøl, Knut. 1941. *Saga og folkeminne* (Oslo)

Ljungkvist, John and Per Frölund. 2015. "Gamla Uppsala: The emergence of a centre and a magnate complex", *Journal of Archaeology and Ancient History*, 16

Loyn, H.R. 1984. *The Governance of Anglo-Saxon England 500–1087* (London)

Lund, Niels. 1986. "The armies of Swein Forkbeard and Cnut: Leding or li(th)", *Anglo-Saxon England*, 15

Lund, Troels. 1929. *Dagligt liv i Norden i det sekstende aarhundrede* (Copenhagen)

Lunde, Øivind (ed.). 1986. "Tre norske middelalderbyer i 1970-årene", *Fornminnevern og utgravingsresultater Hamar-Oslo-Tønsberg. Riksantikvarens rapporter*, 12

Magnell, Steinar. 2009. "De første kirkene i Norge. Kirkebyggingen og kirkebyggerne før 1100-tallet" (University of Oslo)

Matthew, H.C.G., Brian Harrison and Lawrence Goldman. 2004. *Oxford Dictionary of National Biography* (Oxford)

McGlynn, Sean. 1994. "The Myths of Medieval Warfare", *History Today*, 44

McGuigan, Neil. 2015. "Neither Scotland nor England: Middle Britain, c.850–1150" (University of St Andrews)

Megaard, John. 2017. *Hvem skapte Heimskringla? Forfatterne bak Snorres kongesagaer* (Oslo)

Merback, Mitchell B. 1999. *The Thief, the Cross and the Wheel: Pain and the Spectacle of Punishment in Medieval and Renaissance Europe* (London)

Moberg, Ove. 1941. *Olav Haraldsson, Knut den store och Sverige: studier i Olav den heliges förhållande till de nordiska grannländerna* (Lund)

Morris, Marc. 2014. *The Norman Conquest* (London)

Morten, Øystein. 2013. *Jakten på Olav den hellige* (Oslo)

Munch, P.A. 1853. *Det norske folks historie, første deel, 2. bind* (Kristiania)

Myhre, Bjørn and Ingvild Øye. 2002. *Norges landbrukshistorie 1. Jorda blir levevei* (Oslo)

Myrvoll, Klaus Johan. (2014) "Kronologi i skaldekvæde. Distribusjon av metriske og språklege drag i høve til tradisjonell datering og attribuering" (Universitetet i Oslo)

Nedkvitne, Arnved and Per G. Norseng. 2000. *Middelalderbyen ved Bjørvika. Oslo 1000–1536* (Oslo)

Neidorf, Leonard. 2012. "II Æthelred and the politics of the Battle of Maldon", *The Journal of English and Germanic Philology*, 111.4

Neidorf, Leonard. 2016. "Archbishop Wulfstan's Ecclesiastical History of the English People", *English Studies*, 97.2

Nordal, Guðrun. 2002. "Snorri and Norway", in *Reykholt som makt- og lærdomssenter*, ed. Else Mundal (Reykjavik)

Orchard, Andy. 2011. *The Elder Edda: A Book of Viking Lore* (London)

Orning, Hans Jacob. 2015. "Hvorfor vant kongene?" *Historisk Tidsskrift*, 94:2

Orning, Hans Jacob. 2015. "Festive Governance: Feasts as Rituals of Power and Integration in Medieval Norway", in *Rituals, Performatives, and Political Order in Northern Europe, c.650–1350*, ed. Lars Hermanson, Wojtek Jezierski, Hans Jacob Orning and Thomas Smaberg (Turnhout)

Pentz, Peter. 2013. "Skibet og vikingerne", in *Viking*, ed. G. Williams, P. Pentz and M. Wemhoff (Copenhagen)

Poole, R.G. 1991. *Viking Poems in War and Peace: A Study in Skaldic Narrative* (Toronto)

Price, Neil S. 2002. *The Viking Way: Religion and War in Late Iron Age Scandinavia* (Uppsala)

Price, Neil. (2020). *The Children of Ash and Elm* (London).

Price, Neil S. and Stefan Brink. 2008. *The Viking World* (London)

Pullen-Appleby, John. 2005. *English Sea Power c.871–1100* (Hockwold-cum-Wilton, Norfolk)

Pye, Michael. 2015. *The Edge of the World. A Cultural History of the North Sea and the Transformation of Europe* (New York)

Rando, Juan Carlos, Harald Pieper and Josep Antoni Alcover. 2014. "Radiocarbon evidence for the presence of mice on Madeira

Island (North Atlantic) one millennium ago", *Proceedings of the Royal Society B*

Reuter, Timothy. 1991. *Germany in the Early Middle Ages 800–1056* (New York)

Reynolds, Susan. 1994. *Fiefs and Vassals: The Medieval Evidence Reinterpreted* (Oxford)

Reynolds, Susan. 1997. *Kingdoms and Communities in Western Europe, 900–1300* (Oxford)

Richards, J.D. 2004. *Viking Age England* (Stroud)

Roesdahl, Else. 1998. *The Vikings* (New York)

Roesdahl, Else and Anne Kroman. 1996. *The Arabian Journey: Danish Connections with the Islamic World Over a Thousand Years* (Århus)

Rumble, Alexander R. 1994. *The Reign of Cnut: King of England, Denmark and Norway* (London)

Sahlins, Marshall D. 1963. "Poor man, rich man, big man, chief: Political types in Melanesia and Polynesia", *Comparative Studies in Society and History*, 503

Sandwich, Kent Archaeological Assessment Document 2004.

Sawyer, Birgit. 2015. "Sigrid Storråda: hur och varför blev hon til?", *Historisk Tidsskrift*, 94:2

Sawyer, Birgit and Peter Sawyer. 2004. "The Making of the Scandinavian Kingdoms", in *Die Suche nach Ursprüngen: Von der Bedeutung des frühen Mittelalters*, ed. Walter Pohl (Vienna)

Sawyer, Peter. 1968. *Anglo-Saxon Charters: An Annotated List and Bibliography* (London)

Sawyer, Peter. 1971. *The Age of the Vikings* (London)

Sawyer, Peter. 1982. *Kings and Vikings: Scandinavia and Europe, AD 700–1100* (London)

Sawyer, Peter. 1987. "Ethelred II, Olav Tryggvason, and the conversation of Norway", *Scandinavian Studies*, 59:3

Sawyer, Peter. 2001. *The Oxford Illustrated History of the Vikings* (Oxford)

Schjødt, Jens Peter. 1999. *Det Førkristne Norden: Religion og mytologi* (Copenhagen: Spektrum)

Schove, D.J. 1986. *A Chronology of Comets and Eclipses, AD 1–1000* (Woodbridge)

Schreiner, Johan. 1927. "Olav den helliges siste regjeringsår", *Historisk Tidsskrift*, 6:5

Schreiner, Johan. 1927. "Olav den hellige og nabolandene", *Historisk Tidsskrift*, 5:7

Schreiner, Johan. 1927. "Sigvat Skald", *Historisk Tidsskrift*, 5:7

Schreiner, Johan. 1967. "Olav den Hellige og Norges samling", *Rikssamling og kristendom. Norske historikere i utvalg I*, ed. Andreas Holmsen and Jarle Simensen (Oslo)

Schreiner, Johan. 1927. "Studier til Olav den helliges historie", *Historisk Tidsskrift*, 5:7

Scott, Ida. 2016. "Kongs- og lendmannsgårder i Viken ca. 800–1240: i et rikssamlingsperspektiv" (University of Oslo)

Searle, Eleanor. 1988. *Predatory Kinship and the Creation of Norman Power, 840–1066* (London)

Selnes, Arulf. 1995. *Vandring langs gamle veifar: fra sagatid til nær fortid* (Trondheim)

Sigurðsson, Jón Viðar. 2003. *Kristninga i Norden* (Oslo)

Sigurðsson, Jón Viðar. 2007. "The appearance and personal abilities of goðar, jarlar, and konungar: Iceland, Orkney and Norway", in *West over Sea: Studies in Scandinavian Seaborne Expansion and Settlement before 1300*, ed. Beverley Ballin Smith, Simon Taylor and Gareth Williams, *The Northern World*, 31 (Leiden)

Sigurðsson, Jón Viðar. 2008. *Det norrøne samfunnet: vikingen, kongen, erkebiskopen og bonden* (Oslo)

Sigurðsson, Jón Viðar. 2011. "Kings, Earls and Chieftains. Rulers in Norway, Orkney and Iceland c.900–1300", in *Ideology and Power in the Viking and Middle Ages: Scandinavia, Iceland, Ireland, Orkney and the Faeroes*, ed. Gro Steinsland, Jon Vidar Sigurdsson, Jan Erik Rekdal and Ian B. Beumermann, *The Northern World*, 52 (Leiden)

Sigurðsson, Jón Viðar. 2012. "Et fælles hav: Skagerrak og Kattegat i vikingtiden", *Nordlige verdener* (Copenhagen)

Sigurdur, Nordal. 1973. *Snorri Sturluson* (Reykjavik)

Skre, Dagfinn. 2013. "Money and Trade in Viking Age Scandinavia", in *Economies, Monetisation and Society in the West Slavic Land*, ed. Mateusz Boguaki and Marian Rębkowski (Szczecin)

Skre, Dagfinn and Frans-Arne Stylegar. 2004. *Kaupang. The Viking Town* (Oslo)

Skaaning, Poul. 2010. *Knud den store: drømmen om Nordsøimperiet, 1014–1066* (Højbjerg)

Skaare, K. 1976. *Coins and Coinage in Viking Age Norway* (Oslo)

Snædal, Thorgunn. 2004. *Svenska runor* (Stockholm)

Sogge, Ingebjørg. 1976. *Vegar til eit bilete: Snorre Sturlason og Tore Hund, Skrifter Nordisk institutt, Universitetet i Trondheim* (Trondheim)

Spejlborg, Marie Bønløkke. 2014. "Anglo-Danish connections and the organisation of the Early Danish Church: Contribution to a debate", *Networks and Neighbours*, 2.1

Stafford, Pauline. 1997. *Queen Emma and Queen Edith: Queenship and Women's Power in Eleventh-century England* (Bodmin)

Steen, Sverre. 1934. "Fartøyer i Norden i middelalderen", in *Handel och samfärdsel under medeltiden*, ed. Johannes Brøndsted and Adolf Schück (Stockholm)

Steen, Sverre. 1934. "Veiene og leden i Norge", in *Handel och samfärdsel under medeltiden*, ed. Brøndsted, Johannes and Schück, Adolf. (Stockholm)

Steen, Sverre. 1967. *Langsomt ble landet vårt eget* (Oslo)

Stefansson, Jon. 1909. *The Vikings in Spain From Arabic (Moorish) and Spanish Sources* (London)

Steinsland, Gro. 2000. *Den hellige kongen: om religion og herskermakt fra vikingtid til middelalder* (Oslo)

Steinsland, Gro. 2005. *Norrøn religion: myter, riter, samfunn* (Oslo)

Steinsland, Gro. 2012. *Mytene som skapte Norge* (Oslo)

Stenton, F.M. 1971. *Anglo-Saxon England* (London)

Stephenson, I.P. 2007. *The Late Anglo-Saxon Army* (London)

Storli, Inger and Torbjørn Alm (eds). 1995. *Ottars verden* (Tromsø)

Stylegar, Frans-Arne. 2015. "Eastern Imports in the Arctic", in *Scandinavia and the Balkans: Cultural Interactions with Byzantium and Eastern Europe in the First Millennium AD* (Newcastle upon Tyne)

Stylegar, Frans-Arne. 1996. "Roskilde 6, langskipet fra Viken", http://arkeologi.blogspot.com/2011/10/roskilde-6-langskibet-fra-viken.html, 2 March 2021

Stylegard, Frans-Arne. 2015. "Jomsborg og jomsvikinger mellom arkeologiog historie", *Fund&Fortid*

Svanberg, Fredrik. 2003. *Decolonizing the Viking Age* (Lund)

Sveinbjarnardottir, Guðrun. 2002. "Reykholt, a Centre of Power: The Archeological Evidence", in *Reykholt som makt- og lærdomssenter* (Reykjavik)

Thompson, Simon. 2017. "Configuring Stasis: The Appeal to Tradition in the English Reign of Cnut the Great", in *The New Middle Ages*, ed. Michael D.J. Bintley, Martin Locker, Victoria Symons, Mary Wellesley (New York)

Turville-Petre, Gabriel. (1981). *Speculum norroenum : Norse studies in memory of Gabriel Turville-Petre*, ed. Dronke, Ursula (Odense)

Tveito, Olav. 2013. "Olav Haraldsson: misjonær med 'jerntuge'", *Historisk Tidsskrift*, 92:3

Tyler, E.M. 1999. "'The Eyes of the Beholders were Dazzled": Treasure and Artifice in Encomium Emmae Reginae', *Early Medieval Europe*, 8

Van Houts, Elisabeth M.C. (ed. and trans.). 2000. *The Normans in Europe* (New York)

Vince, Alan. 1990. *Saxon London: An Archaeological Investigation* (London)

Weibull, Lauritz. 1911. *Kritiske undersökningar i Nordens historia omkring år 1000* (Lund)

Whaley, Diana. 1991. *Heimskringla: An Introduction* (London)

Whaley, Diana (ed.). 2012. *Poetry from the Kings' Sagas 1: From Mythical Times to c.1035. Skaldic Poetry of the Scandinavian Middle Ages 1*, ed. Diana Whaley (Turnhout)

Williams, Ann. 1999. *Kingship and Government in pre-Conquest England c.500–1066* (Houndmills)

Williams, Ann. 2003. *Æthelred the Unready: The Ill-Counselled King* (London)

Williams, Gareth, Peter Pentz and Matthias Wenhoff. 2013. *Viking* (Copenhagen)

Williams, John. 1871. *Observations of Comets, from BC 611 to AD 1640, Extracted from the Chinese Annals* (London)

Williams, Thomas J.T. 2015. "Landscape and Warfare in Anglo-Saxon England and the Viking campaign of 1006", *Early Medieval Europe*, 23.3

Williams, Thomas J.T. 2010. "Alfred's Wars: Sources and Interpretations of Anglo-Saxon Warfare in the Viking Age", in *Warfare in History*, ed. Ryan Lavelle (Woodbridge)

Winroth, Anders. 2012. *The Conversion of Scandinavia: Vikings, Merchants, and Missionaries in the Remaking of Northern Europe* (New Haven and London)

Wormald, Patrick. 2001. *The Making of English Law: King Alfred to the Twelfth Century. Volume 1: Legislation and Its Limits* (Oxford)